MW01643967

TWO ROYAL WOMEN

TWO ROYAL WOMEN

NORMAN KING

WYNWOOD™ Press
New York, New York

Poem on pages 135-36 is copyright © John Betjeman and reproduced by permission of Curtis Brown Ltd.

Library of Congress Cataloging-in-Publication Data

King, Norman, 1926–
Two royal women.

Bibliography: p.
1. Elizabeth II, Queen of Great Britain, 1926– —Family. 2. York, Sarah Mountbatten-Windsor, Duchess of, 1959– . 3. Diana, Princess of Wales, 1961– . 4. Great Britain—Nobility—Biography. 5. Great Britain—Princes and princesses—Biography. II. Title.
DA590.K48 1989 941.085'092'2 [B] 89–5305
ISBN 0–922066–06–X

Copyright © 1989 by Bill Adler Books, Inc.
Published by WYNWOOD™ Press
New York, New York
Printed in the United States of America

TO BESSIE

Ma . . .
I should have kissed you more
. . . and argued less

CONTENTS

TWO ROYAL WOMEN

I

THE PRINCESS OF WALES AND THE DUCHESS OF YORK

1

DIANA AND FERGIE

IT WAS REMINISCENT OF THE FAMOUS SCENE IN *MY FAIR LADY*—LIZA Doolittle at the Royal Ascot, all traces of her accent thoroughly sanitized by Professor 'Iggins, all corners of her personality rounded off to a smooth velvety finish, seeing her horse in the race lagging, and breaking out irresistibly to urge him on with that cockney blare: "Move your bloomin' arse!"—only this time it was the real thing.

And the players? Well, they were—ulp!—real royalty!

The headline-making occasion occurred ironically enough at that very same Royal Ascot—the major social event of the English royalty season. It is, as Cecil Beaton demonstrated in designing the costumes for the musical *My Fair Lady*, the event at which one dresses in one's very best costume, wears one's very best smile, and walks in one's very best and most sedate fashion. No horsing around.

Of the best-dressed royals present in the 1987 season were Diana, the Princess of Wales, wife of Prince Charles, heir to the throne of England, and Sarah, the duchess of

York, newly wed wife of Prince Andrew, now the duke of York and—uh, let's see—fourth in line of succession to the throne of England.

Diana, just twenty-six years old, and Sarah—called "Fergie" by the world press even if the nickname did annoy the duke—twenty-seven, were in high spirits. High in spite of the fact that Diana and Charles had been recently rumored by Fleet Street—England's opposite number of America's famed "media"—to be ready to break up their marriage of six years.

Under their hats and inside their exquisite costumes, wearing gloves and carrying umbrellas to combat the incipient weather always a threat in England, the princess and the duchess (although both women in fact are princesses since they are married to princes of the realm) were strolling serenely along through the bright, brilliantly dressed crowds, nodding occasionally to a known acquaintance and absorbing the wide-eyed stares of all onlookers, when quite suddenly the poltergeist of Liza Doolittle surfaced in—of all people!—Princess Diana.

Feeling that her progress was being impeded by a good friend, a male, dawdling in front of them, Diana lifted her umbrella and stroked it squarely against his behind. He jumped, of course, turned indignantly, saw who it was—and bit his tongue properly.

Diana giggled, leaned forward, and gave him a conciliatory peck on the cheek. Red-faced, he turned and tried to make the best of a bad thing. Diana, now dissolved into giggles, rejoined her companion, the duchess of York, and both continued on their way, consumed with hilarity.

Gasps from all about them were the order of the day. The top-hatted and expensively groomed gentlemen of the realm and their exquisitely coiffed ladies—a large percentage of them blue bloods of royal birth—winced in elegant concern. Heads were averted. Eyes gazed at the heavens. Blood congealed.

There was more to come. Spotting Princess Michael of Kent, one of the snootiest and least fun loving of the Windsors, in the royal box, Diana waved wildly, gave a cool wolf-whistle, and turned to Fergie in mocking, open-mouthed awe, crying out loudly enough for everyone around her to hear: "Isn't that *Princess Michael?*"

Princess Michael, quite rightly, turned white with rage.

With their spirits still bubbling high, the two princesses strolled through the crush of the highest ranking of their loyal subjects in the royal enclosure, turning heads and exchanging an occasional nod with the well-off and genteel lucky enough to rate attention.

Making their way through the concentration of the best and brightest in the commonwealth, Diana and Fergie finally mounted to the royal box, their irrepressible spirits not yet exhausted. In fact, the clowning and high jinks continued unabated. Fergie, not exactly a nymphlike figure of a woman, suddenly leaped into her sister-in-law's lap, clinging to Diana and refusing to be dislodged, until Princess Anne, another sister-in-law, would deign to drop in for a short chat with them.

The fever of rebellion still running high, Diana stood up to smooth out the wrinkles in her clingy yellow dress, finishing the act with a shake of the royal bum in charming imitation of a professional stage stripper. That delighted Fergie and dissolved her into giggles.

The horse races went on, of course, and the two young royals, chatting happily with each other in the box, watched for a while. But soon even the rather muted excitement of the spectacle palled on them, and they foraged about for something to *do.*

Finally, with a sigh, Diana turned to Fergie, and was overheard to say: "Let's go to the Turf Club—and get drunk!"

Thus the theories of Henry Higgins, care of George Bernard Shaw, were proved to be altogether too true.

There is a human being inside every titled aristocrat fighting to get out. That day Diana and Fergie—a creditable princess and a newly made but just as creditable duchess (and princess too)—had broken free and made history. Well, history of a *sort.*

It didn't end with the Royal Ascot, however. The two royal friends were quite busy elsewhere—in tandem and sola.

There was, for example, the widely advertised television charity event broadcast in London as "The Grand Knockout Tournament." Largely a product of the theatrical genius of Prince Edward, the younger brother of Princes Charles and Andrew and brother-in-law to the duchess of York, it was a comedic outing reminiscent of the Keystone Kops, with titled personalities dunking each other in cold water and dressing up as vegetables and wearing other outrageous costumes.

The duchess of York at one point was cavorting about in an old-fashioned getup from the middle ages as a kind of scullery wench—making up to big movie stars and other celebrities involved in the frolic.

Later Fergie was seen gushing over singer David Bowie like some goggle-eyed teenager as she presented him with the Silver Clef Award, a music honor of some sort. She even confessed, in most unduchesslike terms that "You are one of my favorite stars, and I love all your records."

But it wasn't only the irrepressible Fergie who was making headlines. It was Di as well.

Take the early part of the summer, during a polo match at Windsor. The Princess of Wales had gone along with Prince Charles to the match in which he was to play. She was there to keep him company and to cheer on his team.

They drove down in Charles's 1970 Aston Martin convertible, an $80,000 present from the queen herself. He had got it on his twenty-first birthday, and considered the car a priceless item—as indeed it was.

Anyway, during a lull in the action, the usual photographers were clamoring for Diana to pose for them, and she did. To oblige them, she climbed up on the hood of the car, hitched one leg over another, and smiled charmingly. At this point the Prince of Wales appeared in the distance, staring, and then moved quickly forward in a frenzy.

Pushing up to the crowd, he cried at his wife: "You can't sit there!" He began waving his arms. "Get off!" He lunged forward through the crowd. "You'll dent the bodywork!"

Diana, startled, pulled herself together as best she could and slid off the expensive hood, straightening out her dress as she did so. She said nothing, but her eyes were bright and dangerous.

Charles immediately pushed her aside to inspect the metalwork for damages, gazing closely and intently at the surface of the hood. Finally he backed away and declared with satisfaction that the car was apparently all right. He turned to her, smiled, and departed for the match.

She said nothing. When he had gone, she became a bit less grim, hitched up her dress, and climbed back on the hood, crossed her legs again, and pretended that nothing had happened.

The photograph got into the papers—along with the tongue-lashing Charles had given her.

There was a capper to that incident. Two days later Charles crumped up the car in a minor accident in Windsor near the castle. This prang did indeed put a dent in the convertible's smooth finish, and the Prince of Wales had to cough up $1,600 of royal money to get the wrinkles ironed out. No report on who won the polo match.

But Diana's big gaffe was not in poking backsides with umbrellas or in seating the royal bum on expensive metal. It involved her friendship with a man named Philip Dunne, a twenty-eight-year-old investment banker and bachelor. This *faux de passion* took place during a period of time when Prince Charles was away from home—first in the Outer Hebrides doing farm work, and then in Botswana's Kalahari Desert studying the Bushmen.

While he was away, Diana was squired about to concerts, stage shows, and a posh Mayfair club called Annabel's without him on the scene—or even backstage. The crucial event was a weekend Princess Diana spent with Dunne at Gatley Park, Dunne's family estate. A reporter found out about it, and it was billed as a "romantic liaison" (read, "extramarital affair") between Diana and Dunne. After that weekend, Diana was reported to have attended a rock concert with him—at least, so said the *Daily Mail.*

However, it turned out that this latter tidbit was a mistake: Princess Diana's escort was actually Major David Waterhouse, an officer of the Life Guards, and hardly anyone to be having a "romantic liaison" with the heir apparent's wife.

In fact, it was later reported that Di's weekend with Dunne was hardly the twosome it was hinted to be. Dunne's girlfriend—a photographer named Katya Grenfell—was present at all times during the weekend. If anything, it was Diana who was the outsider to whatever hot affair there was between any others.

Well!

All these individual items would cause no alarm normally, especially in England where Fleet Street is always on the watch to point out foibles of the royal family. However, lumped together, these manifold tiny items added up to a bit of undigestible hash.

And it was the press, of course, that began the wrist slapping and the scolding.

Quite swiftly, indeed!

"WE ARE NOT AMUSED," bleated the *Daily Mirror,* describing the Royal Ascot escapades with unconcealed relish. The

Sun took another tack, going after Diana for her "weekends" away and her various escorts in town while Prince Charles was off: "FLIGHTY DI IS FLIRTING WITH DANGER."

The *Sunday Times*, commenting on the television show in which the duke and duchess of York, Princess Anne, and Prince Edward participated, wrote: "The royal family has become so used to being treated like a soap opera that some of its members are beginning to act as if they are in one." In other words, it was " 'Dallas' at the Palace," as *Newsweek* humorously headlined a piece on the royal events generally.

Jean Rook of the *Daily Express* wrote: "It has been a suicidally silly season for the younger royals."

The biggest item that came out of the various reports in the press had to do with Sarah Ferguson, the new wife of Prince Andrew, and not with Diana, the rather settled-down mother of two children and wife of six years.

"I think Fergie probably has a great deal to do with the antics we've been seeing," intoned Harold Brooks-Baker, the managing director of *Burke's Peerage*, the arbiter of all things royal and titled. "Everyone likes a laugh, but things have gone too far."

There was no official palace response to the newspaper comments, an incredible turn of events to Americans who are used to televised equal-time responses even to such proclamations as State of the Union addresses. Instead, the palace set up a photographic opportunity to watch the royal family at a school outing for Prince William, Diana's five-year-old son. There, Diana carried on as the perfect wife and mother, with no ruffle out of place. Then Queen Elizabeth opened Parliament, with Charles and Diana both in attendance.

The queen, however, was said, behind the scenes, to be "very sad" over the situation in general. So, apparently, were some supporters of the monarchy—and certainly many of those who aren't.

The *Sunday Times* editorialized: "It is the single biggest weakness of today's royal family that it is still too closely associated with the very upper classes, often of the more stupid sort, and some recent behavior has served only to remind everybody of this."

Somebody at the *Times* suggested the royals should "get a job."

From the day she was engaged to Charles, it was obvious that the age gap in the relationship between him and Diana might eventually become a problem. Those twelve years were difficult to span even during the courtship months. Once married, the gap seemed to widen. It was the arrival of Sarah Ferguson—the duchess of York—in court circles that helped pull Diana up out of the doldrums into which she had begun to sink after the quick arrival of child number one and the subsequent arrival of child number two.

Never really comfortable in associating with the clannish members of the House of Windsor and becoming rapidly bored with the heir to the throne's interest in very serious subjects—music, architecture, and even gardening—Diana found Fergie's lighthearted approach to life a tonic that seemed to lift her out of the depths.

The fact of the matter was that it had been the Princess of Wales herself who was instrumental in helping to "arrange" the courtship of Prince Andrew and Sarah Ferguson. Diana and Sarah had known one another for some time and had always gotten along famously together.

The young and inexperienced Diana—who had married as a teenager—was in need of companionship in the royal circle into which she had been precipitously tossed and to which she had been confined by the "marriage of the century." Fergie could well serve the post of confidante to the queen-to-be—probably better than anyone else Diana knew. Not altogether royal in blood and in attitude, and certainly sophisticated and knowledgeable in the ways of the world—something Diana had been prevented from experiencing—Fergie was an obvious lifesaver who might help keep the Princess of Wales from drowning in deep dignity.

"Fergie has pointed Diana toward a world she left behind when she married Prince Charles," one Diana-watcher said. "For the first time in her life she is meeting interesting and attractive people her own age."

One of them, of course, was Philip Dunne, the son of Thomas Dunne, the Lord Lieutenant, or queen's representative, of Hereford and Worcester. Diana had met Philip at a party in 1981, when Prince Andrew celebrated his twenty-first birthday. Fergie had skied with Dunne in Verbier, Switzerland, and it was largely through her influence that Diana began seeing him again. At parties and other affairs.

In spite of the gossip that came out of their meeting, Diana only danced with Dunne a few times at a wedding reception held for a mutual friend, the marquis of Worcester. Charles was present at the affair himself. Later, the mistaken report that Diana and Dunne were together alone at Gatley Park fueled the flames of innuendo.

"The stories flying around lately are just crap," a friend of Dunne declared. "Philip is simply not having an affair with Diana."

Nevertheless, because she was the Princess of Wales, any action she involved herself in was doubly explosive if at all suggestive. Like Caesar's wife, the Princess of Wales must always be "above suspicion."

"They can't keep her locked up," wrote Ingrid Seward, editor of *Majesty* magazine, "but she does have to be a bit careful."

What royalists were fuming over was Diana's lack of discretion. And they began pointing their finger at Fergie for her "bad influence" on the Princess of Wales.

"I think it's very clear that Fergie, unknowingly, with her sense of fun and her general youthful attitude, good humor, and other things, is undoing much of the good work that the Queen has done," Brooks-Baker declared. "She and the others have to realize what their jobs are all about."

Once the finger of blame was pointed in her direction, the duchess of York took it to heart and tried to do something about it. But of course she had endured a trying year at best. The first commoner to marry one of the princes of the realm in this century, she had been involved with all the hassle and tribulations of the first-year adjustments to wedded life. She had been moved from one level of life to another as well—from that of commoner to that of royalty.

"She is constantly under strain," one of her close friends said. "Individually, Sarah gets on extremely well with virtually everybody in the royal family, but when she's with them all, she just can't relax. Every word has to be watched, every gesture, even the way she dresses."

The main problem during those crucial, trying months was that her husband, Andrew, the duke of York, was required to carry on his naval duties away from home, with only weekends open to join his wife. And not only that, but he preferred to visit his family at Balmoral and Sandringham, rather than stay exclusively with his wife.

"She complains about this," one observer said, "but he says not to be silly that these homes are big enough for the two of them to be able to get away from the others."

In spite of these mines strewn about her in her first year of marriage, the duchess of York was able to maneuver through them. Although she had been stung at first by the wisecracks of the press about her weight—she was simply of another shape than Diana—she managed to reduce considerably from a blowsy size 14 to about a size 10. And she changed her hairstyle to conform more to what the well-dressed London sophisticate would sport.

She also began paying more attention to her own looks. Red-headed and freckle-faced, she began sitting under a sunlamp once a day in order to put on a patina of golden Bermuda glow that made her look more glamorous and improved her image in front of the camera lens.

But why all this fuss?

The question *really* was—as Ray Alan put it recently in *The New Leader*—"How useful is Britain's monarchy?" In other words, was it really needed?

His conclusion was that while it was expensive—more costly than the presidential regime of any democracy of Britain's size—it *was* indeed successful. "Snobbery and conformism established the titled idler as a model," he wrote. "What little criticism the British media publish of the royal family is usually personal and superficial. Anne may be described as equine, Charles weak, and Diana an anorexis stick-insect intent on dominating Charles, yet major issues and basic principles are generally avoided."

In fact, until television, the royals themselves were generally avoided, and if anything, put at a distance from the public. They were made remote, as it were, from the common folk. When Elizabeth was crowned queen, she reminded Alan of "everyone's favorite librarian."

On television, Elizabeth soon became a star. And now, with Charles settled in as heir apparent—conceivably forever—with no need for further publicity, it became the lot of Diana, first, as Princess of Wales, then later and just recently, Sarah Ferguson, as the duchess of York, to become the stars—not as *royals* exclusively but as the very important links between the English commonality and the royals.

To put it another way, Diana and Fergie were established to become the windows on the royals—windows through which the rest of England and the world at large can look in at royalty. It was Diana and Fergie who were flesh and blood, flesh and blood just like the rest of us. Through them we glimpse that other world we once read about in fairy tales and love stories.

That is what makes both of them a part of us. It is what makes it possible for us to cross over to that remote world of royalty and see what makes it tick.

It is unlikely that royalty will be wiped out in England in our day. It was wiped out once—during the time of Oliver Cromwell and his son Richard—but it never stuck. Even during the 1930s there was a possibility that royalty would sink. There was a plan afoot when King Edward VIII abdicated so that he could marry a divorced American woman to create the post of president of a Republican Britain if and when the Labour party won power and abolished the monarchy. The duke of Windsor had been promised the job of president of that new Republican Britain.

It just didn't happen.

It is even less likely to happen today—now that the whole concept of royalty seems acceptable to the masses all over the world, largely through television as a bridge between the high and the mighty and the common folk.

But of course the two worlds badly needed a link.

And the link became people like Diana, this beautiful, modellike creature, a clothes horse, and the mother of two beautiful children, and Fergie, this outgoing, effervescent, bouncy commoner who even learned to fly a helicopter—two windows through which we can see the royals and feed on their royalty.

But in order to visualize these living "windows" more clearly, it is necessary to see where they came from, how they were selected by royalty to become part of them, and where their future lies.

And so:

Here's looking at Diana and Fergie!

II

LADY DIANA

2

HARD BEGINNINGS

DIANA FRANCES SPENCER WAS THE THIRD OF FOUR CHILDREN BORN TO Edward John Spencer, Viscount Althorp, and Frances Roche Spencer. The event occurred on July 1, 1961. The future Princess of Wales was born at Park House, a residence on the royal estate at Sandringham, which the Spencers rented from Queen Elizabeth II. Spencer had been equerry to King George VI for two years—from 1950 to 1952—and to Queen Elizabeth for two years—from 1952 to 1954.

What's an *equerry?* The word originally referred to an officer of a prince or a king charged with the care of his master's horses—hence the remains of the Latin root *equus* in the word. Of course, the horsy sense of the meaning was lost many years ago. It became a word used in the British royal household describing the office of the person in attendance on the sovereign or any of the sovereign's close relatives.

The position hints at closeness to the royal family—not only physical closeness, but psychological closeness as well. And not only was the Spencer family close to the royals, but Diana's mother, born Frances Roche, was the daughter of Ruth, Lady Fermoy, Dame Commander of the Royal Victorian Order and Lady of the Bedchamber of the Queen Mother. In spite of the quaintness of the titles, Frances Roche Spencer was simply a member of the court.

In addition, the Spencer family also boasted of another Dame Commander of the Royal Victorian Order. She was Diana's paternal grandmother, Lady Cynthia Hamilton. Thus both of Diana's grandmothers were close to the royal family, involved in personal service.

Because of all these intimate ties in the Spencer–Roche family lines, it was not at all unusual for the Spencers to be renting their home on the royal estate at the time of Diana's birth. Her father had not yet become the eighth earl of Spencer; Diana's grandfather, Albert Edward John Spencer, the seventh earl of Spencer, was still alive and thriving at Althorp, the Spencer estate. Eventually Althorp would be inherited by her father and she would spend some of her teenage years there.

At Sandringham, the queen's residence, only a low stone wall separated Diana in her youth from the four offspring of the royal family: Prince Charles, Princess Anne, Prince Andrew, and Prince Edward. At the time of her birth Charles was a teenager, away at public school—"public" in Britain means the same as "private" in America.

By a quirk of fate, the Spencers had the only heated swimming pool in the vicinity. For that reason the Windsor clan would frequently swarm across the stone barriers to join their neighbors for a swim in the pool during the coldest winter weather. Charles, as the oldest, was usually the leader in these forays. The age difference between him and Diana—twelve years—created an automatic, quasi-generation gap; a dozen years may not technically be a generation, but it was close enough to that during those early years to be almost unbridgeable. And so Prince Charles and Lady Diana were too far apart at that time to be together on any kind of "equal" or companionable level.

It was Prince Andrew—only two years older than Diana—who became her favorite playmate among the royals. Sometimes she would wind up with Prince Edward, who was even younger than she. The important thing was that the queen knew Diana and she knew the queen—intimately enough to call her "Aunt Lilibet." Life on the royal estate, in a rented residence or not, was free and easy—within the strictures of tradition and class.

And so Charles and Diana did not know each other by much more than name and sight really, until both were quite grown up—in 1977 or thereabouts, some eighteen years later. Nevertheless, Diana was born in the same kind of titled atmosphere that Charles was. As well as he, she was born to wealth and privilege, separated from the rest of us by that invisible barrier that is difficult to ignore and impossible to leap.

Make no mistake, she was not *sheltered,* nor was Charles. But she was more or less *protected* within a class and a culture of a specific nature, hermetically sealed from the pressures of everyday life that others must face.

What made Diana's ties even closer with the royal family was her father's substantial and close friendship with both Philip, the duke of Edinburgh, and the late King George VI (Elizabeth's father).

Diana Frances Spencer was an entirely normal, bumptious youngster. Even as a baby she was, in the words of her father, "a superb physical specimen." She was also a superb genetic specimen. The family tree of Lady Diana is impeccable, at least from the standpoint of the royal family.

In fact, Diana is related distantly to the man she would later marry; she and Charles are seventh cousins. The link and mutual ancestor was Henry VII, a Tudor monarch of the sixteenth century. In the words of Brooks-Baker, he of *Burke's Peerage,* "Lady Diana descends five times from Charles II, four times on the wrong side of the blanket and one on the right side."

The humor in the wordage does not suggest that Brooks-Baker was kidding. In fact, having a bastard ancestor in those days was something of an honor—and not what it came to be considered later. In his day (read, night) Charles II produced dozens of aristocratic lines both legitimate and illegitimate.

Brooks-Baker: "Out of twenty-six dukes in England today, five of them are direct descendants on the wrong side of the blanket of Charles II. This applies, too, to several marquises and earls."

Many stuffy researchers do not admit even *one* legitimate link between Diana and Charles II. However, it is obvious to the experts that Diana quite probably has even more royal blood in her veins than does Prince Charles. Generally speaking, she had four ancestors who were mistresses of English kings. Three were linked to Charles II, the son of Charles I; the fourth was linked to James II, Charles II's son.

Why all that promiscuity?

Charles I lost his head when the English aristocracy rose against him and set up an experimental, religiously oriented dictatorship called a "republic" under Oliver Cromwell. After Cromwell's son Richard was unable to keep the dictatorship going, Charles I's son was restored as king and the Stuart line recommenced after that brief hiatus of dictatorship that distinguished itself in history mostly for its roundheads and rump parliaments.

As a kind of countryside backlash against the puritanical repressions of the Cromwells, the English went on a spree of almost compulsive philandering. The result was a life-style that produced illegitimate lines of England's aristocracy that extend right up to the present.

The first of Charles II's paramours in Diana's family tree was Lucy Walters, with whom the king became intimate in 1648. Their son was born in 1649, and was proclaimed duke of Monmouth. Others included in that branch were several earls of Lucan, and members of the Bingham family.

The second and most active of Charles II's paramours in Diana's family tree was Barbara Villiers, the duchess of Cleveland. Married to Roger Palmer, she became the king's favorite about 1659, before he was restored as king. After the Restoration, Charles created an earldom of Castlemaine in Ireland, making Palmer, Lord Castlemaine; there he was more or less exiled. Barbara Villiers Palmer stayed with the court as Lady Castlemaine. The king had at least five children by her. The branch from which Diana sprang included several dukes of Grafton, a marchioness of Hertford, and an admiral.

The third of Charles II's paramours was Louise de Kéroualle, the duchess of Portsmouth. Her branch included several dukes of Richmond, countesses, marquises, several dukes and duchesses, and more than one duke of Abercorn. Her period of favor peaked about 1671, and was soon done.

The fourth paramour in Diana's tree was Arabella, the daughter of the first Sir Winston Churchill. She was a favorite (read, mistress) of James II, the son of Charles II. She bore him a daughter. Several steps down in its branches the Churchill family joined the Barbara Villiers family.

Arabella Churchill had a brother, Sir John Churchill, the first duke of Marlborough. It was Sir John who had become intimate outside his marriage with none other than Barbara Villiers, after she had ceased being particularly intimate with the king.

Lady Castlemaine by that time was rich enough to hire male courtesans to supply her own rather inexhaustible sexual needs; young John, not yet knighted nor made duke of Marlborough, was just starting out in politics. He became one of Barbara's bought-and-paid-for male—well—prostitutes.

One story had it that Churchill was once forced to make an undignified retreat through Barbara's window when the king arrived unexpectedly in her boudoir. Charles heard the commotion and leaned out the window, spotting Barbara's half-naked lover in the bushes.

"I forgive you," the king shouted down, "because you do it for your bread."

Diana Frances Spencer was descended from both Arabella Churchill's line and from Sir John Churchill's line. The duke of Marlborough's line merged with the Spencer family to produce in 1710 an earlier Lady Diana Spencer—foreshadowing our own twentieth-century one. *She* married the fourth duke of Bedford. The present Lady Diana came from the line of her brother, John Spencer of Althorp.

And so not only was Diana steeped in royal blood, but in common blood of a superior sort as well. The first Winston Churchill was the father of John Churchill, the first duke of Marlborough, a family that flourished at the end of the seventeenth century, and reemerged with flying colors in the twentieth century to lead England against the forces of Hitler.

Thus Diana shared a common ancestry with Winston Churchill, whose middle name, of course, was the same as hers: Winston *Spencer* Churchill. She was actually Sir Winston's cousin.

Even in the eighteenth century, the Spencers continued to liaise with royal lines. Two daughters of the first earl of Spencer made notable conquests of royal favorites. Georgiana, the duchess of Devonshire, known to history as the

"Duchess of Dimples," carried on a most successful affair with one early Prince of Wales, the man who eventually became George IV. Her sister Henrietta once boasted in her diary: "In my fifty-first year I am courted, follow'd, flatter'd, and made love to, en toutes les formes, by four men."

One Spencer escaped the family tradition and converted to Roman Catholicism. He was George, the brother of the third earl of Spencer. He became Father Ignatius of the Passionist Order. Those who knew him considered him a saint. The order has prepared a proposal to consider him for beatification—a step toward eventual Roman Catholic canonization.

Diana Spencer was also distantly related to Bertrand Russell, the philosopher and sociologist, as well as former Prime Minister Sir Alec Douglas-Home.

Nor were her ties restricted to England. Through her great-great-grandfather Frank Work, who was a dry-goods clerk in Chillicothe, Ohio, she could trace a number of American lines. Work became a millionaire when his stores began making big money; later he became a stockbroker working with the Vanderbilts on the exchange.

Work married Ellen Wood; it was Ellen Wood's mother who provided all the "interesting" relatives. George Washington was an eighth cousin, several times removed. Through Ellen Wood, Diana was also related to several other American presidents: John Adams, John Quincy Adams, Millard Fillmore, Rutherford B. Hayes, Grover Cleveland, Calvin Coolidge, and Franklin D. Roosevelt.

She could even trace her lineage outside political lines to Henry Adams, the famous historian of the famous American Adams family, and to Noah Webster, the man who put his name to one of America's best-known dictionaries. She was the seventh cousin of Humphrey Bogart, and the eighth cousin by marriage to Rudolf Valentino. She also had a line to Lillian Gish.

Frank Work's daughter Fanny (her real name was Frances, Diana's middle name) provided the link to European aristocracy when she married James Boothby Burke Roche. James Roche was the third Baron Fermoy. His marriage incensed Roche's father, a Yankee-hating Englishman, who remarked: "International marriage should be a hanging offense."

Sure enough, Fanny Work's marriage to Roche deteriorated. Her angry father, as much as anglophobe as her father-in-law was a yankeephobe, declared that he would prevent her and her children from inheriting his fortune unless they promised never to return to Europe to live or marry Europeans.

Only one of the children, Edmund Maurice Burke Roche, the elder of a pair of twins, defied the father's ukase and went back to Britain to claim the Fermoy title. Win it he did, and he married Ruth Sylvia Gill, whose daughter was Frances Ruth Burke Roche.

Frances Roche was Diana's mother; Edmund Roche, an American, her maternal grandfather. Thus Diana Frances Spencer was born one-eighth American.

"The real aristocracy in this country is that which existed before the Industrial Revolution, when lots of people who owned factories were given titles," Brooks-Baker has noted. "There are only about 150 families that fall in this category." The Spencer line is one of the "real aristocracy."

In spite of all that blue blood flowing through the veins of Diana, Brooks-Baker, the arbiter of lineage, summed up her heritage with a slightly lifted eyebrow, referring to the Spencer family directly: "There is nobody in her family of any great importance. They are nice people who live in beautiful houses and have the good fortune to be related to almost every member of the aristocracy."

And that was the background that made Lady Diana most suitable as a candidate for the hand of Prince

Charles—a one-eighth American Englishwoman who was brought up in a beautiful house and was, above all, a "nice person." With all that hanky-panky in her remote background, it should not be astonishing that she should go in for pranks of the sort that were endearing her to the public but were making her a target of the royals and of the arched-eyebrow supporters of the monarchy.

As for her father, Edward "Johnny" Spencer was educated at Eton College. He attended the Royal Military Academy at Sandhurst, before becoming an aide-de-camp to the governor of South Australia for three years in the 1940s. A millionaire many times over, he kept most of the assets of the family tied up in the estates and in art treasures the Spencer line had built up over the centuries.

In 1954, in one of the most glittering high-society events of the year, "Johnny" Spencer married Frances Ruth Burke Roche in Westminster Abbey. At eighteen, the bride was the youngest woman to have been married there in fifty years.

The Spencers had four children. Lady Diana was number three. Number one was Lady Sarah, and number two, Lady Jane. Number four was a younger brother, oddly enough named Charles, born three years after Diana.

All three Spencer girls inherited the title "lady" at birth; Charles was the Viscount Althorp, meaning that he was and is the heir apparent to the title of earl of Spencer and the direct heir to the Althorp fortune—which is considerable.

Historically, the first Spencer was Sir John Spencer, of Wormleighton in Warwickshire, who purchased the immense estate at Althorp in 1506. He was knighted by King Henry VIII, and was said to have been a "noble housekeeper, liberal to his poor neighbors, and bountiful to his tenants and servants." He claimed direct descent from William the Conqueror's steward, Robert Despencer. The "De" was dropped to make the name seem more Saxon than Norman, and hence more fashionable, as the years advanced.

This early Spencer amassed a considerable fortune by herding sheep on the extensive lands at Althorp. His son, William, married a merchant's daughter with holdings in Suffolk. On the death of his father-in-law, warehouses of gold, satins, tapestries, furs, velvets, and fustian were discovered—fustian being a kind of cotton cloth popular in those days. These treasures were immediately added to the Spencer coffers.

The estate itself, with its grounds and mansion, was altered and refurbished by the second earl. Since then, a large number of works of art have been added to the treasures of the house. Sir Joshua Reynolds painted the portraits of three generations of the family. The Marlborough Room today contains works by Reynolds and Gainsborough. In the dining room there are large canvases by Salvator Rosa and Guercino. In the yellow drawing room there are four portraits by Rubens.

The furnishings of the house include French and English furniture, with a collection of Oriental and European porcelain. Most of the rooms have been remodeled during the past several years. Althorp is one of Britain's best-kept houses, concentrating in its contents the best of five homes owned at one time or another by the Spencers.

All these sumptuous surroundings were Spencer-owned, but Diana did not grow up amidst them. Althorp was a far-off never-never land to her. Her home was the rented estate at Park House. It was only later that she would move to Althorp—on the death of her grandfather.

At Park House she began her life under the tutelage of a governess, Gertrude Allen. Diana, her governess recalled, was always "a very conscientious child." At least, she was a child who would always try, even if she failed.

Others who were around her in those early years remembered her as a girl with bright blue eyes and that typically English peaches-and-cream complexion. They noted too that Diana was a practical child, a bouncy type, a person who would help do things around the house. "She would always be the first to put a log on the fire," a friend was once quoted in the *Sunday Times.*

Diana looked back on those years with a typically sunny remark. "A lot of nice things happened to me when I was in nappies."

Plans were under way to send Diana to a state-run primary school when she had reached the proper educable age. There she would be able to mix with village children and play with them as one of them.

But at the age of six, Diana found herself quite suddenly in the eye of a very bad storm.

The Spencer marriage, which had begun with such fanfare and hope, was fatally riven and soon began to fall apart. The fourth Spencer child—Charles—was only three years old at the time. It was then that Frances Roche Spencer decided she simply could not go on with it any longer. She needed to get away—away from her husband *and* from her children.

Quite suddenly one day she vanished. One of the servants remembered that she was simply not there anymore.

What had happened was simple enough, even if it was not exactly the traditional thing for a woman married to a title to do. Diana's mother was bored with life at Park House. She wanted the excitement and whirl of London society. At a party she had met a man named Peter Shand-Kydd, happily married with three children. Shand-Kydd was the heir to a wallpaper fortune, and the owner of a number of cattle and sheep ranches in Scotland and Australia.

Frances, Diana's mother, and Peter continued meeting in London during her constant trips to town. She fell in love with him, and he with her. They set up house in

London, where Frances's children came occasionally to visit.

Soon Peter's wife found out about the affair and sued for divorce. She won, not only the divorce, but custody of the three children of the marriage. Frances Spencer was named adulteress.

The upshot of this was that Diana's father forbade his children from visiting their mother in London—indeed, from seeing her at all. Annoyed at this, she sued for custody of her four children, assuming that the courts would award them to her.

In turn, Diana's father countersued for divorce, naming his wife adulteress in the Shand-Kydd affair. That was in June 1968. Shortly after that, Diana's longtime nanny, Gertrude Allen—called Ally in the family—left the Spencer household. She had good reason to. She had been nanny to Diana's mother; she sided with mother against father in this action.

Sarah and Jane, the two older Spencer daughters, were desperately unhappy over the marital mess. Shattered would be a more apt term. It was thought that Diana, because of her youth, should have been more or less protected from the trauma of the occasion, as would young Charles. This, however, was not the way it worked out.

Of all the four Spencer children, it was Diana who was the most upset emotionally by her parents' divorce. She began to indulge in mood swings from highs to lows within moments, and from lows to highs again. Her highs were bright and happy highs; her lows were moody, quiet, and depressed.

At the time of her mother's "disappearance" Diana was six years old. She was attending a private coeducational day school called Silfield, in King's Lynn, near Park House. She began to cut up in school, taking out her inner frustrations on the teachers and the children around her.

Her home life was also in turmoil, with her father trying his best to keep things going in spite of his inner distress. Diana began to react in different ways. Her father would hire a new nanny to take care of the children. Diana was an expert at getting things her own way—especially in manipulating her nannies into doing what she wanted them to do.

When they didn't. . . .

Diana had a style about her. She enticed one nanny into the bathroom on some pretext, only to dash off and vanish. Quite possibly she was reenacting her mother's "disappearance"—or so a psychologist might say. The unfortunate wretch tried to punish Diana, only to find herself locked in the bathroom by the mischievous girl!

It took a great deal of yelling and pounding on the door before she was finally let out, to appear sheepishly in front of her deliverer—Diana's older sister Sarah.

None of these nannies lasted very long. Another one was aroused in the early morning by Diana, only to find that her clothes had been taken away from her bedroom, leaving her unable to dress. She found them out on the roof after searching almost everywhere else—and had to climb out and get them.

No one really won these battles of the wills, except perhaps Diana. Although she was always considered shy, during these traumatic years she developed a will that was almost cast iron.

The Spencer divorce itself, which continued in the courts from June 1968 to April 1969, was vicious and abrasive. There were bitter arguments over the custody of the children. Frances was desperately trying to gain control of her four children; "Johnny" was trying to prevent it.

Witnesses from both sides of the family were called on to testify in court. Press coverage was enormous. Both families were split down the middle, some Fermoys sympathizing with Johnny and others sympathizing with

Frances, some Spencers sympathizing with Johnny and others with Frances.

The most serious break was that between Diana's mother and her grandmother, Ruth, Lady Fermoy. Her grandmother considered Frances's action as almost treasonable. In effect, Diana's grandmother "cut off" Frances totally. They would never speak to each other again. In the two families there were the "royalists" who supported Lady Fermoy and the "others" who supported the divorcée Frances. It was all a very nasty scene.

The notoriety of the trial and its settlement shattered the family and the people in it. Custody of the children eventually went to the Spencer side of the family. Sarah and Jane were allowed to decide for themselves whether they wanted to spend their school holidays with their father or mother. The younger children, Diana and Charles, lived with their father and divided their school holidays between him and their mother, who lived in London.

It was at this time that Diana was transferred to Riddlesworth, a private girls' boarding school about fifty miles away in Diss, Norfolk. There she began to settle down, finding the atmosphere much more rewarding than it had been at home with all the tension and malice.

Still, the divorce had left its scars on her.

She constantly made reference to the fact that she was sick and tired of being young and a "baby." "I can't wait to grow up like her," she told one of her nannies, referring to her older sister Sarah.

In fact, Sarah was Diana's role model in those years. Even with all the tension around the Spencer place, Sarah was the most adventurous of the three sisters, the most volatile, and the most fun loving. Sarah was the leader. Diana was the follower—as many middle children are.

Mary Clarke, who acted as nanny during part of those

tempestuous years, described the effect Sarah had on Diana:

> Diana looked up to [Sarah]. Though I was able to keep Diana in control during my years as her nanny, I couldn't depend upon her to be well-behaved when Sarah was nearby. Life was never dull around them: Sarah was always daring Diana to do forbidden things. When guests came to lunch, she would try forcing Diana into a giggle fit. It always worked—Diana *always* giggled, especially when nervous.

The Princess of Wales as we know her today was being molded in those teenage years. Now the leader she had looked up to in her older sister is no longer needed; but anyone who has a sense of impish fun will provoke her—to giggle, to poke with an umbrella, to pose for photographers.

Diana was never very good with her books and studies. She simply did not have the ability to concentrate on any one thing long enough. The obvious solution to this problem was to involve her in outdoor activities. One of her favorites was swimming. She always loved to be in the water.

In the pool at Park House she would torment her father. There was a slide alongside the pool that deposited the slider down into its shallow end. The top of the slide overlooked the deep end. Diana loved to climb to the top, yell at her father, "Watch me!" and then, instead of sliding, she would dive headfirst into the deep end of the pool.

Mary Clarke recalled a traumatic event that occurred during her stewardship over Diana. "I took [Charles and Diana] for a pony ride in the park. On the way back to Park House, Diana's pony tripped, and Diana fell. It looked as if no harm had been done, but we all rushed

Diana to the doctor. He confirmed that nothing was broken."

Yet two weeks later, Diana had her arm in a sling; she had apparently fractured her arm when she fell from the pony. Diana's mother had put the sling on; it was during a period when Diana was allowed to visit her just after the divorce was granted. The situation became even more tedious when Diana's mother immediately instituted a second claim for custody of her children—on the basis that Diana was not being handled properly by her father! It came to nothing.

But Diana never felt secure enough to try riding a horse again. Obviously her dislike of riding was not because she had fallen once, but because so much unpleasantness had been unleashed between her parents over that minor incident.

The divorce affected her undoubtedly more than she could ever measure. She confided in her nanny at the time: "I want to fall in love, get married, and have lots of children. But I'll never marry unless I'm really in love. If you're not sure you love someone, you might get divorced. I never want to get divorced."

Diana was then "a pretty child with shoulder-length brown hair and rosy cheeks that blushed easily." She gave the impression of shyness, but that was only a cover for her strong-willed nature. It was something she had inherited from her mother. In spite of the impression of shyness she gave, she made friends easily.

Diana's mother was the first of her parents to remarry. Frances Spencer settled down in London with Peter Shand-Kydd. He had a home in England and a cattle farm located in an isolated area of the Isle of Seil, in the Firth of Lorne just off the west coast of Argyll in Scotland.

When she would leave her father to go to see her mother in London, Diana would tell her nanny, "Poor Daddy. I feel so sorry leaving him on his own!" But then, on the way home from London, she would tell her, "Poor Mummy. I feel so sad leaving her on her own." It did not seem to occur to her that her mother, who had remarried, was not alone at all.

"The most distasteful part of my job," Mary Clarke said later, "was when I had to pick up Charles and Diana after they had spent half of their school holidays with their mother. Lady Frances would always act coldly toward me. She rarely acknowledged my presence. She disliked me because she felt I was taking her place in her children's affections. No matter what she did or how she acted, however, I'd have to bite my tongue and be tactful."

Nevertheless, Diana soon settled down and accepted the split life of her parents with some equanimity.

III

SARAH FERGUSON

3

THE ONCE AND FUTURE DUCHESS

ALMOST TWO YEARS BEFORE THE BIRTH OF DIANA FRANCES SPENCER, ON October 15, 1959, there was born to Major Ronald Ferguson, an officer in the Life Guards, and his wife, the former Susan Fitzherbert Wright, a second daughter, Sarah Margaret. She saw the first light of day at the private Welbeck Clinic in London's Marleybone, and then within a few days she was returned to the Ferguson home. The Fergusons then lived at Lowood, a residence in Sunninghill, a village near Ascot, about thirty miles southwest of London, where both the young Ferguson daughters—Sarah and Jane—grew up.

Although *somewhat* wealthy, though never a millionaire, Major Ferguson—a captain at the time of Sarah's birth—did not bring up his daughters with the proverbial silver spoon in their mouths. Nevertheless, the family line tended to intertwine with the royal line in ages past and even, for all practical purposes, at the present time as well.

Sarah's paternal grandmother, Lady Elmhirst, the granddaughter of the sixth duke of Buccleuch, was the cousin of Princess Alice, the duchess of Gloucester, an aunt by marriage to Queen Elizabeth II. It was through Lady Elmhirst that the Fergusons could trace their ancestry back to the Royal House of Stuart—no surprise to anyone familiar with the background and family tree of Sarah's great friend-to-be, Diana Spencer.

In point of fact, Sarah Ferguson could even claim distant relationship to the future Lady Diana Spencer; both had similar backgrounds and their family lines coincided during the days of King Charles II. If Diana had four ancestors linked, however dubiously, to kings of England, Sarah had three. The truth was that they were the *same three* mentioned in relation to Diana's family tree.

The first was Lucy Walters, who was the mother by Charles II of the duke of Monmouth. Monmouth became the first duke of Buccleuch. Sarah was in fact the great-great-granddaughter of the sixth duke of Buccleuch through her father, who was also descended from Thomas Lennard, the earl of Sussex, and his wife Anne.

Follow this next carefully: it is the second link to the Spencer line mentioned above.

Anne, the wife of Thomas Lennard, the earl of Sussex, was the eldest natural daughter of our old friend Barbara Villiers, the duchess of Cleveland. Charles II was *probably* Anne's father, although she may just as easily have been the daughter of Philip Stanhope, the earl of Chesterfield, or even Roger Palmer, the earl of Castlemaine!

From that line came several earls, barons, and viscounts, with Brigadier General Algernon Ferguson, Sarah's great-grandfather, marrying Margaret Brand, the daughter of Henry Brand, the second Viscount Hampden.

The *third* link to the Spencer line was the notorious duchess of Portsmouth—Louise de Kéroualle, whose son by the merry monarch became the first duke of Richmond.

That line merged with the earls of Leicester and the viscounts Powerscourt. Sarah's maternal grandmother, née Doreen Wingfield, was the daughter of Merwyn Wingfield, the eighth viscount Powerscourt. Thus Sarah's mother was the granddaughter of the eighth viscount, descended from King Edward II through his fifth son, Edmund of Langley, an earlier duke of York!

As if that lineage isn't tangled enough—with all its links tenuous at best through illegitimate relationships—there's a more important one in Sarah Ferguson's actual *legitimate* and undisputed connection with royalty: through her father.

Thus: The duke of Monmouth's grandson and heir, the second duke of Buccleuch married Lady Jane Douglas, eldest daughter of Charles Boyle, Lord Clifford, and Lady Jane Seymour. Lady Jane's father, William Seymour, the second duke of Somerset, was the heir of Edward Seymour, the earl of Hertford and his past wife, Lady Catherine Grey—Seymour's grandparents. Lady Catherine Gray was the youngest sister of Lady Jane Grey, the nine-days Queen of England; Lady Jane was beheaded in 1554, and her sister, Catherine, died in the Tower of London in 1568. Lady Jane Grey was heiress and granddaughter of Mary, Queen of France, and later duchess of Suffolk, the younger daughter of Henry VII and Elizabeth, daughter of Edward IV.

Hey, now, that wasn't so hard, was it?

Here's the bottom line. Sarah Ferguson is directly descended from the first Tudor and the first Yorkist kings; her descent is shared by the Queen Mother and the Princess of Wales.

The sixth duke of Buccleuch—if you're still with us—was Sarah Ferguson's great-great-grandfather. He married Lady Louise Jane Hamilton, the daughter of the first duke of Abercorn. This duke's forebear, the first earl of Abercorn, was a grandson of James Hamilton, the earl of

Arran, governor of Scotland from 1543 to 1554 during the minority of Mary, Queen of Scots. He was the great-grandson of James II, King of Scots. Through his English mother, Queen Jane, James Hamilton was thus the great-great-grandson of Edward III of England.

And that is the final branch in the lineage to be traced. The Ferguson link with royalty can be seen to be legitimate as well as illegitimate—a link the frequency of which is astounding amongst the English gentry.

As for the Fergusons themselves, they lived well—no doubt about that. The life-style of young Sarah was never that of a typical English commoner. Sarah grew up in a fairly large household, composed of a cook, a gardener, and a nanny.

One of Sarah's first nannies was a Finnish au pair girl in her twenties. Ritvu Risu once described Sarah and her sister, Jane: "My first impression of the [Ferguson] children was that they were so well behaved. They never caused the slightest trouble. Sarah was always my favorite. She was just so good and gentle, even as a little girl."

Sarah was always "my little Redhair" to her Finnish nanny. Even in Sarah's early years she displayed, according to her nanny, the traditional fiery nature of the stereotypical redhead.

Indeed, even though the younger sister, Sarah tended to dominate Jane.

"She was much more lively than Jane," her nanny observed. "She was full of energy and had a great sense of humor. Jane was more ladylike while Sarah was something of a tomboy."

From the beginning, Sarah was a part of the "horsy" set in England—through the talents and skills of her Life Guards–officer father. In the course of his career in the British military, Ronald Ferguson had risen to a position of commander of the Sovereign's Escort of the Household Cavalry, following directly and comfortably in the footsteps of *his* father, Colonel Andrew Ferguson, who had served with distinction in World War II.

During the postwar years, especially in the 1950s, Ronald Ferguson had become recognized as one of the better polo players in England. Prince Philip, Queen Elizabeth II's consort, was impressed with his athletic skills and sought him out for help in his own favorite sport. It was no surprise that the two of them—on the strength of their interest in and dedication to polo—should become good friends.

In 1966, Major Ferguson's father, Andrew, died, and Ronald inherited Dummer Down House, a beautiful brick manor built in the Georgian style, surrounded by eight hundred acres of lush farmland on twelve hundred acres in rural Hampshire, just southwest of Basingstoke.

Ferguson took this opportunity to retire from the Life Guards after twenty years' service to take over the running of his large estate. He moved his family down to Hampshire, and it was there that Sarah and Jane began to enjoy the more relaxed country life that is the usual perk of the beautiful and titled people of England. It was not long before Ferguson became deputy chairman of the Guards Polo Club at Smith's Lawn, Windsor, probably the country's most distinguished polo club.

On Ferguson's retirement from the Life Guards, Prince Philip seized the opportunity to appoint him his own polo manager. With Prince Charles's interest in polo on the increase through the years, it was not long before Ferguson was also helping out the heir apparent's efforts in the sport. Eventually Ferguson became the Prince of Wales's polo manager, while still holding the reins of the Guards Polo Club at Smith's Lawn.

It was his proximity to the royal family that put members of his immediate household in touch with the royal line—through mutual interest in horses and those sports that involve riding.

In 1970, for example, when Sarah was ten years old, a picture taken by one of the queen's photographers shows Sarah and her husband-to-be in the distant future—Prince Andrew—engaged in what might be a brief conversation on the grass at Smith's Lawn. The queen is seen standing nearby listening to a very young Prince Edward and Lady Sarah Armstrong-Jones—his cousin—laughing together over something.

"Our families would meet and, naturally, the children would play, like any other children," Sarah's mother explained later. "They wouldn't really understand what royalty meant at that age."

She went on to explain a little more fully that Sarah and Andrew really did not see much of each other until they were both in their teens. At that time, they might bump into one another at the polo matches more or less by accident.

But that was much later. By now Sarah was going to school in Hampshire—enrolling at Daneshill School, in nearby Basingstoke. This was a coed preparatory school—preparatory in the sense of preparing for more advanced work. Although she was never a sensationally brilliant student, she managed to do better academically than her friend-to-be Lady (and later Princess) Diana. Sarah was better known for her high spirits than for her high marks. She did excel at sports, especially tennis and swimming.

Naturally, because of her father's expertise in horses, Sarah took up riding early on and became adept at the sport. From the beginning of her life, Sarah had been close to horses. Almost as soon as she could walk, she had been taught to ride on the Ferguson family pony. Then, when she was ten years old, Sarah was given her first pony. From both her mother and her father—who were excellent riders—she inherited a natural ability to ride and a love of horses.

Her father noted that she was always a fierce and

competitive person, and he was able to mold these character aptitudes into effective ridership capabilities. Before she reached her teen years, Sarah was an accomplished equestrienne.

"She used to go absolutely straight and take crashing falls, and would sit on the ground beating it with frustration," her father said of her. She knew why she had fallen; she knew what she had done wrong. And she did everything immediately to correct those faults. She learned to ride at gymkhanas, pay clubs, and junior trials.

She was so good, in fact, that she was selected to represent Daneshill at the All-England Schools Championship held each year at Hickstead.

After graduating from Daneshill School, Sarah Ferguson enrolled at Hurst Lodge, a girls' boarding school in Ascot—one of those marvelous countryside red-brick boarding places with a reputation for art and drama. Sarah had no talent for art, but took ballet lessons even though she favored modern dance over it.

Nor was she so bad at this time in her studies. Actually she took six O levels (ordinary level tests): Art, English Language, English Literature, Spoken English, French, and Biology. But of course she starred in sports.

She was popular—a leader. In 1976 her peers and the school staff selected her to be joint "head girl" in her senior year. She was also made netball captain. But being elected head girl was an important achievement for her. Her father congratulated her on her election, assuming that she had proved herself "responsible."

But Sarah had doubts about that. "No," she told him shortly. "I was so uncontrollable they had to make me head girl so I would start behaving!"

It was fun to be alive in those days and pleasant to live in the countryside. But the good life was unfortunately to be short-lived for the Fergusons. When Sarah was thirteen, just beginning her second year at Hurst Lodge, her mother met and fell in love with an Argentinian polo player named Hector Barrantes.

Barrantes was a charismatic outdoor type—a professional sportsman expert in the art of polo playing. Settling easily into the role of a kind of "polo bum," Barrantes made the most of his riding and playing skills and became one of the best players in the world. By keeping himself always in shape and continuing to play, he turned into one of those mercenary poloists—hiring himself out to rich amateurs to bolster up their polo teams during the season.

Sarah's mother thought enough of Barrantes to consider marrying him. And when he asked her, the Fergusons agreed to split up. The divorce was short and sweet—amicably arranged and almost civilized in every way. The former Mrs. Ferguson then became the current Mrs. Barrantes and moved with the Argentinian polo superstar to settle down on her new husband's ranch some five hundred miles south of Buenos Aires. The breakup occurred in 1974.

Sarah and her older sister, Jane, were devastated at this turn of events. For someone without both feet on the ground and a solid personality rooted in independence and self-confidence, it would have been the finishing blow. But the two Ferguson youngsters were able to cope.

"Neither of them were difficult children, and I think the crisis had more effect on Jane than on Sarah," Ferguson later said. "Sarah didn't openly react to her mother's departure, and I don't think it changed the way she was. But of course she was *affected* by it."

Ferguson admitted that "it was a trauma, a bit of a fright, to put it mildly, for everyone. It meant that at that vulnerable age, they didn't have Mother, so Father took over and did his best."

Yet Sarah's friends at Hurst Lodge remembered her as a jokester who used to slip salt in the sugar bowl to bring on howls of misery by the unsuspecting, and even loved to get up illegal midnight snack fests in the dorm.

"She was our gang leader," said Susan Clapham, one of her classmates. "If we were up to something we shouldn't have been, Fergie was usually behind it."

Even at that age, she had become "Fergie" to those who knew her; "Sarah" was almost a forgotten word in her life.

Somehow the three remaining Fergusons survived the divorce and subsequent readjustments in their family life. Not being particularly introverted psychologically, Sarah was able to turn her frustrations and doubts into positive action through her interest in sports. She was never one given to brooding; and this personality trait helped get her over those crucial years.

It is ironic that two fast future friends—the Princess of Wales and the duchess of York—should have suffered such similar teenage traumas in their growing-up years.

Did it strengthen them? Or weaken them? Or simply roll off their backs, like water off a duck's?

"I've never actually heard either the Princess or Sarah talk about the bustup of their parents' marriages," a friend of Sarah's said. "But when the subject of divorce came up once in connection with someone both Sarah and Diana know, there was a definite freeze in the conversation. I don't think either of them likes to be reminded of something that was very hurtful."

Sarah had grown up close to her father. She had taken up his interest in horses and in riding. And she had always been interested in sports like tennis and swimming.

Diana too had been close to her father. But unlike Sarah, she had never been particularly interested in horses or in riding—whether this was caused by the trauma of falling off a pony at an early age or simply by an inability to acclimate herself to the sport is not known and can only be speculated upon.

But both young women were molded in the same kind of crucible of early life: a well-off background, life among the beautiful people, and the nastiness and subsequent disruption of their lives by a divorce.

As for Sarah, she was able to continue in school as a modestly average student and at the same time seemed astonishingly able to fortify herself against any reversals that might come her way in the future. She was a child of adversity—one who used that adversity to strengthen her own defenses. And so was Diana, although her own reactions to the setback at the time seemed a bit less mature than Sarah's.

What happened to Sarah was that she became much closer to her father than she had ever been before—although they were never physically or psychologically apart at any time, of course. But she found herself spending more of her days with him at Smith's Lawn and with the polo crowd that frequented the place.

She found herself rubbing shoulders now with members of the royal family, so that she became a familiar figure among them. It was inevitable that she should come closer now to the crowd in which Lady Diana moved—even though Lady Diana was not in any way a lover of horses or of riding.

Besides, Diana was almost two years younger than Sarah—and was still struggling her way through school. She was *not* having an easy time of it.

IV

LADY DIANA

4

CHARLES AT ALTHORP

AT RIDDLESWORTH HALL DIANA SETTLED DOWN SOMEWHAT. UNLIKE MANY educational institutions, happiness was the first priority at Riddlesworth. There were special consolations offered to any of the students who were lonely. And, of course, Diana—without a mother—was one of them.

Headmistress Elisabeth Ridsdale remembered that Diana was good at games and particularly excelled at swimming—those years in the heated pool at home had not been lost on her—and that she was not as unhappy a girl as might be expected from her tumultuous background.

"I always remember how awfully sweet she was with the very little ones," the headmistress recalled. Diana even won a prize for effort while at school.

But soon Riddlesworth was behind her. At thirteen Diana changed schools and went to West Heath, a boarding school far away from Norfolk near Sevenoaks in Kent.

Kent is southeast of London, Norfolk northeast of it. Diana was now about a hundred miles from home in West Heath.

This school was a much more disciplined place than Riddlesworth. Nevertheless, Diana had no trouble fitting in. There were about 130 boarding students, each of whom was allowed to develop and mature at her own pace. The emphasis of the training was to develop character and build a young woman's confidence in herself.

In these teenage years Diana was not a terribly attractive teenager—nothing like the leggy, slender, and bosomy woman she became in her more mature years. She wore bangs then, and shoulder-length hair. But she was healthy and happy, anyway—and not a person one would call "beautiful" or even "pretty" in the normal sense.

From somewhere she had inherited a very sunny, indestructible disposition and a cheerful, beaming attitude toward life. Her mood swings had moderated, if not entirely disappeared. She did tend to get the giggles, but she was always ready with a helping hand for any chore that needed to be done. Her giggles came from that earlier period of her life.

Of the people at home in Park House, she thought mostly about Prince Andrew. In fact, she let it be known at school that she had a crush on the queen's third child. Other students recalled that Andrew was the one Diana considered as a would-be suitor. Their ages were almost the same.

She never mentioned Charles.

After all, Charles was an old man to her. She and her friends at school occasionally referred to him as old "Jug Ears." But Prince Andrew—ahah! He was only two years older than she was. And he was a very handsome young man—even at that age. Nothing stuffy about him!

Yet by one of those odd coincidences that occur in real life even more frequently than in fiction, it was a photograph of Prince Charles that hung above Diana's bed on the wall of her dormitory room. It had been presented to the school by a newspaper publisher whose granddaughter was one of the pupils. The picture was a blown-up photograph of Charles's investiture as Prince of Wales in 1970.

Diana was good at art. She learned how to dance without any trouble at all. Physical things never seemed to daunt her; only mental things. She never did really take to books or studies of any kind. Again, it was her cheerfulness and upbeat attitude that impressed everyone who knew her.

"She was always helpful and willing," Headmistress Ruth Rudge of West Heath said of her. She always noticed what needed to be done, and then she did it cheerfully. "The dining room staff liked her a lot because she used to help them with laying tables and cleaning up."

West Heath stressed character building by giving its pupils a sound general education to train them to develop their own minds and tastes and realize their duties as citizens. The schedule was an almost Spartan one. At 7:30 A.M., the rising bell would ring. Lessons would continue throughout the entire day until 7:00 P.M. There was even an extra session on Saturday morning, when all the other kids in England were playing.

According to the headmistress, "Diana always did her best with her lessons. She was on time, rising at seven-thirty, eating her boiled egg, and getting on with her work until seven at night."

Diana's recollection of West Heath was that it was "a thoroughly enjoyable time."

In 1975, while she was still at West Heath, vast changes were taking place in the life-style of the Spencer family. The seventh earl of Spencer died that year and "Johnny" inherited the family estate and all its fortune. That meant that all the Spencer entourage at Park House packed up and moved to Althorp, located in Northamptonshire, somewhat to the southwest of Norfolk, but not too far off.

Life on the Spencer estate was a whole new way of living for the Spencers. Althorp was a national treasure, one of those country homes that had once even been open to the public to poke about in. The eighth earl—for that was the title Johnny Spencer now held—found himself with his hands full. All members of the family pitched in to help, but it was a new and rather terrifying experience.

Although Diana had stayed with the rest of the Spencer family after the divorce, she had always kept in touch with her mother. She would spend most of her free time on the Scottish Island of Seil, at the Shand-Kydd's sheep farm. Her time at home, of course, was spent at Althorp, where the newly transplanted Spencers were trying to cope with the management of the enormous estate.

Help was in the wings. After his divorce, Johnny Spencer had met a woman who was going to make a great change in his life-style and in the life-styles of all the Spencers. That someone was a woman named Raine McCorquodale.

Raine was a divorcée. She had married Gerald Legge, a young officer of the guards, when she was only eighteen years of age. Legge soon became the earl of Dartmouth, making Raine technically the countess of Dartmouth. Legge was a friend of Johnny Spencer; both of them had attended Eton together. Their friendship lasted through their school days and on into their maturity.

But that friendship was not to last forever. Mostly the problem had to do with Legge's wife, not anything Legge or Spencer did. It had to do with Raine McCorquodale's genes, her makeup, her personality.

This woman was a fountain of boundless energy, a do-gooder whose welfare work had made her known from one end of England to the other. In her early twenties she had become the youngest member of the Greater London

Council, from the Borough of Westminster. She was a health nut. She had been wary of seasoned food all her life. In that she took after her mother.

There lay the source of Raine's genes. Her mother too was a whirlwind of energy. Born Barbara Cartland, Raine's mother had begun writing romances in her youth. She then married Alexander McCorquodale, and began a career that was to make her one of the most prolific and successful of all modern romance writers.

Quite suddenly, in her thirties—just before World War II—Barbara McCorquodale divorced Raine's father and married his first cousin, Hugh McCorquodale!

Like mother, like daughter. The inherited Cartland energy suffused Raine with the same kind of—well, some might call it *irresponsibility*—when she was in *her* thirties. It was then that she decided to throw over *her* husband, the earl of Dartmouth, and leave him for his old Etonian schoolmate, Johnny Spencer, the new eighth earl of Spencer.

This was in 1976, just after the eighth earl had taken over Althorp and moved his family into the huge ancestral manse. Raine began seeing him from time to time, and things suddenly heated up between them. It was then that she made the decision that paved the way for her own divorce and all that lay beyond that. That decision was to marry the eighth earl. After all, she felt sorry for him—no woman to help him around the house!

Raine even told her mother, Barbara Cartland: "It is just like one of your books, Mummy. I am wildly in love and there is nothing anyone can do about it!"

And so Raine did exactly what she said she was going to do; she left the earl of Dartmouth and moved into Althorp. Her appearance there was not considered a happy event for the Spencer children. On a scale of 1 to 10, it rang in at about minus 5. Because Diana was away at school, she did not suffer the full impact of the vast changes in the family life-style brought about by this new and disturbing addition to the household.

None of the Spencer children liked the way she had won over their father. They could not understand what he saw in her. There were murmurs from friends of the family to the effect that Barbara Cartland's novels always involved virginal heroines—but that her own life-style and that of her daughter did not quite conform to that same stereotypical pattern.

The earl of Dartmouth and the earl of Spencer forgot their early friendship on the playing field of Eton and struck out at one another fiercely and angrily. In a nasty divorce action, the earl of Dartmouth accused the earl of Spencer. The two men argued it out in court. One accused the other of adultery; the charges made all the gossip columns and increased Fleet Street's circulation for a few days at least. It was once again a rerun of the early troubles when Frances Spencer had thrown over Johnny Spencer for the Australian wallpaper tycoon.

Eventually the judge granted the earl of Dartmouth a decree of divorce because of his wife's adultery "with a man against whom the charge has not been proved."

All this was going on while Diana was away at school. But even worse was in the offing. Within a short two months after the divorce, Diana's father married the daughter of Barbara Cartland. The nuptials were celebrated in a very wee manner, with only two witnesses present. None of the four Spencer children were in attendance. Not even Barbara Cartland was there to take notes for a new novel. When it was over, Raine telephoned her mother to tell her the good news.

The first few months after the marriage were stormy ones at Althorp. An undeclared feud between the new bride and the Spencer entourage—including even the house staff—raged. Raine complained to her mother:

"They won't accept me. Whatever I do is wrong. I just want us to be one close family."

Raine's boundless energy was taking its toll. The story got around that she threw out a number of old family retainers who had been at Althorp for years with the seventh earl. She once again opened the house to the public as it had been open before, offering guided tours through the rooms. Under Johnny's supervision, she started up a souvenir shop in the stables, where trinkets and costume jewelry and china could be purchased, with the coat of arms of the Spencer clan on it. To take care of visitors, a tea shop opened up with a kind of fast-food air about it—a sort of McSpencer's of the Northants.

The Spencer children hated it. Others outside the family sometimes revealed an inherent mistrust of Raine, now the countess of Spencer. At one Northamptonshire dinner table the host sat in silence next to her all during the first course of dinner as she continued to prattle on in her breathless nonstop manner. Suddenly he turned to her and inquired:

"What did you say your name was? Storm?"

"No, Raine," said the countess, somewhat deflated.

"Yes," the host said in that plummy British upperclass throwaway tone. "I *knew* it had something to do with bad weather."

The pressure began to tell on Diana's father. In 1978 he suffered a massive brain hemorrhage and was rushed to Northampton Hospital. The doctors there told Raine that he would be lucky to survive the night.

Now Raine McCorquodale Spencer's boundless store of energy and determination became channeled into one plan of action. She would not let him die. Immediately she chartered a private ambulance to drive him the seventy miles to a London brain clinic.

For hours she sat by him, at his bedside, talking to him and almost physically pulling him back to life again. When one doctor failed to live up to her expectations, she fired him and hired another. She even moved him from one hospital to another to get what she considered would be better treatment.

He remained in a coma for days, but Raine continued to nag at him, willing him to reach out and grasp hold of life once again. From that small beginning, he did bring himself back to life—mostly because of Raine's undying confidence in his ability to defy death.

Nevertheless, it was a long, agonizing recuperation, helped along step-by-step by Raine's unflagging devotion and presence. Without her, he certainly would have died.

By the autumn of 1979, he was cured, the only indication that he had been gravely ill, a slight hesitation in his speech and some blurring of his voice. The earl and countess of Spencer celebrated with a service of thanksgiving in Northamptonshire.

Raine's determination and unhesitating dedication to her new husband, the miracle she had worked for his recovery, was not lost on the dissident Spencer children. One by one, each came to respect their stepmother for what she had done to save their father's life.

It was in 1977, during the period when the Spencers were involved in their internal differences over Raine's accession as mother of the family, that Diana turned sixteen and finished at West Heath without any particular academic success to record.

No one would ever claim that she had blossomed as a scholar at school. She came through with what was charitably called a "middling result" on her O levels. She was not a fool, but she certainly succeeded better at outdoor games than classroom recitations. Her school reports—kept secret from inquiring journalists later—showed that she really had no inclination toward the rigors of a university career. She did win a prize for "service"—an interesting award in view of her later marriage to Prince Charles, whose family motto is *Ich Dien* (I serve).

One teacher remembered her as being "kind and carefree, always the first to offer a smile."

And so when she was through at West Heath, her father told her to forget anything complicated like four years of university study. He said that she could go where she liked—to any finishing school of her desire.

It was at this point that Diana's entire life changed. It so happened that just at the time Diana was trying to figure out what to do with the rest of her life after having finally got out of West Heath Academy there was a hunting party at Althorp. To it came a number of royals, including Charles Philip Arthur George Windsor, or Mountbatten-Windsor—otherwise known as Prince Charles.

Diana found Charles gazing at her with a slight look of puzzlement on his face. But when she came up to talk to him, he knew who she was. He remembered her from the heated pool that he had liked so much at Sandringham–Park House. And they chatted a bit.

For the record, no romance burst into instant flame. Nothing happened at all except that they laughed and talked for a few moments before the hunting horns sounded and Charles took off with the rest. Diana remained on the sidelines, watching some and simply chatting with friends the rest of the time.

Actually, Charles was much more interested in Diana's older sister Sarah—the one who always made Diana laugh—than he was in Diana. What happened directly after the brief encounter between Lady Diana and Prince Charles at Althorp was quite simply that Prince Charles invited Lady Sarah to join him at Klosters in the Swiss Alps for a sojourn of skiing in the prince's picturesque schloss.

But that was to happen later.

It was several months before Diana saw Charles again. As nearly as either of them could remember it, that second meeting occurred at the queen's estate at Sandringham.

Sandringham House, located in Norfolk, England, very near the chilly English Channel, serves still as a favorite residence for the royal family during the winter, in spite of the biting and nasty icy winds that blow in off the North Sea. There the queen and her family enjoy the frequent shooting parties and the riding, as well as afternoon walks and comfortable evenings in front of the roaring log fires.

Diana visited Sandringham that winter on the queen's invitation, in a way more or less celebrating a kind of homecoming herself—to the Park House area, of course. There was a large crowd of people at the royal estate that weekend, but Diana did manage to seek out Prince Charles. She talked to him at some length. She realized that he found himself attracted to her; she was attracted to him, too.

Throwing all caution to the winds, she finally persuaded him to try out a new tap-dancing step she said she had learned. Charles obliged out on the concrete terrace of the mansion, to the amusement of much of the crowd around him. Everyone knew Charles simply didn't indulge in that kind of horseplay.

Charles had fun. Never one to shy away from personal contacts with others—even though he was by nature shy and introspective—he found Diana's ebullience and insouciance irresistible. As for the dance step, it ended in absolute disaster, but the disaster had an element of hilarity in it. They both wound up roaring with laughter at the result.

"He thought she was adorable," one friend of the family recalled. "It was rather like being given a puppy, full of vitality and terribly sweet." The cuddly puppy was, of course, Lady Diana.

Although they talked and laughed and spent some time

together, there was once again no leaping of flame to indicate that a royal romance had been touched off.

Diana talked about her future. She was at a crossroads in her life. She wanted to enroll in a more advanced level of school—but she knew she was no scholar at all. She was thinking, she told him, of going to an exclusive finishing school in Switzerland. Called the Institut Alpin Videmanette, in Rougemont, it carried on the tradition that finishing schools in Switzerland have always cultivated.

In the end, whether Charles concurred, or did not concur, she made the move, and enrolled that winter shortly after her tap-dancing lesson to Charles. At the Institut, Diana concentrated on learning social poise and grace, and also on improving her skiing techniques. She had a fair grasp of French from her days at West Heath, and tried to improve it in Rougemont. Along with the courses in the social graces, she took classes in dressmaking and cooking—mainly French or Swiss in style. But she had made up her mind about one thing. She wanted to spend her time in some career where she could work with children.

Actually, Diana's heart was not yet in her studies. Switzerland was interesting, but it wasn't home. She suffered bouts of homesickness and finally dropped out after a few months and returned to Althorp early in 1978. A family council was held to try to determine what to do with Diana.

The obvious thing was to "come out" in London, that is, be introduced to society as a debutante. The average debut of the young upper-class woman in English society resembles the American system as practiced in New York City, involving an expensive series of parties, afternoon teas, and dances. The typical American "deb" is usually rich and becomes a debutante to establish herself as an acceptable young woman in the marriage mart.

Slightly different, England's system is traditionally a

matter of involved levels of snobbery and one-upmanship that frequently make people enemies for life. Diana Spencer certainly was eligible to be presented as a legitimate member of a very high social order. Even though it was tempting to think of the various advantages of such a debut, Diana eventually decided against it. In that decision she followed the lead of her sister Sarah, who had opted not to be introduced into society in this Victorian kind of fashion.

Even if Sarah had become a debutante, it is doubtful that Diana would have decided to follow suit. She wanted freedom, not only from the strictures of school life, but from those of social status as well. She did have enough credits in her brief school career to get a job teaching younger children of kindergarten age; she decided that she would like to try out her wings in this kind of thing.

After a brief family consultation at which Diana issued her ultimatum against the trappings and tradition of a debut into society, her father decided to go along with her wishes and let her get a job if she wished. He saw no reason—nor did she—to keep up with her studies. She was intelligent, but she was not an intellectual. She thought she would do better by going out into the world and working like most of the young women her age.

With about $200,000, Diana's father purchased for her an apartment in a building overlooking Old Brompton Road in London's Earl's Court, not far from Knightsbridge. The apartment was in an extensive line of buildings called Coleherne Court, dating back to 1901 and 1902, constructed on the former site of Coleherne House and Hereford House. Exclusive and built adjoining a beautiful garden, 60 Coleherne Court proved to be the perfect choice of an apartment in the city for Diana.

The rooms were too large for her to manage herself. She gathered together some friends of her own age and status, starting with Virginia Pitman, whom she had met at West Heath in Kent while she was in school, and then adding Ann Bolton and Carolyn Pride. Ann was a secretary, the daughter of a brigadier general. Carolyn was pursuing a career in music. Virginia had a job mending china.

Although the three of them were career girls pretty much in the mode of the 1970s and 1980s, they were strictly well-educated young ladies from the cream of the English upper classes—not just a group of stenos and typists from the ubiquitous middle classes. Make no mistake about that!

Diana settled in at Coleherne Court, almost immediately landing a job as a part-time cook. She made about $5.25 a serving by cooking for dinner parties. That work didn't last long; besides, it was a lot of labor for very little pay. Diana then got a job working as a nanny for a baby-sitting agency. There she made less than $4.00 an hour. Finally a friend suggested that she get a job teaching young children for a few days a week in Pimlico at the Young England Kindergarten in St. George's Square. There she became a kindergarten assistant, making about $4.00 an hour. But she loved that work and stayed there.

She was maturing quietly into a singularly attractive, poised young woman—quite a step up from the giggly schoolgirl she had been; but her high spirits did not subside at all. She found herself dating various men who were interested in her. It was at this point that she renewed her acquaintance with Sarah Ferguson, whom she had met some time before around the races at Ascot.

Although she liked to go out to dinner at places like the Poule au Pot on Ebury Street, in Victoria, where she would meet groups of young people her age, she did not like to "do the town" in the manner of many of her peers. Discotheques and swinging parties were not actually her style. She was in no way subdued, but she did tend to keep to herself.

Males of all shapes and kinds constantly were in pursuit of her. "Chaps would meet Diana and fall instantly in love," one of her friends said. "Many tried to win her, sending flowers and begging for a date, but she always politely declined."

Most of her dates were one-time things. She did not want involvement. Her friendships were purely platonic; she made that evident to everyone she dated. In a setting like swinging London, that was unusual in itself. But Diana was growing up. Although she appeared unsophisticated and schoolgirlish, she was wise and understanding. But, at the same time, she was quick-witted, warm, and reliable.

She was also very attractive. Long-legged, she stood at least five feet ten inches tall. She was solidly built, but extremely shapely. She had the kind of no-nonsense body dreamed of by the too slender and the too fat. Her complexion was that peaches-and-cream texture reserved exclusively for English women. Her hair was light and thick—but she did touch it up a bit to give more glow to its mousy look.

She chose her friends with great care, selecting a kind of retinue of trustworthy attendants. She was faithful to them, and they to her.

During her first years of freedom, she learned how to drive a car. Almost immediately, she perfected a kind of racetrack driving style, not exactly reckless, but certainly unrestrained. She became involved in three accidents in her Renault during the first months of her driving, none of them, luckily, serious.

As for Diana's relationship with Charles. . . ?

Nothing yet.

V

SARAH FERGUSON

5

A SLOANE RANGER

THE AFFINITY OF THE FERGUSONS TO SMITH'S LAWN AND THE POLO CROWD caused an upturn in the life of Sarah's older sister, Jane. It was there that Jane Ferguson met Alex Makim, a polo player from Australia. After a brief but effective courtship, the two were engaged to be married.

Sarah, who was sixteen years old, was to be chief bridesmaid for her sister at the wedding. Although the occasion was exciting and upbeat, the aftermath was a bit sad for the two remaining Fergusons—Ronald and Sarah—because Jane almost immediately moved to the northern part of New South Wales in Australia to set up a household with her new husband on his remotely located ranch.

Shortly after that, however, things picked up for the family. Major Ferguson had met a pleasant young woman named Susan Deptford, the daughter of a very well-to-do farmer in Norfolk, in whom he took a more than passing interest—in spite of the fact, so it seems, that her name, like his first wife's, was Susan. When he proposed, she accepted him, and the two were married in 1976.

Now Sarah's life once again paralleled Lady Diana's. Just as Diana was the only one of the four Spencer children to get on well with her stepmother, Sarah took to her stepmother in an outgoing, cheerful, and open-armed fashion—quite like a woman able to take things for the best even though they might not be just quite that.

There was no holding back with her stepmother, either. She was grateful for Sarah's acceptance of her.

"It says much for Fergie's big heart," she once said, "that she welcomed me with great enthusiasm as her stepmother. She was very close to her real mother, but she went out of her way to make me feel welcome."

Incidentally, in the years to follow, Sarah's stepmother would give birth to three children—Andrew, Alice, and Eliza—so that in the end the Ferguson family would be composed of five offspring rather than just two.

By the time of her father's remarriage, Sarah was in her last years at Hurst Lodge, trying to figure out what to do next. Unlike Diana, she was a commoner, and needed either to get a job or to get a husband. Perhaps both. And so she took the most logical course to get either or both.

After graduation from Hurst Lodge—she was sixteen at the time—she enrolled at Queen's Secretarial College in London. It seemed the sort of thing one should do.

She did not find it easy to achieve the aptitude with either a typewriter or a pencil to be a good secretary. Nor was she very good at figures. Shorthand? Forget it. In fact, she and a newly found friend, Charlotte Eden—she was the daughter of a Conservative junior minister, Sir John Eden—sat in the back row and pretended to work hard.

The back row was well chosen. Not only were they seated there physically, but they were, as well, by the ratings, in the back row of the class too.

In the confidential school records Sarah Ferguson was described as "bright" and "bouncy." However, she was also noted as "a bit slapdash." The report continued: "But has initiative and personality which she will well use to her advantage when she gets older." And ended with a keynote point: "Accepts responsibility happily."

She was definitely a slow starter. Yet, in spite of this, her character seemed to be forming for the better. Always good at sports, a competitive and imaginative player, she now combined physical skills with psychological charm and charisma. None of the scars of her teenage woes seemed visible. She had managed to turn her life force outward rather than inward—and she was able to present a pleasant, likable, and happy face to the world.

This was the picture that she presented to the royal family—for, of course, because her father was Prince Charles's polo manager, the royals were in constant attendance at Smith's Lawn and Ascot and wherever the polo matches were held. In fact, it was said later that the queen and the rest of the royal family had always liked Sarah. Yet because of her smiling countenance and her athletic build, they tended to think of her as some kind of tomboy—and, quite likely, as just part of the general scenery.

It might be said that they thought of her that way because of a natural tendency to link a daughter with a father; like father, like daughter. That is, a member of the sporting set really, rather than of the titled aristocracy. And that, of course, was indeed true.

For years Sarah had seen and talked to Prince Andrew. He considered her a good friend, because of her proximity to the stables and to the polo fields. But *because* of her link with polo and sports, Andrew never seriously considered her in any romantic light at all. Which was odd in a way, because he considered almost *all things* female in a romantic light from the moment he laid eyes on them.

With Sarah, *that* kind of thing was to come later.

And in a most devious and indirect manner.

In spite of her natural inability to take shorthand, to type, and to handle figures, Sarah made the best of her time at secretarial school, learning to work laboriously at a typewriter, learning to draw up letters in a fairly adequate manner, and discovering how to do all the things that make an office run smoothly. And she made friends everywhere because that was her way.

Soon enough the two-year course at Queen's Secretarial College was over, and the future loomed up, challenging and exciting. What to do? Well—

Sarah had an idea. What she wanted to do was to visit her mother. But her mother was then living on that ranch in Argentina with Hector Barrantes, Sarah's stepfather. How to get down there to see her? A trip alone simply was not feasible. But with a friend?

And so it was she dragooned her best friend at the secretarial school, Charlotte Eden, into planning a long-distance trip to South America to visit her mother and her stepfather—with whom she really had no quarrel. Her own father was not particularly excited about the proposed journey, but he did not prohibit it. Besides, he had enough on his plate handling his *new* family.

Sarah and Charlotte traveled first to Buenos Aires in South America and visited Señor and Señora Barrantes on the big horse-breeding ranch.

Of course it turned out to be just the thing to do at the time. Sarah renewed her acquaintance with her mother and enjoyed the salubrious surroundings of the huge ranch.

"We don't see each other as often as we would like," her mother said at the time, "but the mother-daughter bond is very tight indeed."

It was during this visit with her mother that Sarah met someone who would play a part in her later life. His name was Kim Smith-Bingham. He was an "Old Etonian" spending a few weeks down in Argentina to celebrate the completion of his own schooling. But at the time he and Sarah Ferguson simply met one another and spent a few pleasant hours together.

About this time, Sarah and Charlotte had another of those grand ideas: they were going to make a *fabulous* tour through the whole of the New World of South America—a trip not by plane but by bus!

Any way you looked at it, it was an adventure! First they bussed down to Rio de Janeiro, traveling along bumpy country roads—most of them completely unpaved—with dozens of backcountry peasants and farmers carrying portable livestock like chickens and birds along with them right in the bus!

Then they journeyed all over the country, taking an extended four months to see all the main points of interest, including villages, towns, cities, jungles, plains, mountains, and rivers. Up and down, across, backward and forward, and straight ahead again.

At the end of the trip, they made their way up to the United States for a short visit—without much of any money left—before returning to England.

Exhausted, but fulfilled after a fashion, the two of them split up to look for jobs. Sarah realized she would have to live in London in order to find work, and so she took an elegantly furnished, two-bedroom apartment in a small house in Clapham, a section of South London.

Quite like Diana, she shared this digs. Her roommate was Carolyn Beckwith-Smith, a cousin of Anne Beckwith-Smith, who was soon to be the Princess of Wales's number one lady-in-waiting and close confidante.

Jobs were not easy to come by, but Sarah worked first as an "office temporary" for an agency that was engaged in leasing apartments in Knightsbridge. It was owned by Neil Durden-Smith, the husband of a TV broadcaster named Judith Chalmers. Durden-Smith was also a polo commentator—and it was through this connection that Sarah got the job at a time when jobs were difficult to come by.

Her own particular boss was a man named Peter Cunard. He always remembered Sarah Ferguson for one particular reason.

"She incurred my wrath," he admitted later, "by spending a great deal of time on the phone dealing with her social life, fixing up dinners and nights out." Even so, he admitted that "she was totally reliable, thrived on responsibility, and was totally professional."

But it was only temporary work. Shortly after leaving it, Sarah took on a short-term assignment as a kind of secretary and personal assistant at a Kensington video company. Like the first job, that one didn't last long either.

She then moved to a trendy Covent Garden art gallery, where she kept the books and helped out with the visitors. Her outgoing personality made her well liked by her employers and by the customers as well. She was restless, of course. She was not going to last long there, either.

According to people who knew her, she continued to put her social life well above her business life. She loved to have dinner with friends and go dancing afterward. Annabel's was one of her favorite night spots.

Nevertheless, she visited all the posh discos popular with the lively and artistic crowd, and haunted the boîtes of the rich and the famous—the so-called beautiful people. She liked to have lunches with friends, spending a great deal of time over them. This was the kind of thing that did not endear her to her employers, particularly her immediate bosses who had to exert control over her straying ways.

Pretty soon she got a job in a small public relations firm, doing odd bits of chores and thoroughly enjoying herself. In spite of the fun there, she quit this job and got another with a rival public relations outfit, still looking around for more "meaningful" work.

Eventually she would land a job as "directrice" of a London graphic arts publishing company called BCK—"directrice" evidently because the firm had its main headquarters in Geneva, Switzerland. But that would be later on.

Now there was much more going on. Business and working was one thing—but the *big* thing was to meet all the people who were anybody in town. And, of course, all the important people lived within shouting distance of one another—usually around the up-and-coming area called Sloane Square.

Sloane Square?

Sloane Square is located in West London—any glance at an underground map of the city will show the Sloane stop—and is the established stamping grounds of most of the upwardly mobile and well-connected young professionals in England. These might be considered Britishized versions of America's so-called yuppies—young upwardly mobile, etc. In addition to these young people's professional pursuits, they also loved to party and to shop around the fashionable Sloane Square area.

And it was here that Sarah immediately found herself in demand among the young males and females of the "set"—called, by the media and those in the know, "Sloane Rangers." In short, she became one of the most prominent of the Sloane Rangers during her young formative years and attracted, with her bouncy ebullient style, an endless procession of male admirers.

In her healthy, outgoing way, Sarah Ferguson managed to survive all the affairs she was subjected to, all the rejections that came her way, all the breakups that were part of the love game. It was here in this exciting, upwardly mobile milieu that she renewed her earlier acquaintance with Lady Diana Spencer, who was, exactly like Sarah was, working as a professional woman—in Diana's case as a "teacher" of young children—in London after her school years.

Of course the two of them had known each other since childhood, as has been stressed, but it was not until they were both more or less doing the same thing among the same friends that they found they were much more like each other than they had ever before realized. They found that they got along very well and exchanged confidences whenever they could.

Sarah's bouncy good spirits were the spark that lit up Diana's own sense of humor—and the two of them found that they now seemed to enjoy each other's company much more than in their early years. With less than two years of age separating them they were totally compatible.

Interestingly enough, Diana found that her friendship with Sarah presented no problems at all with her own family. And, when push came to shove—when quite suddenly and astonishingly Lady Diana Spencer became engaged to Prince Charles—the royal family had no objections to her friendship with Sarah, either.

But that would come later.

Meanwhile, as a Sloane Ranger, Sarah Ferguson settled down into the role of an upwardly mobile professional woman in London—and made the most of it in every way that she could.

As for Diana . . .

She was just about to meet The Man in Her Life.

VI

LADY DIANA

6

THE LADY MEETS THE PRESS

PRINCE CHARLES WAS MOVING QUICKLY ABOUT THE WORLD, IN BOTH A political as well as social sense. Diana's sister Sarah seemed quite well entrenched with the Prince of Wales. In fact, their friendship was becoming something for the gossip columnists on Fleet Street to feed on.

"It was quite charming to see the two of them together," a weekend guest at the Spencer home gushed in the *Daily Express*. "They were obviously very fond of one another. One morning Charles was waiting for Sarah at the bottom of the stairs and he greeted her with a kiss. Sarah is quite besotted with Charles."

Diana read that note with some chagrin. And Sarah managed to get into print quite a bit during that period. Later, in an interview in *Women's Own*, she came right out and denied any implication of a romance with the Prince of Wales.

"Our relationship," she insisted, "is strictly platonic. I think of him as the big brother I never had."

She continued to give out words of wisdom to anyone with a pencil and pad and time to take notes. In the *London Sun* she was quoted as saying: "I am very fond of the Prince. He makes me laugh a lot. I enjoy being with him. I adore his love of horses."

She told reporters that Charles made his own dates, contradicting what others said about his having to make them through third parties. Oh, she went on, he might pick up his date in his Aston Martin or invite her to meet him at one of the royal residences. She said that it wasn't always too easy to go on a weekend date at Windsor Castle with him: it involved a suitcase full of clothes.

A typical ensemble, she said, might require a riding habit in the morning, a day dress for lunch, a skirt for tea, and a long dress for dinner. And she revealed that the Prince of Wales should always be addressed as "sir," until, as might happen, he would ask you to call him "Charles."

Also, she pointed out that whenever Charles took someone out to a club or restaurant, one of his detectives was always waiting outside, or hanging around somewhere.

But then came the blockbuster statement, appearing in *Women's Own:* "There is no chance of my marrying him. I'm not in love with him. And I wouldn't marry anyone I didn't love whether he were the dustman or the King of England. If he asked me, I would turn him down."

That statement, in point of fact, was the end of Sarah Spencer's "affair" with Prince Charles. Shortly after that came out in print, she began appearing with him less and less. In a short time Sarah was indeed married to Neil McCorquodale, and moved to Northamptonshire with her new husband to be a gentlewoman farmer married to a gentleman farmer. And it is to be noted that she married into the family of Raine McCorquodale, her stepmother and at one time one of her implacable enemies.

Other women began taking up Charles's time. Diana managed to see him, at a distance, once or twice. In 1978, Diana's other sister, Jane Spencer, married Robert Fellowes, assistant private secretary to the queen since the Jubilee Year of 1977. Fellowes was the son of Sir William Fellowes, for many years land agent at Sandringham. Diana acted as her sister's bridesmaid. Lady Jane had been fashion assistant at the English *Vogue* until her marriage. The couple was married at the Guard's Chapel, London, in April.

A year later, in the summer, Diana saw Charles again when she was invited along with a large party of other guests aboard the Royal Yacht *Britannia* for the Cowes Regatta held just off the Isle of Wight. Between the Isle of Wight and the coast of Hampshire lies The Solent, a narrow strait of icy-cold water. Sailing on a windsurfer out of Cowes on The Solent, Charles found himself quite suddenly and unceremoniously dumped into the water. Diana had grabbed the mast in a fit of fun and tipped it over.

Charles was not amused—at first. But when he realized who had done him in, and how surprised he had been at being ducked, he saw the humor of it and realized that it was quite a special woman who would risk His Princely Displeasure by taking such a chance. However, he very carefully did not let her know how he really felt; she could almost *feel* the icy displeasure with which he studied her. Yet his impression of her was solidifying in his mind.

The next time she saw Prince Charles was at the home of the duke of Richmond in 1980 when the Goodwood House Race Meeting was held. Diana was astonished when Charles came over to her at the ball held during the gala weekend and asked her to dance. They waltzed together but no one seemed to take much notice of it.

In July, Diana became an aunt when her sister Lady Jane had her first baby. The Felloweses were following the royal party at the time, and the baby was born at Balmoral. The Scottish castle is the usual retreat for the royal family during the summer months. Located some five hundred miles away from London in the highlands of Scotland a good nine hundred feet above sea level, the castle was acquired by the crown during Queen Victoria's reign when the property, formerly belonging to the Farqueharsons of Inverey, was sold to Sir Robert Gordon, whose trustees then sold it to Victoria's husband, Albert.

Built of granite in the Scots baronial style familiar to any reader of Sir Walter Scott, the castle has an eastern tower a hundred feet high commanding a spectacular view of Ballochbuie and Braemar to the west, Glen Gairn to the north, Lochnagar and the beautiful valley of the Dee to the south.

The royal family spends a great deal of time at Balmoral in the fall, shooting grouse, fishing for salmon, and attending the regular events associated with the castle, the most important of which is the Highland Games at Braemar.

Helping out her sister with her new baby took up little of Diana's time, although she enjoyed every minute of it. For some reason the Prince of Wales chose not to think about Diana in the romantic setting of the ball at the duke of Richmond's, but instead talked about the ducking she had given him in The Solent. Oddly enough, Charles had mellowed over the months since that ignominious soaking; he reminded Diana of the incident with a twinkle of the royal eye.

Diana hardly knew what to say; she could never anticipate how people would react to her impish pranks. She had lost as many old friends through her ways as she had won new converts. Apparently Charles was going to be a convert. Their amusement and high good humor spilled over onto others at Balmoral during those warm summer days in the wilds of the Highlands.

The courtship that did not exist seemed to be taking on an almost palpable shape.

Charles's high spirits and good humor were not lost on Queen Elizabeth. Later on, when she was making up the early fall list of guests at Balmoral, Charles himself leaned over her shoulder and suggested that Diana Spencer might be a good candidate for the list. The queen nodded sagely. Many of Charles's dates had been invited to Balmoral during other Septembers: the list was almost as long as the royal arm. She dutifully wrote down the name and forgot about it.

And so it was that on September 13, barely two months after Diana's trip to Balmoral to act as baby-sitter for her sister, the phone rang in Diana's Coleherne Court apartment and was answered by Virginia Pitman, Diana's friend from West Heath. She turned to find Diana.

"It's for you. Some man says he's from Buckingham Palace. Obviously it's a joke."

Diana took the telephone and listened. When she hung up she turned to Virginia, who had now been joined by Ann Bolton and Carolyn Pride.

"I'm going to Balmoral for the weekend." She then explained that she was to be the guest of the queen—on her own, not as Lady Jane's surrogate nanny.

There were shrieks of excitement from the three roommates, who knew how Charles's mind worked and who knew what those September invitations *really* meant. The group then got down to some high-level gossip and speculation.

Two days later Diana drove out to Heathrow, the biggest international airport in the world, and there lined up to board the British Airways flight to Aberdeen, Scotland. She was surveyed by a small group of rather seedily dressed men standing by with papers and notes in their hands. This was the skeleton crew of Fleet Street, checking out the manifest bound for Aberdeen. Keeping a journalistic eye on Prince Charles and his romances was a never-ending vigil for them.

Charles-watchers had pursued him for the past twenty years, ever since he had left the royal nest to begin school. His comings and goings were always news, particularly when he was squiring about a new woman. He had gone through a long list of glamorous pesonalities over the years. He was getting now to an age when he was expected to settle down. Yet where was Miss Right? Would he be another Edward VIII—almost forty years old when he married? And—after all—look who Edward had married! And study the consequences!

The press knew where Charles was at all times; it was all written down in the royal schedule. He would be at Balmoral for the weekend. But who would be with him? There were several women he had been dating through the year, but the list had dwindled down to an almost precious few. These names were known to the Fleet Street gang, and to the readers of the tabloids. The watch was kept on the plane to Aberdeen, because it was the obvious way to get to Balmoral by air from London. From the airport there, you simply drove west along A-93 by the River Dee to Banchory, Aboyne, Ballater, and on to the Castle of Balmoral. Anyone boarding a flight to Aberdeen *might* be headed for Balmoral.

Two scribes and three photographers from Fleet Street simply passed up Diana. The manifest had a much more interesting name than D. Spencer; it was D. Sheffield the reporters were interested in. Davina Sheffield had been one of Charles's dates for some time now. D. Spencer was a nobody.

And so she boarded the plane, a Trident jet, without incident. Two hours later she was in Aberdeen. Dyce, the Aberdeen airport, was bustling. Offshore oil drilling in the North Sea had brought the whole area alive with excitement and the smell of big money. Only 514 miles away from Heathrow, it was like a different country.

A man in a green waterproof anorak and tweed suit sauntered over to Diana Spencer at the airport. A well-spoken, quiet, and unassuming young man in his twenties, he was fully armed with a loaded .38 caliber revolver in a leather holster kept well out of sight. Handpicked by Scotland Yard, he was one of two dozen Royal Detectives selected to protect the top ten members of the British royal family.

Since the assassination the previous year of Prince Charles's great-uncle "Dickie"—Lord Louis Mountbatten—by terrorists indirectly connected with the Irish Republican Army, even guests at Balmoral were guarded as they had never been before.

Diana had been told that she would be met there. Quite soon the two were in a green Range Rover parked beside the terminal building. A Range Rover is a jeep-style Landrover. In it they drove westward through the forest of Glentanar until they came finally to the market town of Ballater, then turned off to the entrance to the castle. The driver took Diana to the main door of the turreted building and deposited her there.

It was an exclusive dinner: Queen Elizabeth, Prince Philip, the Queen Mother, Prince Charles, Prince Edward, and Diana. Prince Andrew was away at school. Soon enough Prince Charles, who was seated directly opposite Diana, began talking about the delights of fishing in the River Dee. And he wondered if Diana might not like to accompany him on a fishing expedition the next morning.

She would. And at an early hour the two of them were in the green Range Rover, with Prince Charles's favorite golden Labrador retriever, Harvey, in the backseat. A set of the prince's fishing rods was attached to a rack on the side of the car.

Near a bend in the River Dee about five miles from the

castle, he pulled over and took Diana down to the side of the river. They looked out over the water where it boiled down over hundreds of rocks, making a perfect place in an icy-clear pool to land a good salmon. It was a site, Charles told Diana, favored by the Queen Mother—Charles's grandmother, the wife of King George VI. Even at eighty, she still visited the Dee to indulge in her favorite outdoor sport.

It was brutally chilly. No one else seemed to be outdoors at all. They moved into the open and Charles began casting his line into the water. It was the first time the two of them had ever been really alone, with no one else around. They talked and laughed easily about many things. Diana noticed that occasionally Charles would stop and look across the River Dee to the other bank.

The royal property reached the riverside, but did not extend over to the opposite embankment. Other anglers frequented the far side, at least those rich enough to afford the extremely costly fishing permits. None were in sight that morning. Nothing marred the early moment of the couple in the heady solitude of the Scottish countryside.

Diana and Charles began to share the kind of empathy that can come to a person who suddenly finds someone else of an understanding nature, who is "in tune," more or less, with oneself. They relived some early years when they had barely known one another—when the age gap of twelve years had been all but unbridgeable. They relived recent meetings during which they had spoken a bit to each other—but not much.

Suddenly they found that they were getting to know one another a lot better than they had imagined they might. And there was no longer a platonic friendship involved; there seemed to be something far deeper growing between them. Something that might indeed be permanent.

Charles, wearing thigh-deep waders, was in the water,

and Diana was seated on a bank beside a tree, when suddenly Charles turned red in the face and strode angrily out of the water and up the bank to the Range Rover. He ripped a pair of binoculars from the back of the car and made his way down to the bank where Diana stood in the woods. He focused the glasses on the opposite bank where he could see a man in the trees about thirty yards up from the river.

He handed the glasses grimly to Diana. She looked too. She saw a man with a camera, focusing what appeared to be a long-range lens at the two of them. She handed the glasses back to Charles and quickly turned her back on the photographer. She pulled a compact out of her bag and opened it, using its mirror to study the photographer from her now-concealed position.

It was too late.

Ken Lennox had already snapped the picture that would be immortalized in the press of the world. It was the first picture taken of both Prince Charles and Diana Spencer together. It showed Diana bundled up in a coat, thick brown hair covered by a long-billed soft cap, peering out from under the brim toward the hidden cameraman, and Prince Charles, holding a fishing rod on his right shoulder.

"It's all over," Charles grated out, and waved Diana back through the woods. They got in the Range Rover and drove back to the castle, their early-morning fishing outing in ruins.

But if their angling adventure had died, another adventure of a much more fertile and enduring nature had been born.

The seeds of romance that had been planted that morning during those stolen minutes together were embedded in soil that would nourish and sustain them through many more such crises—leading eventually to one of the most celebrated weddings of the twentieth century.

A word about Charles-watching and royalty-ogling. Because there are so few true monarchies left in the world, the British royal family has always been the focus of interest among its own people. Since the fall of most monarchies—or, at best, their decline—the image of the British royal family has risen in value. The media focuses as much on it as it does on, say, the pope, or the president of the United States, or whatever man is occupying the Kremlin.

From his earliest years, Prince Charles had experienced the constant probing of reporters, the clicking of photographers' cameras, the incessant barrage of questions from impertinent journalists. He had grown up in the middle of the goldfish bowl of royalty.

Diana Spencer had not. That incident on the River Dee was her first brush with the phenomenon. Because of the privacy of the royal woods, she was able to get away from the prying eye of the camera with impunity—almost—after her first bout. But, sadly, she would never again be able to avoid the peering eyes of the world from that Saturday in the Balmoral woods to eternity.

By the time she and Charles had driven back to the castle, the word was out to the world. When Charles accompanied the queen and Prince Philip to the Highland Games that same afternoon at nearby Braemar, the ranks of Fleet Street reporters and photographers had swelled astonishingly, everyone hoping to get a glimpse of the early-morning angler in the woods.

But they had to be satisfied with shots of Charles in his ceremonial tartan kilt and tweed jacket. He had learned how to parry questions and say nothing in such a way that it could not be twisted into something rich and strange.

Diana, quite intelligently, had stayed back at the castle in seclusion from the public. On Sunday night she was driven back to Dyce Airport where she made the flight to Heathrow. By then the members of the press knew who she was and had begun digging up as many of the few known facts about her as they could. The digging had not yet produced much usable material, and the research continued on into the next morning—which was Monday.

Meanwhile, at the Coleherne Court apartment, Diana was on the telephone to Charles at Balmoral shortly before midnight—he had called her for a talk after she arrived from Heathrow—and the two were discussing an upcoming date when Charles wanted her to be with him in Scotland later in the month.

By now Diana knew that things were beginning to heat up. She realized that she was being swept up into a vortex of excitement and drama that would carry her along inevitably, no matter what happened. She had a hint of how it would be, but the hint was nothing like the reality of what was actually to happen.

First of all she knew she must swear her roommates to silence. They agreed not to say anything about the romance, and listened to Diana's story of what had happened on the weekend in Scotland with bated breath. True to their word, not one of them leaked any secrets from that moment on.

On Monday morning Diana drove across town through Chelsea and on to Pimlico where she worked—Pimlico is the area just south of Westminster Abbey and Parliament and on the Thames, not far from Victoria Station—and parked her car in peace and quiet. Her day was a normal one, quite the same as it had been since she had begun working with her fifty charges at the school.

By tea time, when she drove back to Coleherne Court, the researchers and checkers had found out almost all they could about her. There was a photographer waiting to snap her when she got out of her car. That was just a harbinger of what was to come.

Nigel Dempster, whose *Daily Mail* "Diary" was England's nearest thing to the final word on the royal family's doings, wrote a column on September 17 on Lady Diana Spencer.

"Has Charles found his future bride?" he asked rhetorically. The answer, according to Dempster, was that he had indeed. The new romance, he pointed out, was in the very early stages. Anything could happen, of course, to halt it. Dempster, however, was optimistic—that is, he thought it would work out. The lady was Diana Spencer; accompanying the article was a likeness of the possible bride, unrecognizable in a picture taken of her with her eyes cast down.

On the day after Dempster's Monday column appeared, there were almost a dozen journalists and photographers waiting at the Young England Kindergarten when Diana got to work. And they got a picture that certainly made their day.

It was hot, steamy weather. Diana had worn a cotton gingham skirt that looked cool and fresh. When the photographers posed her with some of her young charges during her lunch break, they snapped picture after picture in the garden under the cherry trees. It was all very English-garden enchantment and old-fashioned landscape serene.

The sun was casting a shadow over the garden from a church in St. George's Square. The photographers could see that it was blotting out their light. They asked Diana to move out of the dark and let the sun light up her fair skin and blond hair from behind.

Unsuspectingly, Diana complied. The paparazzi were trying to get a kind of "halo" effect, with the sun making her hair into a blaze of sparkling light around her face.

She picked up one of the children and walked across the playground out into the light with the sun directly behind her. The photographers began snapping and continued without a word to her. What Diana had forgotten was that because of the heat of the day she had not worn a slip under her skirt, or perhaps she had assumed that the flowery cotton print would effectively screen her legs.

It did not. The sun shining through the cotton skirt from behind revealed a very good pair of legs and chic briefs. The photographs appeared two hours later in the first editions of the London evening papers.

There, emblazoned on all the front pages, were photographs of her posing in the bright autumn sunlight, her legs clearly silhouetted through a see-through skirt. The headlines were Fleet Street's idea of coy fun: DI IS BLUSHING one tittered. Another decided on tongue-in-cheek humor: LADY DIANA'S SLIP.

That she was shapely and young and beautiful was without question. But there was such a thing as propriety, especially when she was rumored to be the latest of Prince Charles's female conquests. Diana was still at school when one of the teachers brought in a copy of an evening paper, with the ink still figuratively wet, to show her.

She took one wide-eyed look, put her hand to her mouth, and turned crimson with embarrassment.

Her coworkers were sympathetic, but they could not ease Diana's panic. She realized that she would have to be a little more circumspect with the press in the future.

Besides—what would Charles say? What, indeed, would the *queen* say? *That* was what was important.

Lady Diana's concern over the publication of the picture of her in her see-through dress grew through the night. The next day the Prince of Wales telephoned her at Coleherne Court. She answered, wondering if it was all over.

After a few words of greeting, he mentioned seeing the photographs in the morning's papers. He told her that he had been shocked. Diana closed her eyes and crossed her fingers, the blood draining from her face.

Shocked, he told her, at first—but then he had decided that it was a rather good joke on her after all. He laughed. Diana could feel relief surging through her like adrenaline. She laughed with him, shaking off the tension that had been building in her for a full day.

That telephone conversation led her into a period that Diana could only call heavenly. During the following weekends, Diana and Charles spent as much time together as they could manage—as much of it as possible out of the public eye.

And that privacy was what made the whole thing difficult—sometimes impossible. The press was now onto her, but it could not follow her *everywhere*. She managed to work out a pattern. She spent her working days, four days a week from nine to three-thirty, in Pimlico at the school. There the paparazzi took pictures of her as much as they dared. Even a photograph of Diana getting out of her car to enter her apartment at Coleherne Court was a scoop that made the front page.

From the beginning of their friendship, Charles determined that he and Diana would never be photographed together. He knew that *togetherness* was the epitome of the photographer's craft. It was the only way Fleet Street could present to the public the fact of their relationship.

When Charles would go on to the Beaufort Hunt in Gloucestershire, Diana would be nearby, waiting for him to return. By telephone calls, by prearranged signals, by any kind of subterfuge, they managed to meet in secret rendezvous sites without the press tumbling in advance.

However, Fleet Street had most assuredly not given up the chase, although things calmed down a bit with only an occasional photograph of Diana in the papers with the obvious captions. Not once did anyone catch Charles and Diana together, although there were several narrow escapes.

The media sensed that Diana was going to be a permanent fixture in Charles's life. And she was kept under constant surveillance. In October she was dressed in a sporty green coat and boots and sat in the grandstand at Ludlow racecourse in Shropshire while on the track Charles raced his newly purchased Irish chaser, Allibar.

Even though Charles's real riding game was polo, and his secret passion was fox hunting, he had decided to qualify as a steeplechase race jockey. He had his own string of six polo ponies. The game was hard-riding and exhilarating, both for players and onlookers. Because it was so strictly a blueblood sport, the general public did not flock to its tournaments or really know much about it.

Since polo was not a commoner's game, and since fox hunting was extremely unpopular with growing groups of demonstrators agitating against it, Charles decided to clean up his act a bit. At least, he could appear in public on a horse in something that did not offend the senses of the populist-inclined or the squeamish.

"You can't have everything you want," Charles once said, "even if you feel it does no harm. People's sensibilities count."

As a substitute for the fox hunt, Charles decided to take up cross-country, or steeplechase, riding. To qualify, he had to make several races. In 1978 he began practicing and preparing to ride as a steeplechase jockey.

Steeplechase riding was different from hunting—there wasn't any fox. Basically, it was a kind of fox hunt over jumps that were as hard and as unexpected as those a hunter had to cope with taking out across country after a fox. It was a tough ride over jumps around a circular field, using up about five or six minutes in extremely rough running and humping competition.

In 1980, Charles had purchased a beautiful, well-groomed, ten-year-old gelding named Allibar which he kept in stables in Landbourn under the care of his race-horse trainer, Nicholas Gaselee. What Charles hoped to do was to take Allibar to the Grand Military Gold Cup race at Sandown Park in March 1981. He had four races to ride before entering the Grand Military.

As Diana watched him driving in Allibar that day to a second-place finish in the three-mile steeplechase, she cheered him on, screaming with excitement as he was narrowly beaten. She never let on that she was there *with* Charles to the members of the press who were keeping their eyes on her. Both had driven to the racetrack in separate cars. When the race was over, Diana made her way by herself to her car, and only later on met him surreptitiously in the evening to celebrate his near victory with champagne and good food at the home of one of Charles's lifelong friends.

Going out together and pretending not to be with one another became a day-to-day game with the two of them.

When Princess Margaret—Charles's aunt—celebrated her fiftieth birthday on November 4 with a big party at the Ritz Hotel, Charles had not one but *two* guests: Diana on one side and—surprise!—Jane Wellesley on the other.

Jane Wellesley had been one of Charles's steady dates for many years, a potential fiancée the press had considered in the running for a long time. Gossips were wondering if Charles had tired of his "new" girlfriend; was he returning to Lady Jane? Or was he simply playing the old shell game, using Lady Jane to take the heat off his *real* love, Diana?

However, once the evening was on, rumors circulated that Charles could hardly keep his eyes off Diana. Only rumors. The paparazzi were unable to get close enough to them to take a shot that bracketed the prince and Lady Diana together.

But the next day's news stories carried speculation and more speculation. In fact, things were heating up for one simple reason. November 14 would be Charles Windsor's thirty-second birthday. Wouldn't his birthday be a perfect time to announce his engagement to his new heart throb?

It was the *Sun* that finally opened up all stops and predicted flatly that Prince Charles would announce his engagement to Diana Spencer during his birthday celebrations. On Sunday, November 9, the prediction appeared in print for the first time. Actually, almost everyone else had been thinking about it; it was only a matter of putting it on record.

And, of course, the *Sun* wanted to be number one with the news.

Immediately scores of photographers descended on Young England Kindergarten to shoot pictures of Diana. Reporters besieged the apartment at Coleherne Court. Telephone calls came in at all hours, with journalists badgering Diana and each of her roommates with questions and suggestions.

But she would not say one way or another. And because of his prediction, Sir Larry Lamb, editor of the *Sun*, became something of a guru on the coming nuptials. There was so much interest generated in Diana that Independent Television's "News at Ten" devoted a major part of one program to her. Appearing on it in the role of devil's advocate, Nigel Dempster stated flatly that the engagement would *not* be announced at the Prince of Wales's birthday party. He offered to wager one thousand pounds with Sir Larry Lamb that nothing would happen on Charles's thirty-second birthday that Friday.

In fact, the next day he doubled his bet, and on the third day, had four thousand pounds (about eight thousand dollars) at stake.

"What will you do if you are proved wrong?" Dempster was asked.

"I shall end it all," he remarked serenely.

Then, to the excitement of the world and to the consternation of Nigel Dempster, on the day before Prince Charles's birthday, Diana Spencer suddenly disappeared.

Absolutely *disappeared* from the face of the earth!

Reporters hastened to Sandringham Castle, where Prince Charles would celebrate his birthday with a party in the heart of the family. Charles was out horseback riding, ready for the hunt. The Fleet Street scribes huddled around waiting for him to return. It was icy cold, with the wind blowing in off the North Sea.

When he did return from the hunt, Charles simply gave them stares and silence when they asked him about Diana. No one could get a glimpse of Diana Spencer. Even from *inside* the Sandringham mansion there was no leak. It was apparent that she was *not* there.

Then where *was* she?

Number Two Fleet Street Surveillance Group stood guard outside the Coleherne Court digs. They telephoned her roommates. Sorry, Diana was not in. Her Renault was parked outside, but she wasn't anywhere nearby. She proved to be, as the *Times* reporter wrote, "as scarce as last season's grouse."

Diana's three roommates, giggling in the beleaguered rooms above the street, peered down at the unhappy journalists, and one of them took a photograph of them milling about in total disarray, like a defeated army rallying around to beg scraps from the populace.

Meanwhile, the only thing the photographers could come up with was a picture of one of London's finest hanging a parking ticket on Diana's Renault.

At Sandringham, Charles celebrated his birthday party in complete secrecy, surrounded only by members of his immediate family. Outside in the windy winter's bitter chill, laden with the smell of the North Sea, members of the press shivered in cars trying to keep warm by smoking and idling the engines. It was a dreary Friday night.

Eventually, from wherever she was hiding out, Diana telephoned Charles at the mansion and wished him a happy birthday. The presents she had purchased at Harrod's had to wait until later for delivery when she could hand them to him without the ubiquitous journalists in attendance.

Unfortunately no one had taken up Nigel Dempster on his bets; the *Sun* had no comment to make about its erroneous prophecy.

Where had Diana been? Simply in seclusion far from her own apartment *and* from the royal family. Probably at home in Althorp.

In spite of the frustration of the *Sun* and its public, the press continued to keep a watchful eye on Diana. The Coleherne Court apartment was under constant siege. When Diana drove around the block, she would be followed. Not until the middle of November would the pressure be off. It was then that Charles would leave for a three-week royal tour of India. Fleet Street *knew* it could not get a shot of him with Diana during that hiatus.

The night before he was to leave, Diana somehow managed to slip away from the reporters and drive out from London to Highgrove, a sumptuous Gloucestershire mansion situated in 346 acres of rich farmland in the tiny village of Doughton close to Tetbury. Charles had recently purchased it after Diana had approved it as a possible future residence.

There she spent Saturday night with Charles. The house was still in the throes of refurbishing. It was almost the same as camping out. The only others present were two caretakers who had worked for the Macmillans; the Harold Macmillans had owned the estate before Charles. They stayed on to manage the place for Charles.

Charles and Diana said their good-byes there and Diana drove back to the city. With her roommates, she sat later that night in front of the television set in the apartment watching the prince's ceremonial arrival at Delhi Airport.

Now, with the Prince of Wales out of the country, the press shifted into high gear once again. The strategy was to focus all eyes on Lady Diana. A story came out in the *Sunday Mirror* that Prince Charles had twice smuggled Lady Diana aboard the royal train to indulge in secret "love trysts." There was a great deal of elaborate detail in the story, all of it completely cooked up by imaginative scribes.

The tryst was supposed to have taken place the night of Princess Margaret's birthday party, when Diana and Charles had been with her in the ballroom of the Ritz Hotel in Piccadilly.

Diana was reduced to tears by the publication of the false story. She knew there was not a word of truth in it, but she could not deny it since denial always hinted at guilt. She did not know what to do. In any event, she actually did nothing.

She had daily telephone conversations with Charles in India. The connections were absolutely dreadful, but the two could hear one another. One night Diana told him, with some emotion, about the scurrilous story of the train tryst. She was so overcome by shame as she repeated it to him that she suddenly burst into tears.

Charles blew up. He immediately reached the queen and told her how the story had affected Diana. The queen acted. An item appeared in the next day's papers.

"There is not a word of truth in it!" said Michael Shea, the press secretary to the queen at Buckingham Palace. A retraction of the story was demanded by the palace. Although the request for the retraction came from the Prince of Wales, the spokesman at the palace said that the queen also "wished this to be done."

It was done.

Nevertheless, the "love tryst" wasn't the only incident. Journalists now began to make up stories of interviews with Diana. She gave none, so any that appeared were a total invention. She was quoted about her intimate feelings for Charles and about how she missed him.

Cleverest of all the plots was the rumor circulated that Lady Diana Spencer was merely a "cover" bride; the *real* bride-to-be was Princess Marie-Astrid of Luxembourg, who had been mentioned previously as the intended for Prince Charles—erroneously as it later proved.

According to the newly polished-up story, the whole Diana Spencer "affair" was simply a gigantic ploy to divert Fleet Street and the public from the complicated and elaborate negotiations now going on to prepare for a marriage between a Roman Catholic Princess and a Protestant Prince. And so on and so forth.

Diana read these stories and listened to these rumors with growing disbelief. What kind of a life was she facing? Would it be possible to go through with it all, even if the prince *did* ask her to marry him? Probably not.

The siege at Coleherne Court continued day and night. Later in November, Diana, feeling despondent over the increasing furor about her relationship with Charles, climbed into her red Mini Metro to go to work. This new car was a gift from Charles; he had presented it to her in early November before leaving for India.

Diana was worried about her driving; she had already gotten three speeding tickets. When she pulled away from the curb this time, a half dozen press cars took out after her, in full pursuit, like some kind of mad Western posse in a grade B movie.

Grimly determined to lose her pursuers, Diana drove off through London in the general direction of Mayfair rather than Pimlico—Mayfair being to the northeast rather than to the east. Finally she shook them off. She parked the car and wound up in tears on a bench in Berkeley Square, where she was comforted by a friend. It was most uncharacteristic of her to burst into tears so soon after her breakdown with Charles on the phone.

The cynical journalists, startled over the effect of their pursuit, got together and penciled a note to her.

Later they slipped it through the sunroof of her car as it stood parked near St. George's Square.

"We didn't mean this to happen. Our full apologies."

Mean to or not, the pressure was beginning to tell on Diana. When a housewife from Lancashire went on the BBC's popular "Today" show with a special song for her, she did not know what to do. The words, in part, went:

"Diana divine, my sweetheart sublime."

The woman's idea was to encourage the romance, to persuade Charles to pop the question.

He had not proposed as yet. Diana could not forget what her sister Sarah had said about Charles. Although she had been quoted in a magazine, she had told Diana as well. "Charles," she said, "is a romantic who falls in love easily." And, the implication went, out of love just as easily.

Diana began to wonder if the feeling she had for Charles was simply a one-way street. Was it, in fact, nothing more than an adolescent crush on the Prince of Wales? as the American newsmagazine *Time* put it. Or was it, as the same periodical went on, a crush that had blossomed into a serious mutual adulation?

Meanwhile, on the other side of the world, Charles was having his own thoughts about his future. At a reception for him in Delhi, he was chatting with a group of three reporters from home about international trends and social problems. In the middle of the conversation, without shifting gears at all from the small talk and trivia that usually occupied such dialogues, suddenly—

"Diana's a very nice girl, you know," he said in an offhand manner, apropos of absolutely nothing.

The reporters turned to him, somewhat startled, but trying to hide it. Prince Charles, they knew, was a master at holding back any kind of talk about his personal feelings.

"All this," he went on, "has been something of a strain for her, you know."

The reporters, one of whom was Harry Arnold of the *Sun,* hemmed and hawed.

"At times it has reduced her to tears," Charles said, "but she has coped magnificently."

None of the journalists knew that she had been weeping because of the press chase through the crowded London streets.

Charles continued as the reporters simply stared at him with their mouths hanging half open.

"You must not rush me," he told them. "If I get it all wrong, you will be the first to criticize me in a few years' time."

Get what wrong? Good Lord, they wondered, could he be talking about marriage to Diana Spencer?

"It's all right for you chaps. You can live with a girl before you marry her, but I can't. I've got to get it right from the word go."

Although she was in the midst of the controversy surrounding the *Sunday Mirror*'s fake story on Prince Charles's tryst with Diana, Queen Elizabeth had simply carried out her son's wishes the best way she could. It was she, of course, who had talked to Michael Shea, the palace press secretary, even though it had been Shea who actually wrote the letter of reprimand to the newspaper in question.

Charles had told the queen nothing at all about how he really felt about Diana Spencer. Still, he had never told her much about any of the girls he went out with. Although he was thirty-two years old, she had never really reprimanded him about his lengthy bachelorhood.

There were articles in all the newspapers about Diana Spencer and Prince Charles. The American press was now taking up the hue and cry. THE SPORT OF CHARLIE WATCHING,

Time magazine headlined one story. "Has the Bonnie Prince picked his future Queen at last?"

Meanwhile, Charles had communed with himself during an extended period in the Himalayas and had come back to civilization for the trip back to London.

The Lockheed 1011 Tristar in which he was a passenger touched down at Heathrow Airport late on the night of December 14. As he hurried out, shaking hands with the members of his staff who had come to meet him, he learned that the queen wanted to see him.

Tell Charles, the word had come from the palace, to see the queen as soon as he was free.

It seemed pretty obvious to Charles that she wanted to talk to him about Diana—and about what he was going to do about himself and about Diana.

Yet he did not want to see the queen right away. There were other and more important things to think about. He wondered how long he could avoid the coming confrontation. He gave no promises to anyone and hurried home to Buckingham Palace.

In spite of the urgency of the queen's command, Charles avoided sitting down with her for some time to discuss the situation between him and the Lady Diana. In fact, it was not until the Christmas holidays that he finally got around to it.

Traditionally the royal family celebrates the Yule season at the royal house at Windsor Castle. Diana was not present—not because she was not invited but because she had caught a bad case of the flu and was sent from London to Althorp to recuperate.

And so,it was at Windsor Castle,the epicenter of the royal legend and of regal reverence, as was only fitting, that this most absolutely *important* subject of Charles's intentions of marriage—if, indeed, he had any—should be dutifully explored. The queen thought he did so intend. She had already made her own feelings known to her associates.

"Even I don't know what's going on!" she had admitted with a toss of the head.

The discussion opened in private. Both parents were at Charles to make up his mind. Actually, Charles *had* made up his mind, he told them. However, he did not really know *completely* about Diana's mind. He told them he had made a tentative approach and she had not turned him down. But she had not really said yes, either.

Could he get her to make a definite commitment? they wondered.

Charles demurred. He did not want to leave her with a feeling of being trapped. Some observers felt that Charles had considered himself badly burned when one of his recent steadies, Anna Wallace, had suddenly become engaged to another man right at the height of her relationship with Charles. He did not want to look an utter fool if his feelings for Diana Spencer were not totally reciprocated. He finally admitted that he did indeed feel it was time to sit down with her *quietly* to discuss the matter.

The queen began to fidget and wondered what kind of "perfect setting" was needed in order to pop the question.

What was needed, Charles told his mother and father, was a chance to have a few intimate moments with Diana, the kind of moments that were so hard to arrange for any member of the royal family. There was always the press, and the public, and the people in the royal entourage.

The duke of Edinburgh finally asked his son specifically what he *did* want.

Would his mother invite Diana to Sandringham to join the family for the New Year? She would then be recovered from her case of the flu. Perhaps in the euphoria of the Christmas holidays he could finally bring the situation to a satisfactory conclusion.

Yes, the queen told her son. But this time, she insisted, he must not linger too long over the decision. He must bring it to a close. "The idea of this romance going on for another year is intolerable for everyone concerned."

It was a royal command.

Charles telephoned Diana and invited her to the yearly pilgrimage to Sandringham estate—at New Year's and afterward. It was traditional that the press left the royal family alone during these weeks of the holiday. The queen felt secure in the knowledge that the royal residence would be free of the Fleet Street crowd, at least through January.

But these were not normal times. The fever of excitement that had stirred in the media during the closing months of 1980 had heightened to a fever pitch by January. An enormous crowd of journalists and photographers swarmed over the estate, sitting in cars and gazing at the royals through long-range glasses.

Pheasant hunting became an impossibility. The queen, distinctly annoyed because she had promised Charles that he and Diana would have relative peace and quiet, spoke directly to a group of newspaperpersons at one time. "I wish you would go away!" she snapped in no uncertain terms.

On New Year's Day, Prince Charles strolled out and smiled at a group of photographers who began taking pictures of him.

"I wish you a very happy New Year," he told them with a glint of ice in his blue eye. "I hope your editors have a particularly nasty one."

Charles's youngest brother, Prince Edward, came out one morning and shouted at the photographers who crowded around him: "Watch out. You might get shot!"

It was a prophetic note. The following morning a report surfaced in the papers that one of the shotguns of the royal hunting entourage had been discharged dangerously close to some of the camped-out scribes. Pellets had been heard to rattle down on the roofs of some of the cars.

The time arrived for Diana to come to Sandringham—and that called for paramilitary tactics. Misdirection, actually. One weekend near the end of January, Diana, who had finally recovered from the flu and was staying and working in London, let her roommates drop the information—Charles's disinformation—that she would be going home to Althorp for the weekend.

She started out in her red Mini Metro, stopping off at Kensington Palace, where her sister Jane lived. The reporters then headed out for Northampton and Althorp. Diana borrowed Jane's silver Volkswagen Golf. In it she drove out to Norfolk, where she followed the back roads and drove into Sandringham through a remote entryway unfamiliar to the waiting and eagle-eyed contingent. By now the Fleet Street crowds had begun to thin out. The lack of news had deterred some editors from spending the big money necessary to keep their corps continually on the wait.

No one discovered that Diana was there. She and Charles sat down alone without any pressure on them. It was, as the queen had promised, the place for them to be quite alone together.

What happened at that meeting was more in the manner of a progression in their relationship than any special decision. Nor did Charles ask Diana to be his wife. But she was assured that he would, when she had had enough time to think about it. She told Charles she wanted to take a trip to Australia. Her mother spent the winter months in Australia on one of her husband's sheep ranches. Diana wanted to talk over things with her mother and spend some time with her. She was about to make a momentous decision, and she wanted to know what the woman nearest to her thought about it.

"Go ahead," Charles urged her. "Think the whole thing over in Australia." He said he understood exactly what she was going through.

To effect Diana's escape from Sandringham at the end of her stay, Charles had devised another ploy involving the royal family. On Sunday, Prince Philip and Princess Anne's husband Captain Mark Phillips went on a pheasant shoot. One out of three of the photographers tagged along.

Charles got in his car and drove out of the gate; the Charles-watchers followed immediately, hopeful that Charles might be going to meet Diana. Charles led them to the dog kennels on the estate, where he fed his golden Labrador retriever Harvey to the clicking of many cameras.

The real target was at that moment driving out the back way in the borrowed silver Volkswagen Golf. Lady Diana Spencer was home in London by noon.

The royal family ate lunch at the King's Head, a local pub in Norfolk. Charles strolled by the group of journalists after lunch and grinned at them.

"There's no one here. I wish you'd all go away."

Diana was to leave for Australia on Friday, February 6, and the night before she was invited to join Charles for a farewell party at his private quarters at Buckingham Palace. She drove over from Coleherne Court in a long evening gown and warm coat, carrying a small evening bag. She was waved through the gate by the officer on duty at the security check at about eight o'clock.

She then ascended the stairs to the small three-room apartment kept by Charles at one corner of the palace. Actually, she had visited his quarters before. He was dressed tonight in a dark suit, sitting on a sofa near the small round table set for supper. He seemed nervous; Diana had no particular idea why.

Even she was not her usual cheerful, relaxed self. After a bit of small talk they began awkwardly to eat. A candle in the middle of the table flickered between them. It was as they sat there after the end of the meal that Charles finally asked Diana officially to be his wife. He said that he did not expect an answer from her right away. He wanted her to think it over carefully. He knew that by marrying him she would have to give up her own comfortable life-style and become a part of something else again—the royal family. She should have time to consider her future.

What he expected her to say was that she wanted a little time to think about it, that she would have to go away somewhere to deliberate, perhaps to talk to her mother before deciding and all that.

Diana fooled him.

She looked across the flickering candlelight at him, her eyes bright, and said that of course she would marry him. She told him that she had made up her mind quite a bit before to do so. She knew that she was deeply in love with him. She could think of nothing lovelier than being his bride.

Somewhat surprised, but extremely overjoyed, Charles leaned over and kissed her.

Shortly after that Diana left for her apartment. She could scarcely contain her excitement. Virginia Pitman recalled that night with amusement.

"Diana just sat on the bed beside me and said she was going to marry Prince Charles. There was a big smile on her face. We started to squeal with excitement and then we started to cry."

Ann Bolton remembered it a bit differently. According to her recollection, Diana strolled into the kitchen and found her and Virginia there. "I'm engaged," she said simply. Carolyn Pride was in the next room and learned the big news through the door.

"We knew how much in love the two were," Ann said later. "But when she told us about the engagement, it completely threw us. We started running all over the place, laughing and shouting."

Diana simply sat there in a kind of pink haze.

Finally they had sense enough to break out the champagne and began to celebrate.

Charles was busy celebrating too. The first thing he did was the gentlemanly and traditional thing. He telephoned Diana's father, the eighth earl of Spencer, to ask him for permission to marry his daughter—a somewhat quaint tradition dating back many years among the well-to-do and seemly.

The earl later reported that Charles had even called him "sir" during the dialogue, another piece of old-fashioned business. After Charles had asked him the question, the earl pondered a moment and then burst into laughter. So did Charles.

It was a somewhat ridiculous encounter for the year 1981. In fact, the earl later said that he had been expecting news of some kind ever since before Christmas. "I realized Diana was in love." Of course he gave his consent immediately, telling Charles that Diana was a wonderful girl, and that Charles was a lucky man.

Later the earl thought about the matter in a television interview, and let a twinkle show in his eye. "I wonder what he would have said if I had said no?"

Diana's roommates and the Spencers were, of course, sworn to secrecy, although it was difficult to contain the information once they were apprised of it. Friends might well have guessed it from their expressions. But the news did not leak out as it might have been expected to.

Almost immediately, Diana was in the air flying to Australia. She had expected enormous crowds of paparazzi at Heathrow. Amazingly, there were none. In fact, no one even knew she was on the flight; at least, no one who could bruit the news about. It was not until she had landed in Sydney and debarked from the Qantas flight that she was recognized.

The press put two and two together and guessed that she was visiting her mother at the Shand-Kydd sheep farm. Almost immediately the farm became a kind of Sandringham-down-under, with journalists and photographers milling about looking for Diana Spencer.

Normally it was a quiet, remote spot, where no one ever bothered to come unless invited. Its very remoteness was the reason the Shand-Kydds spent the winter weeks in the summer weather there. Now, with the media in Australia carrying headline stories of Diana's arrival there, the local reporters were all on hand to try to get coverage of her visit.

Diana wanted complete seclusion. Her mother engineered it for her. "My daughter is not here," she kept telling the inquisitive members of the press. "You have got the wrong continent. She is in the sun somewhere, but not here."

When Diana did not show up, the journalists one by one were called in by their editors. No use wasting money if her sighting was a mistake.

Finally Diana was able to go out in dark glasses and covering head scarf to picnic and sunbathe at a nearby beach. During the weeks she stayed there, she had long conversations with her mother. It was now not a matter of making up her mind about marriage, but simply a matter of discussing the possible pitfalls and problems of living in the royal fishbowl and exposing herself every moment to the world at large.

The first time Charles telephoned Diana to talk to her there was an amusing altercation between him and whoever answered the phone. The Shand-Kydds had become tired of fobbing off journalists and had a temporary staff of men from the sheep farm on the phones to tell all callers that "Diana is not here."

One of these assistants was on duty when Charles put through his call from Buckingham Palace. "Who is this?" asked the Aussie operator.

"This is the Prince of Wales," Charles told him.

"Oh, sure," said the sheepman waspishly in a kind of Crocodile Dundee accent. "And I'm the queen of the May."

"No, look, I really am," Charles protested. "I want to speak to Lady Diana Spencer."

"Sorry, mate," said the sheepman. "Nice try, but no cigar."

And he hung up.

Charles did have another private number to call, and he did so, somewhat irritated. During one of these telephone calls from opposite ends of the earth, Charles and Diana discussed her return to London. Now that the engagement was official, if secret, it had to be announced. And it should be announced only after Diana had returned home. With her stay in Australia planned for three weeks, she would be coming back about the end of February.

However, if Diana didn't mind, Charles had a plan. Prince Andrew's birthday was February 19. Would it be possible for Diana to schedule her return to coincide with Andrew's birthday party? Charles's military mind was once again at work.

Prince Andrew was training at that time as a helicopter pilot at the Royal Naval Station in Cornwall, three hundred miles southwest of London. With the pressure off Diana and Charles, it would be obvious that the press would be on hand for a royal or nonroyal celebration of Andrew's birthday. Either way, it would be a story with pictures and plenty of glamour.

Prince Andrew had grown up to be a most attractive, good-looking, and photogenic individual. "He's the Robert Redford in the family," Charles often said. Andrew had always proved himself to be a dashing escort to the young ladies. In fact, he was known far and wide in England as "Randy Andy." As such, Prince Andrew was always good for a couple of columns of hot copy on a cold day.

With that fact in mind, Charles wondered if Diana might not like to arrive on his birthday. Fleet Street would, perhaps, be decoyed away from Heathrow and she could get in quietly.

Diana did not want to arrive from the other side of the earth in London, frazzled and half dazed from jet lag, to be surrounded by yammering journalists waving copy pads, microphones, and cameras in her face. She agreed wholeheartedly to Charles's plan. She would have liked, perhaps, one more week in the sun, but she knew too that the pressures were increasing on Charles about the announcement of the engagement. Secrecy had been maintained so far, but it was obvious that the truth might leak out at any moment now. A leak like that could ruin the effectiveness of the official announcement.

Besides, Charles told her that her sapphire engagement ring was ready. She had selected the design from a Garrard's catalogue before leaving for Australia. The oval sapphire was surrounded by fourteen perfect diamonds set in eighteen-carat white gold. Once she began wearing that, of course, there was no possibility of concealing the fact of her engagement.

When the day came to leave Australia, Diana bid good-bye to her mother and stepfather, and flew back to England, to arrive at Heathrow February 19, a Thursday, as planned. Once again Charles's familiarity with military tactics had provided a cover for Diana. She slipped easily through the crowds at Heathrow, without any sighting by the Fleet Street gang.

That night there was a formal gathering of the royal family at Windsor Castle. This was one of the most important meetings of the entire season. Almost all the members of the royal family were present: the queen, the duke of Edinburgh, the Queen Mother, Prince Andrew, Princess Anne, Captain Mark Phillips, and Princess Alexandra.

It was the night when the royal decision would be made about the announcement of the engagement of Prince Charles and Lady Diana. After the cat-and-mouse game Charles and Diana had been playing with the press, it was obvious that something had to be done. The announcement *must* be made. The sooner the better, was the consensus.

In fact, Diana was having narrow escapes every day now—and it was felt that it would be unfair to subject her to the merciless grueling of Fleet Street all alone. There had been a near call just recently. She had been under almost constant siege by journalists and photographers. The most persistent were Kenny Lennox, a photographer, and James Whitaker, a writer, of the *Star*.

Whitaker had been with Lennox when the *Star* photographer had shot the very first sighting of Diana at Balmoral—and had continued to dog her footsteps during the months that followed.

He was gracious, persistent, but at the same time serious about getting *news*. The rumors were continuing that the engagement had been proclaimed and the date set. When was it to be announced? That Friday?

One night Diana simply gave up and invited Whitaker inside the hallway of Coleherne Court. They stood in the halls and sat at times on the stairs—talking for about an hour and a half. They talked about the imminent announcement of the engagement, and they even talked about Diana's feelings for Charles. Everything.

"Throughout the whole of that highly emotional midnight chat," Whitaker wrote later, "Lady Diana managed to retain her sense of humor. And although she was clearly worried she also remained marvelously calm and controlled. . . . When it came to the crisis, there was nothing shy about Di."

At the end of the talk, Diana laughed and said: "That

was quite a conversation. One day you and I will have to write a book about it all."

Whitaker, who had guessed that the announcement would be made soon, kept his promise to her and did not write about it.

The date selected at the meeting in Windsor Castle was Tuesday, February 24, at 11 A.M.

Now word went out to the select few who would know ahead of time. Margaret Thatcher, the prime minister, and her staff at 10 Downing Street and other top cabinet ministers were told. So was the archbishop of Canterbury, Dr. Robert Runcie, the man who was going to perform the ceremony. Word also went out to the heads of the British Commonwealth all over the world.

Vibrations were beginning to hum through all of Fleet Street. *Something* was up. On Monday calls came in to Buckingham Palace press officers; but no one would confirm anything. At five o'clock, Lady Diana Spencer drove her car to Buckingham Palace. A freelance photographer standing at the gate snapped her picture, and made a modest fortune later with the prints.

Later on that night, Diana moved into a bedroom at Clarence House, the home of the Queen Mother. The mansion was located some five hundred yards from Buckingham Palace off St. James Street in Piccadilly. Diana was to be guest of the Queen Mother between the time of the announcement and the wedding—at least that was what would go out to the press and to the public.

Yet almost immediately the pressure of her position became evident. She could no longer live with the three roommates with whom she had shared so many months of fun and friendship. There were tears in her eyes—tears of happiness and regret—when she packed up her things at Coleherne Court and said good-bye, at least for the time being, to her three friends.

"For God's sake, ring me up," she said, as she left. "I'm going to need you!"

On the way into Clarence House, after a hectic drive across town, Diana had to fight through a crowd of photographers and journalists who were mobbing the place for shots of her and for any new personal information. With the emotional pressure of the Fleet Street chase off, and the game of cat-and-mouse over, Diana turned halfway up the steps, faced the press, smiled radiantly, and waved her hand to them in what seemed already to be a regal manner.

Because of her gracious appearance on the steps that day, Diana's stock rose with the Fleet Street crowd—although it had never been low—and she was from then on an established favorite.

Even on the first day of her stay at Clarence House, Diana had to drive back to Coleherne Court to pick up some things she had left there. And she waved again to the Fleet Street watch both at Clarence House and at her old digs. Then, later that day, she had lunch with the queen. Charles was off in his Range Rover, shopping in the country for a race horse to replace Allibar, who had been put down after a nasty fall.

Actually, Diana would stay at Clarence House only two days, and would then move into a special suite for her in Buckingham Palace, on the same floor as Charles's suite. Discreetly, Diana's things were moved into Buckingham Palace and her suite fixed up for her coming residency. But none of this information would come out until months after the wedding and the honeymoon.

About the announcement—

What else?

There was a leak. There was *always* a leak of some kind.

Tuesday's London *Times* scooped Fleet Street and the world with a statement that this would be the day. The

Times was right, of course. The guessing game was finally over.

At 11:00 A.M., the word went out from Buckingham Palace, just as the *Times* had said it would. These were the words:

> It is with the greatest pleasure that the Queen and the Duke of Edinburgh announce the betrothal of their beloved son, the Prince of Wales, to the Lady Diana Spencer, daughter of the Earl Spencer and the Honorable Mrs. Shand-Kydd.

Charles and Diana were engaged!

Within moments of the official announcement of the engagement of Prince Charles and Lady Diana—made verbally by the Lord Chamberlain at the beginning of a routine awards ceremony at Buckingham Palace—there was immediate applause from those assembled at the affair. Reportedly the queen smiled radiantly.

Outside the palace, some of the curious had gathered in anticipation of the announcement, alerted by the notice in the *Times,* and as they mingled with the usual crowd of curious in front of Buckingham Palace, there were cheers.

Diana's father, an avid amateur photographer, was among those waiting outside Buckingham Palace. After all, he *knew* what was going to happen. He spent the next few minutes snapping pictures of crowd reaction to the announcement. HMS *Bronington,* commanded by Prince Charles during his naval career, fired a congratulatory salvo.

London pubs celebrated with millions of pints of ale hoisted in toasts to the royal couple and to the Prince of Wales. Almost immediately a record company in London began peddling copies of a new song entitled "Diana Divine."

In Parliament, Prime Minister Margaret Thatcher interrupted a political discussion with the announcement. There were cheers from both sides of the House.

"It's good news—the country needs it," said one Londoner.

"Yes, it's true at last—and about time!" That from a newsdealer in London's Piccadilly Circus.

In the stock market, the shares of Wedgwood, the china firm, rose almost immediately, with stockbrokers anticipating a large influx of foreign tourists and consequent sales of their products.

London's merchants began rubbing their hands in hopes that there would be sales galore of every type of merchandise, including jewelry and artifacts designed in commemoration of the coming nuptials.

Roy Stephens, managing director of Selfridges, one of the country's biggest stores, was ecstatic. "It is good news for us because it will bring in a lot of foreign visitors."

Immediately the London Tourist Board was quoted as saying: "You probably won't be able to get beds in London for love or money before and after the wedding day." The word went out that probably a million extra visitors would pour into Britain from all over the world to view the royal wedding; the board hoped for a record year in touristry.

By now hordes of staid Britons were swarming around the park outside Buckingham Palace. The first real confirmation to those watching was the arrival of the band of Coldstream Guards, bundled up against the bitter chill in their distinctive scarlet uniforms. They went into a pop song of the 1960s titled "Congratulations" and the forecourt of the palace resounded with their music.

Champagne corks popped everywhere—in palace offices, on the royal estates, in office buildings around the city, in country manors, in the homes of the middle class, even in some of the more exclusive clubs and restaurants around town.

When reporters caught up with the earl of Spencer

outside Buckingham Palace, still snapping pictures, he gave them a few brief words about his daughter. "She's very good-natured," he said. "Publicity doesn't worry her." He explained that his daughter was a very practical girl, "a good housekeeper." He also said that as a baby she was a "superb physical specimen." That brought chuckles from the Fleet Street gang. At five feet ten, with long legs and a perfect figure, she was *still* a "superb physical specimen."

A Buckingham Palace official was even persuaded to describe her as "a girl of charm and sweetness," later pointing out that she could make Prince Charles laugh even when he fell off his horse.

Already, hairdressers were beginning to retool to keep pace with the "new" hairdo—a short, perky "Lady Di" haircut. Similar in its image-making potential to the recent Dorothy Hamill hairdo of America's Olympic Gold-Medal skating champion, the Lady Di had become the trademark of the future queen of England.

Couturiers and clothes manufacturers were in their back rooms already designing variations of the "everyday" type of dress favored by Diana Spencer: corduroy culottes, high-necked blouses, easy cardigans, and flat shoes.

The two principals in this international drama meanwhile were trying to face up to whatever ordeal confronted them in the immediate future after the furor of their romance died down.

The reaction of Prince Charles was predictable. "Thank heavens!" he said, laughing with the paparazzi who were surrounding him. It was a sigh of relief; no longer would he have to worry about headlines speculating about a royal wedding. Now it would finally happen and no more false stories would have to be made up by imaginative tabloid scribblers.

But the most unnerving and daunting ordeal of all was the scheduled appearance of the two newly engaged lovers on a five-minute television dialogue with two hard-nosed reporters—a brief interview that would finally unite both Prince Charles and Lady Diana together in front of the cameras for all the world to see.

As expected, Prince Charles took the lead during the dialogue, because Diana was not used to speaking in public. After all—she was still a nineteen-year-old teenager! He told the two interviewers that he was absolutely delighted at the engagement.

"I'm frankly amazed that Diana is prepared to take me on," he admitted with a rueful smile.

When asked directly how she felt, Diana responded: "Absolutely delighted, too, blissfully happy. With Prince Charles beside me, I can't go wrong. It's what I wanted, what I want."

One of the interviewers leaned forward and asked Diana if she was indeed in love with the prince. "Of course!" Diana shot back.

"Whatever 'in love' means," Charles wisecracked with a macho grin.

When asked where they had met, Diana picked up the questioning. "I first met him in November 1977." Not quite right, but fairly close. "Prince Charles came as a friend of my sister Sarah for a shoot. I never saw Prince Charles before 1977." No? She had seen him, of course—many times. At Sandringham, when she lived there. It didn't really matter. "I was always paired with Prince Andrew," Diana giggled.

The giggle had become an integral part of her personality. In fact, it made her own happiness that much more obvious to the viewers who watched her. The joy was simply bubbling up in her; because she was not used to public appearances, she had the charm of a natural-born star.

Charles pondered when actually they had decided to get engaged. "It was about three weeks ago, believe it or not, just before Diana went to Australia." He went on to say that he decided then that he would let her have a chance to think over his offer so she could either accept it or turn it down before she returned. "But she actually accepted!" Charles went on with a dazed smile.

Once in Australia, Diana explained, there were quite a lot of telephone calls.

"So many telephone calls from the press in Australia," Charles continued, "saying they were Buckingham Palace or me. When I called, the man said, 'How do I know who you are?' I said, 'Well, you don't, but I am,' in a rage."

No date had been set for the wedding, the pair told their inquisitors. They planned to live down in Highgrove in Gloucestershire, and also in London of course.

How did Diana like being in the public eye? "Naturally quite daunting," she told the questioner. "But I hope it won't be too difficult."

Charles turned to her with a warm smile. "You like people, which is a great thing."

As for their age difference, Diana passed it off casually. "Never really thought about it."

"I haven't," Charles said, "I mean, it's only twelve years. Lots of people have got married with that sort of age difference. I always feel you are as old as you think or feel you are. I think Diana will keep me young. That's a very good thing. I shall be exhausted."

The interview was flashed all over the world; from that moment on, Diana was totally in the public eye, never to leave it. Completely unsophisticated, natural, and in her own way, regal already, she had stolen the show from an old professional, her fiancé, Prince Charles. But in more ways than one, it was her day.

During that first week, Diana's mother flew in from Australia, posing for pictures at Heathrow and answering questions posed by newspersons. As she strode across the airport with the journalists in tow, one of them commented on her speed and gait. She admitted that she had good long legs like her daughter. The photographers snapped pictures and agreed.

Mother and daughter met at a secret place for dinner that night, to let down their hair and fill in any gaps that might still remain in their intimate confidences. There were other meetings with relatives on both sides of Diana's family.

The wedding itself, finally scheduled for July 31, was put into the hands of Lord Maclean. In his capacity as Lord Chamberlain, Maclean was in charge of the queen's household and master of pomp and ceremony.

An assistant, Lieutenant Colonel John Johnston, handled an extensive staff of thirteen assistants; in their hands were the plans for the carriage processions and the lists of the protocol to be observed among the thousands of guests at the wedding. Indeed one observer suggested that the logistics of controlling such an enormous concentration of the world's most influential and titled people was tantamount to the deployment of a tactical unit for a typical NATO war game.

Meanwhile, the public outside was getting to know Diana better. The immediate excitement resulting from her romance with the Prince of Wales had subsided. People were now able to think more rationally about what it all meant. And the reactions now began cluttering up the news columns. All kinds of comments came not only from the aristocracy but from the man in the street as well.

"She's lovely, isn't she?" the countess of Longford commented; she was a biographer and intimate of British royalty from way back, and her reactions counted for a great deal. "Marvelous complexion, blue eyes, well-brushed hair. Not sophisticated, but he [Charles] didn't want that. He wanted love. And she doesn't butt in and interrupt him the way the duchess of Windsor used to do with the duke."

Even more supportive was William Borders, a correspondent for the *New York Times* in London, in a long appreciative story on the engagement.

> It is not overstating the case to say that this appealing young woman, who will be known as Her Royal Highness, the Princess of Wales, will help to determine the future of the British monarchy, an ancient institution that depends enormously on the personalities and public images of its leading players.
>
> Just as the institution can be damaged by bad behavior—witness Edward VIII's abdication and Victoria's prolonged period of reclusiveness following her husband's death—it can be greatly enhanced by what is publicly perceived as proper behavior on the part of the royal family.
>
> Not only are dignity and probity essential, but so is a certain aloofness, a quality that it will be Diana's task, as much as Charles's, to preserve.

He could not have known what Princess Diana would be up to a few years later at the Royal Ascot—and yet he hit the nail right on the head with that last paragraph.

Along with the acclaim, there were genuine sour notes. "We're in for six months of mush," growled William Hamilton, an antimonarchist member of Parliament.

In America, the *Nation* grumbled in similar fashion:

> Overnight, the national press dissolves into a swamp of schmaltz. The BBC newsreaders adopt an unctuous tone and set their faces in to a permanent smirk. Party leaders vie with one another in loyalty contests, and the groveling Olympiad is usually won by Labor. Babes are taught to lisp a new name, and what name could come more trippingly than Lady Diana Spencer?

Christopher Hitchens went on to criticize the Prince of Wales by saying that he had chosen for his bride "a girl nearly half his age, who was born on one of the royal estates, who has never passed an examination at any of her many schools, who has never emerged from the warm bath of snobbery in which the English upper crust marinate their offspring and who giggles when referred to as a puppy or a brood mare."

Then, to sink in the barb even further: "One searches for ways to brighten up this picture. I can think of two. By the time the wedding bells ring out, there will be three million unemployed people in Britain who will badly need a splash of color in their lives. And my old chum her stepbrother has, after a long wait, finally and suddenly succeeded in raising a loan from his bank."

In turn, Diana had thought about the working press of Britain, and she came up with this comment. "I love working with children," she said on one occasion when she was asked about Fleet Street. "I have learned to be very patient with them. I simply treat the press as though they were children."

Touché!

"The press made Diana's life difficult," her father once said, "but she behaved very well. It has proved to be a test, though it wasn't meant to be, and she came through with flying colors. I couldn't have done it myself at nineteen. I would have collapsed."

However, the assaults of the paparazzi continued. One weekend shortly after their engagement was announced two French photographers were arrested by police for trespassing on the grounds of Charles's estate in Gloucestershire. The photographers claimed that they thought the couple might be there. They weren't.

Descriptions and estimates of Diana continued to come out strong for her. "She's the sort of person who will follow [Charles's] lead, will stand by him and won't rebel," said a friend of the family. "She fits in perfectly with the royal family's—and with Charles's—old-fashioned conservative values," wrote Robert Lacey, a royal family biographer.

"She's a great girl for a giggle," said one friend in a newspaper quote.

Diana was developing a bit more understanding about her position. With everyone around her in public calling her "Shy Di," and "Di," she began to inform them that her name was really "Diana."

She did have a sense of what was proper. "Di" didn't fit in with her concept of herself.

"She's reserved rather than shy," a schoolmate told a reporter. "She's got her own ideas, and she isn't easily swayed by what people say. She's got a lot of go in her."

Another friend noticed that she was carrying herself differently after her bout with the press. "She never used to put her head down. She was literally ducking the press."

Magazine writers immediately began describing her from head to foot. They pointed out that her nails were short, her hair, blond-streaked brown, thick, and well club-cut. She was a jogger by instinct—hiking in the country for miles on her "long legs," bicycling and skiing too. In Australia, it leaked out, she had spent days swimming and surfing at a beach near the Shand-Kydd sheep ranch.

Her posture was good, but inclined slightly to round shoulders and flat shoes. Although she had been described as "sweet," most writers decided that she wasn't really "sweet" in the sense of "soft." Even with her discretion and humor, a friend pointed out, there was also a certain toughness and determination in her.

In fact, her natural giggle had turned more than one reporter in her favor. She had a gentle voice, not, as one writer put it, the "upper-class British bray that can carry across three counties." Youth, humor, vitality—they could go a long way to help alleviate Charles's sense of responsibility. Despite his well-known jauntiness, love of pranks, and wisecracks, he was quite a serious man underneath. About responsibility, Diana was quoted once as having said: "I will just take it as it comes."

But fitting herself to the life she must lead was not easy. From time to time her trials and tribulations, usually suffered in silence, surfaced. At one public recital she sat for a long time during a sixty-five-minute program. Later, at a buffet supper, a woman saw her gently rubbing her side, and asked her if she had a sore back.

"No, not at all," Diana replied with a smile. "It's just that I've got pins and needles in my bottom from sitting still too long. I've never had pins and needles in my bottom before in my life!"

She was learning the hard way—and so was her body—how to be a member of the royal family. The others had coped with it all their lives. She was only beginning to learn to cope.

But with the arduous tasks there were fun times. After visiting a school with Charles, she was approached by a young eighteen-year-old, holding out a golden daffodil to her from the other side of a police barricade.

"May I kiss the hand of my future queen?" asked Nicholas Hardy.

Diana took the daffodil, looked at it and looked at the young man who had offered it. Smiling prettily, she extended her hand. "Yes, you may."

After the buss, a friend with the young man laughed. Diana giggled characteristically. "You'll never live this down!" she told him.

One habit not much noted up to the time she "went public" with her future on the line was the fact that Diana Spencer bit her nails when she was agitated. It became apparent to the world when she showed off the enormous engagement ring that Charles had given her.

Although Diana got most of the press coverage just after

the announcement of the engagement, Charles was doing rather well himself in the public eye. "The Prince has sown his wild oats and now is ready to settle down," wrote Robert Lacey.

"He won't fool around," Anthony Holden decided. "He's quite a religious chap. Like Bertie [Queen Victoria's son, who became Edward VII upon his mother's death in 1901] he will probably have to wait until he's a grandfather before he becomes king. But unlike Bertie, he is sober and conservative."

"There's something old-fashioned and Victorian about his circle of friends who slap him on the back and call him 'Wales' as they drink Pimm's at country estates," Lacey noted.

Holden found him "out of touch with his own age group." In fact, "He grew up in a world of older people, and it shows in his style of dress."

Oxford historian Lord Blake had a more upbeat impression of Charles. "He's the right sort of person for a modern monarch—hard-working, buoyant, and cheerful, with a deep sense of purpose."

Charles's particular qualities were best summed up some years ago by Lord Mountbatten, his great-uncle, so tragically assassinated. When someone suggested to him that it was lucky for Britain to have a man like Prince Charles as heir to the throne, Mountbatten snorted: "Lucky! It's a bloody miracle!"

VII

THE PRINCESS OF WALES

7

THE STUFF OF DREAMS

"Let's all in love and friendship hither come
Whilst the shrill treble calls to thundering Tom,
And since bells are for modest recreation
Let's rise and ring and fall to admiration."
These lines are taken from a ringer's rhyme
Composed in Cornwall in the Georgian time
From the high parish church of St. Endellion,
Loyal to King Charles the First and Charles the Second,
And through the Georges to the Prince of Wales,
A human, friendly line that never fails.
I'm glad that you are marrying at home
Below St. Christopher's embracing dome;
Four square on that his golden cross and ball
Complete our own cathedral of St. Paul.
Blackbirds in city churchyards hail the dawn,
Charles and Diana, on your wedding morn.
Come college youths, release your twelve-voiced power

Concealed within the graceful belfry tower,
Till loud as breakers plunging up the shore
The land is drowned in one melodious roar.
A dozen years ago I wrote these lines:
"You knelt a boy, you rise a man
And thus your lonelier life began."
The scene is changed, the outlook cleared,
The loneliness has disappeared.
And all of those assembled there
Are joyful in the love you share.

—Sir John Betjeman, Poet Laureate

Wednesday, July 29, 1981, turned out to be beautiful, in spite of a bit of overcast that threatened to turn the whole day into a bleak and gray event. By 9:40 on the wedding morning, it was estimated that nearly a million people had lined the route of the procession from Buckingham Palace to St. Paul's Cathedral, a distance of some two miles. The streets had been specially washed for the event, and gleamed in the early sunlight. In their homes, over three-quarters of a billion people were tuned in to watch the full panoply of the British monarchy.

"We haven't got much any more in this country," said one spectator along the processional route, "but we do have our monarchy. It's a big part of what gives us self-respect."

At St. Paul's, the workmen had already laid a 652-foot red carpet down the center aisle. In the forecourt of the cathedral, nine tons of sand had been spread to keep the royal carriage horses from slipping.

At Buckingham Palace, the Guard of Honour assembled, provided for the affair by the Prince of Wales's Company, 1st Battalion Welsh Guards. Inside Buckingham Palace, members of the British and some foreign royal families began to assemble prior to their departure for the cathedral across town.

The crowned heads of Europe included King Olav of Norway, Queen Margrethe of Denmark, King Carl Gustaf of Sweden, Queen Beatrix of the Netherlands, Grand Duke Jean of Luxembourg, King Baudouin of Belgium, Prince Franz Joseph of Leichtenstein, and Princess Grace of Monaco.

At exactly 10:14 they entered a line of black Rolls Royces at Buckingham Palace and left to follow the processional line: down the red-brick Mall through Admiralty Arch, across Trafalgar Square, down the Strand and Fleet Street, and finally up Ludgate Hill to St. Paul's.

Following the crowned heads were the five bridesmaids—Lady Sarah Armstrong-Jones, Miss India Hicks, Miss Catherine Cameron, Miss Sarah Jane Gaselee, and Miss Clementine Hambro—and the two pages—Lord Nicholas Windsor and Mr. Edward van Cutsem.

Exactly on schedule the first horse-drawn carriage of the procession, the one carrying the queen, left the palace at 10:22. She rode in an open, semi-Landau drawn by four handsome grays, accompanied by the duke of Edinburgh, in the full-dress uniform of Admiral of the Fleet. Dressed in aquamarine, the queen seemed tense as she waved to the crowds; by contrast, Prince Philip seemed to revel in the ceremony. Even Princess Anne seemed in a good humor under her yellow hat. The Queen Mother was cheerful and smiling.

The queen's group of eight carriages was led by a squad of mounted police and four divisions of the Sovereign's Escort of the Household Cavalry—twenty-four Life Guards wearing their scarlet ceremonial jackets and white-plumed helmets and twenty-four horsemen of the Blues and Royals in blue jackets with plumes.

At 10:30 the queen's procession was followed by the bridegroom's procession, escorted by Life Guards, with

Charles riding beside his brother Prince Andrew in the State Postillion Landau, built in 1902 for Edward VII, his great-great-grandfather. Charles was dressed in a specially tailored Royal Navy "Number One" uniform; Andrew was in full dress. As they approached the waiting crowd, cheers reached a high crescendo.

Charles and Andrew were smiling and waving at the crowd, exchanging what appeared to be light banter. In Andrew's possession was the ring with which his brother would wed Lady Diana. It was made of Welsh gold, the same that furnished wedding rings for the Queen Mother in 1923, the queen in 1947, Princess Margaret in 1960, and Princess Anne in 1973.

And now for the climax:

At 10:35 Lady Diana Spencer appeared at the palace with her father, riding in the traditional Glass Coach, originally purchased by George V for his coronation seventy-one years before. She rode unveiled so the crowds could see her and her dress.

The dress was made of ivory pure silk taffeta and old lace, embroidered with tiny mother-of-pearl sequins and pearls. It had a lace flounce around the neck. The full skirt was worn over a crinoline petticoat, with a sweeping train, twenty-five-feet long, trimmed with embroidered lace.

The "something old" in the bridal gown was an antique lace stitched around the neckline; the "something borrowed," a Spencer family tiara; and the "something blue," a blue bow sewn into the waistband, along with a tiny gold horseshoe for luck.

In her hand Diana carried a bouquet of British-grown flowers, with a center of gardenias held up by golden Mountbatten roses to honor the memory of Lord Mountbatten, surrounded by lily-of-the-valley and white freesia, with a cascade of white odontoglossum orchids and stephanotis. There was also a sprig of veronica from the bush on the Isle of Wight which had been grown from Queen Victoria's wedding bouquet.

Meanwhile, the crowd of twenty-five hundred guests were taking their seats inside St. Paul's Cathedral, waiting for the moment when the door would open to admit the bride and groom.

Among the earliest arrivals were Diana's mother, Mrs. Shand-Kydd, and Diana's former roommates at Coleherne Court, who sat together in the front row. Also present were Lady Spencer; Prime Minister Margaret Thatcher with Mr. Denis Thatcher; Nancy Reagan; several former prime ministers, and Crown Prince Hassan of Jordan. The King of Tonga had brought his own chair, better proportioned for his formidable size than the cathedral chairs.

Finally the great west door was thrown open and the ceremony was imminent. Upon the arrival of the queen, she was welcomed by the lord mayor of London, who symbolically surrendered his pearl-encrusted sword to her. This ceremony dated back to the time of Elizabeth I. The queen touched the hilt of the sword, and then entered the great cathedral through its west door to be greeted by the archbishop of Canterbury, scheduled to conduct the wedding service—his first since becoming archbishop the year before.

As the organ began the rondeau from Henry Purcell's "Abdelazar," the queen began her walk down the aisle. Meanwhile, Charles had arrived at the top of the red-carpeted cathedral steps, where he turned to flash a kind of "last smile" at the crowd around him, and then entered the cathedral with his brothers, Andrew and Edward. As he walked down the aisle he had the typical somewhat bemused look of any groom about to take the most important and irrevocable step of his life.

Soon Charles's entourage was in place in front of the altar along with the queen. Everyone but the bride was now in place—when the sudden fanfare of twelve trumpets announced her arrival.

As Diana stepped out of the large-windowed Glass Coach, her glamorous gown with its twenty-five-foot train followed her as she moved up the steps, aided by her bridesmaids. Glancing around and smiling, Diana asked her father with a mischievous gleam in her eye: "Is he here yet?" Then she turned and went inside.

Jeremiah Clarke's "Trumpet Voluntary" blared as she proceeded down the aisle to join the groom on the dais, with the choir then singing Purcell's hymn, "Christ Is Made the Sure Foundation."

The bride and groom moved together and touched hands, and exchanged loving, warm glances, and for the moment the enormous spectacle became intimate and almost breathlessly personal. Even the television cameras caught the emotion.

"Dearly beloved, we are gathered here. . . ." It was the Very Reverend Alan Webster, the dean of St. Paul's, who delivered the familiar words, winding up with the traditional challenge: "If any man can show any just cause why they may not lawfully be joined together, let him now speak, or else hereafter forever hold his peace."

Silence.

Charles flicked away a sudden tear. It was now the archbishop of Canterbury's turn to ask the bridegroom and bride if they were prepared to love, comfort, honor, and keep one another in sickness and health. In an earlier meeting, both Charles and Diana had agreed that the traditional "obey" be dropped from the ceremony in the light of modern mores.

The 1928 version of the old 1662 prayer was adopted, with the bride omitting the promise to "obey." That pledge was inserted in the vows during the Middle Ages, when not only was the bride expected to obey, but to be "bonny and buxom in bed and board" as well!

Dr. Runcie had agreed to the change. "It's a bad thing to start your marriage off with a downright lie."

There were flubs in the ceremony. Diana agreed to take "Philip Charles Arthur George" to be her wedded husband, rather than the real "Charles Philip Arthur George" who stood at her side. Charles fluffed the line, "and all my worldly goods with thee I share," saying "and all thy goods with thee I share," apparently meaning that he would share everything of hers with her rather than anything of his.

But both of them were loud and clear when they said, "I will," and as their words sounded on the loudspeakers outside the cathedral, a loud and ringing cheer went up from the crowd.

After the promises, Charles placed the ring on Diana's finger, declaring in a clear voice: "With this ring I thee wed." The bride did not place a ring on the groom's finger; double-ring ceremonies were not in accordance with strict Anglican practice, nor with royal tradition. Later, she would do so privately.

"I pronounce you man and wife."

With that, Diana's veil was flung back and Charles embraced her and they kissed.

The archbishop began his address.

"Here is the stuff of which fairy tales are made: the prince and princess on their wedding day."

He ended his peroration in this manner:

"This is our prayer for Charles and Diana. May the burdens we lay on them be matched by the love with which we support them in the years to come. However long they live may they always know that when they pledged themselves to each other before the altar of God they were surrounded and supported not by mere spectators but by the sincere affection and active prayer of millions of friends.

"Thanks be to God."

After more prayers, the royal trumpets sounded a fanfare and the newlyweds signed the register—bold and clear. "P. Charles" and "Diana Spencer." The "P" before Charles's name signified "Prince (of Wales)."

New Zealand Maori soprano Kiri Te Kanawa sang Handel's aria "Let the bright Seraphim" and the chorus, "Let their celestial concerts" from *Samson.*

The queen stepped forward to sign the register as witness. Prince Charles bowed to her and the Princess of Wales—who had become a princess the moment she became Charles's wife—dropped a deep curtsy to her.

Sir Edward Elgar's "Pomp and Circumstance No. 4" resounded through the cathedral. By the time the couple had arrived outside on the steps in front of the crowd, Sir William Walton's "Crown Imperial" was echoing through St. Paul's. Showers of rose petals filled the air and the city of London resounded with the ringing of bells.

The streets erupted in a frenzy of jubilation as the newly married couple drove back to Buckingham Palace in the Glass Coach, and a rain of rice, confetti, and rose petals fell on them from upper windows all along the processional route.

At 1:15 the newlyweds made their ritual appearance on the balcony of Buckingham Palace. The reaction of the crowd was tumultuous. Cries of "kiss, kiss, kiss" echoed in the courtyard. Charles and Diana smiled, chatted with each other, held hands, waved, but that was all.

"They are trying to get us to kiss," Charles told Diana.

"I tried to ask you," Diana smiled.

"Well, how about it?"

"Why ever not?"

And they did.

It was the first public kiss on the palace balcony, and the first time any members of the royal family had ever kissed on demand for a crowd of their subjects.

There were cheers and whistles from the crowd. Somebody broke out a huge banner and waved it above the sea of heads: LOVE IS CHARLIE AND DI.

After the kiss became part of history, the bride and groom retreated into the palace for the wedding breakfast—called "breakfast" even though it was going to start at two in the afternoon. And a huge and tasty feed it was.

Centerpiece of the wedding breakfast was an enormous five-tiered cake, baked by Chief Petty Officer David Avery of the Royal Navy. Actually the cake weighed 224 pounds, 49 pounds of which was marzipan and ivory-white icing. The thing stood four and a half feet high. It had a "little rum added"—"Just for flavor," as CPO Avery pointed out. "You don't want people to get paralytic."

The 120 palace guests also feasted on lobster-sauced brilla, chicken breasts stuffed with lamb mousse, and strawberries and cornish cream. Plus, of course, champagne.

Of the wedding guests, at least 2,380 of the 2,500 invited were not selected for inclusion at the wedding breakfast. A palace spokesperson said: "The rest will simply have to go and get lunch somewhere else." Among "the rest" were Nancy Reagan and Prime Minister Thatcher, who had lunch at the Bank of England with a notable army of other dignitaries also lumped in with "the rest."

Meanwhile two of the wedding guests were out in the courtyard taking part in a typical royal family stunt. They were Charles's brothers, Andrew and Edward. From the staff they got hold of a dozen blue-and-silver balloons emblazoned with the Prince of Wales's emblem, begged, borrowed, or stole a lipstick from one of the ladies-in-waiting, and began to rig the royal carriage in which Charles and Diana were to ride to Waterloo Station after the breakfast.

With the lipstick, Andrew scrawled JUST MARRIED across a placard on the back of the buggy, and Edward drew in two hearts and arrows. When Charles and Diana hurried out into the courtyard to leave, the wedding guests threw rose petals onto them as they made their way toward the Landau that would take them to the train. The newlyweds saw the balloons and the hand-lettered sign, laughed it off, and climbed into the open carriage.

At a signal, the coachman started up the open Landau and guided it out of the courtyard and through the palace gates toward the waiting crowd. When it finally appeared outside in view of the crowd, another cheer went up, with some laughter mixed in. It was obvious that the Prince of Wales was holding his new wife's hand on his knee as they began the slow and leisurely ride through the crowds to Waterloo Station across the Thames.

Charles and Diana "looked like a couple of nine-to-fivers heading for a week at Brighton," one observer along the route opined.

Television cameras followed them every step of the way. At Waterloo Station, their own private train was waiting for them to take them on to their immediate destination in Hampshire. For a brief moment the two lovers stood hand in hand at the station after disembarking from their carriage. Lord Maclean, the organizer of the wedding, was waiting for them on the steps of the train. It was at that moment that Diana, impulsive as it was her nature to be, leaned over and gave the Lord Chamberlain a most enthusiastic kiss on the cheek.

Then the bride and groom climbed quickly into the train and in moments it was on its way. The television cameras followed its departure determinedly, knowing that there was to be no more live coverage of the bridal couple for some time. The train continued northward into the Hampshires for a two-hour ride. When it pulled onto a siding, Charles and Diana drove to Broadlands, the country estate of Charles's great-uncle, the late Lord Mountbatten.

It was there, in the first-floor suite of two bedrooms,

that the newlyweds were to spend the first three nights of their honeymoon. For trivia buffs, the same private suite had been used as a honeymoon hideaway for the queen and Prince Philip after their wedding in 1947.

The only sad note in the arrangement, of course, was the fact that Lord Mountbatten would not be present to celebrate with the young married couple. But Charles had long ago faced up to the fact that in his line of work there were many negative elements as well as positive ones.

The fact that he and everyone like him walked with death constantly if not at his side at least within hearing distance had long ago become part of his philosophy and outlook. Diana had only begun to realize that she too was an all-too-visible target for extremists; she was trying to get used to the idea that her name was now on the IRA's hit list. But why dwell on the drawbacks, when the most important thing in life right now was love and marriage? They would have their happiness now and face the future with renewed vigor and the sense of strength revitalized by their constant companionship.

When the Prince and Princess of Wales arrived at Broadlands, journalists and photographers, as had been expected, were standing around the locked gates of the estate, trying to winnow out scraps of information about them. The River Test flows along the edge of the estate; it was expected that Charles would be fishing there perhaps on the following morning. Would he appear?

In the end it developed that Charles would *not* appear to fish at all during his stay there. He had more important things to attend to.

In London there was dancing in the streets, as well as in many outlying districts of Great Britain. The queen and Prince Philip came out on the night of the wedding to a do at Claridge's given by Lady Elizabeth Shakerley. Lady Elizabeth termed the affair, which featured music by Lester Lanin and other entertainers, a "rout," having researched history to find that in the eighteenth century a typical nuclear-age "blast" was called a "rout."

"I don't dare do something with caviar and lobster because I can't afford it," she explained as she noted the menu. "I am having scrambled eggs and bacon from seven-thirty on." Claridge's was hardly the place to save money, but the rout was most successful anyway.

Princess Margaret, the queen's sister, put up her feet on a pair of chairs and had herself a good rest. Her niece, Princess Anne, the sister of the groom, celebrated the night in traditional fashion, appearing next morning at a Royal Navy ceremonial apologizing for her fogginess.

"Please excuse me if I sound somewhat different today, but I am suffering from a hangover after a very enjoyable wedding—but it is a lot less painful than normal ones."

In Broadlands the honeymoon was just beginning.

While the rest of the world slowly settled back into its usual routine, Diana and Charles were finally alone with each other. For once the press decided to let Their Royal Highnesses have a few days to themselves. Besides, Broadlands was an easy place to secure.

Rising in a leisurely fashion, the newlyweds would walk hand in hand along paths on the estate that led down to the River Test. There were many things to talk about, they found, things that they had not been able to discuss before.

"They looked very happy," said the man in charge of their privacy. He was Chief Superintendent Alan Lemish, head of the New Forest division of police. "We are trying to give them total privacy until they leave Broadlands for Gibraltar on Saturday."

Most of their time was spent in the large swimming pool, or beside it, lying in the sun together near the water, and then getting up to swim up and down the pool together and singly.

Nothing bothered them. It was really the first peace and

quiet either of them had experienced together since the day they had been photographed at Balmoral and their intimacy had been shattered.

Soon enough the first phase of their honeymoon was over, and the time came for them to leave Broadlands. On Saturday morning, three days after the wedding, they rose early and drove over with their detective escort to Eastleigh Airport near Southampton. There Charles took control of the turbo-prop Andover, one of the three airplanes in the Queen's Flight, taking off without delay for the seven-hour hop to Gibraltar. Although he did not actually sit at the controls for the takeoff, Charles did man them for a part of the long airflight.

It was an uneventful trip and the two newlyweds were quite soon disembarking from the Andover at Gibraltar Airport. There they readied themselves for the drive through the streets of Gibraltar Town to Algeciras Bay about a mile and a half away.

Even at the airport it was obvious that they were not going to be neglected. The crowd was milling about against the hurricane fences as they entered the open brown Triumph that was to take them to the royal yacht *Britannia*. Cheers went up as they passed through the gate and into the streets of the town. The air resounded with shouts; it was brilliant with waving Union Jacks, pennants, flags, and the sky was thick with confetti. Balloons were going up everywhere.

Diana had never seen the place before. For anyone not familiar with Gibraltar Town, its red telephone booths, blue-uniformed bobbies, trim little pubs, and red, white, and blue banners seemed more like England than some parts of England itself.

As they drove along, Charles could be seen clearly. He was wearing a plain business suit. Diana was wearing a loose-fitting white dress with a floral pattern. "Rule Britannia" played as they drove slowly along through the crowded thoroughfares, waving at the hysterical crowds.

Diana never failed to marvel at the sight that greeted her in Algeciras Bay. It was the royal yacht *Britannia,* almost an enclosed seagoing resort complete with swimming pool, ballroom, chapel, theater, and a dining room that seated forty.

The craft was all brilliant with color and glitter now, her hull a swath of royal blue, red, and gold, with a royal coat of arms on the bow and the royal cipher on the stern.

When Charles and Diana alighted from their open Triumph, the day was already beginning to fade into twilight. The bay was aglitter with the blaze of the setting sun and the colors of the *Britannia.* Spanish fishing boats from the area dotted the bay, simply watching the spectacle of the royal departure.

Their Royal Highnesses mounted the gangplank, and almost immediately the order was given to set sail. Soon the 12,000-horsepower twin-shaft turbine engines were turning to push the yacht out of the harbor and past the North Mole.

Prince Charles and Princess Diana were standing hand in hand on the afterdeck as the sun sank into the west and the strains of "Rule Britannia" once again faded in the distance on the shore. Soon land was almost out of sight and the yacht began to move along in its own graceful, ponderous way, pitching only slightly to the Mediterranean's easy roll.

In spite of the enormous contingent of staff and seamen required to run the huge yacht, Charles and Diana were able to spend a great deal of time alone during the two-week cruise scheduled for the *Britannia.* They took complete advantage of the various forms of entertainment on the ship and used the swimming pool as much as they could.

It was in those quiet summery days that they really got to know one another. The courtship had been hectic and dramatic and a strain up to that point. Particularly so for Diana—the teenager who had captured a crown. Now she was able to indulge in that intimate, comfortable type of relationship open to almost any woman in the world but her.

As they grew closer, the *Britannia* steamed its way in a serendipitous fashion around the Mediterranean, passing along the coast of Algeria, of Tunisia, of southern Italy, and then up into the Greek islands.

The yacht made no stops during the first days of the cruise. Charles and Diana talked about music, about art, about literature, and found that they did indeed share the same love of light music, soft lights, and beautiful flowers. There were sundry things they did not share interest in, of course.

Diana learned that she had married a man who was extremely tender and considerate. Her enthusiasm for life and marriage was sharpened by Charles's obvious and total affection for her.

She found that even when she began nattering about this and that her husband's attention did not waver. And he put up with the many things she did that he might look upon as slightly over the "proper" line of royal tradition. Perhaps the twelve years' difference in their ages had mellowed him to the extent that he was willing to support her against anyone else who might object.

No one on the royal yacht seemed to object. One day after Diana had been swimming in the pool she and Charles mounted to the bridge—she still in her bikini. The eyes of the crewmen bulged. One seaman later said, "I can tell you, it was difficult not to stare. She *really* has a great figure."

Diana retained, and actually honed, her irrepressible sense of humor during those cruise days. She happened to walk into the officer's mess one afternoon at the same time the crew was returning from the showers, naked except for towels draped carelessly around their hips.

"I'm afraid you shouldn't be here, Ma'am," said a highly embarrassed crewman politely.

Diana turned not a hair. "It's all right. I'm a married woman now, aren't I?"

She was indeed.

The *Britannia* made its first touchdown on the island of Ithaca, one of the northernmost of the Greek islands in the Ionian Sea. It was on the sixth day of the cruise, August 7, and they anchored about one mile off the coast at eight o'clock in the evening.

The newlyweds were put ashore in a secluded cove for a swim. There was no problem with security; a boat belonging to the Greek Navy stood on patrol until they had finished.

From Ithaca they sailed to a privately owned island identified as Gramvousa, where they once again swam in a cove out of sight of the world. That island was much less populated than Ithaca.

By August 10 they were anchored off the island of Thera (Santorin) in the Aegean Sea, off southern Greece, in a group of islands called the Cyclades. Two days later the *Britannia* was anchored off Port Said, Egypt, at the tip of the Sinai Peninsula, at the head of the Suez Canal.

On the evening of August 12, President Anwar el-Sadat of Egypt and his wife, Jihan, arrived on the deck of the royal yacht by helicopter from Alexandria to spend the evening and dine with Charles and Diana. The premiere of Greece, George Rallis, had been invited as well, but was forced to cancel out on the dinner because, as he put it, of a "heavy workload."

The dinner with the Sadats was actually the Princess of Wales's first evening as hostess for an event of a ceremonial nature in her new role. It was a festive occasion. Diana and the president's wife struck up a lively acquaintance.

When the Sadats left the yacht, Diana impulsively leaned over and kissed her on the cheek.

On August 14 the royal couple landed at Port Said and were driven to the Egyptian military airport close by. There they boarded a British RCAF VC-10 to be flown back to Britain.

They arrived at Lossiemouth Airbase and from there drove down to Balmoral Castle. The temperature was almost forty degrees cooler than on the Red Sea, where they had climbed aboard their aircraft. It was fitting that they should be at Balmoral for a reunion with the royal family; it was there, on the River Dee, that they had fallen in love with one another.

Shortly after their arrival at the castle, they appeared Sunday at Crathie Church, Diana in a two-piece dark blue suit, white polka-dotted blouse, and a wide-brim hat. The Right Reverend Andrew Dory spoke in his sermon, fittingly, of bringing forth fruit.

Buoyed by their rest on the yacht and by the isolation and peace of Balmoral, Charles and Diana even decided to hold an informal "photographic opportunity" session for the paparazzi. Once again, Charles and Diana were throwing aside precedent in the exigencies of modern media coverage. Most photos of princes and princesses were taken by the royal photography staff and sent out to the press after being carefully screened. But this session at Balmoral was to be a free-for-all, with Charles and Diana available for informal and formal poses, together and singly.

The session was an unqualified success—not only for the photos it produced, but for the public relations impression it created in the minds of the cynical newspeople.

"I can tell you one thing," a seasoned journalist said. "[Charles] was totally captivated by Diana. He came back from that honeymoon more deeply in love than he ever thought he could be."

In a short session, Charles and Diana answered questions put to them by Fleet Street. It had been much bruited about in the press that she could not even boil an egg. And so someone asked if she could cook breakfast yet.

"I never *eat* breakfast," she responded with a smile.

When the chatting was over, the members of the press corps brought in a bouquet of carnations and handed it to Diana.

She accepted graciously. "Thanks. I suppose these are on expenses?" That is, paid for on the expense account.

Shortly after the inordinately productive press session, Charles and Diana visited the Braemar Highland Games, a classic sporting event held each summer near Balmoral Castle. The queen and duke of Edinburgh were there as well. Charles and Diana were with them in the royal box.

Suddenly the band began playing the national anthem, "God Save the Queen."

Charles leaned over close to Diana to whisper something. No member of the royal family ever uttered a word during the playing of the national anthem. But Charles was still under the euphoric spell of the honeymoon. He said in her ear: "They're playing our song."

Startled, Diana gave him a quick, disbelieving glance, and then tried to stifle the giggle that rose in her throat. Even though she had been working a great deal with the Queen Mother on controlling that irrepressible giggle, she had not yet succeeded. She began to laugh, ducking her head to stifle it.

Charles gripped her hand hard, trying to help her.

The queen was not amused. She simply pretended it had never occurred. But the message—delivered strictly in a stony glance and in a beam of penetrating light between them—got through to Charles. It would never happen again.

But Diana was too natural to avoid all gaffes. At a Scottish ball later on, she found that the dancing had tired her feet. She got to her seat after a dance and kicked off her shoes and turned to the person sitting nearest her.

"My feet are killing me. My shoes are new and they hurt like crazy."

And got wide press coverage—and good points—for her spontaneity.

During the excitement and the dramaturgy of the wedding, there had been some disgruntled voices raised about the monarchy and its affluence. A Welsh writer named Jan Morris wrote a scathing indictment in a letter to the *Times,* describing his "sense of revulsion and forboding at the ostentation, the extravagance and the sycophancy" surrounding the affair. Jan Morris had been known as James Morris before a sex-change operation several years before. No one paid much attention to—to Morris.

After a visit to Wales the royal couple returned to London in time to be present at the opening of Parliament. Wearing a white satin and chiffon gown and diamond tiara, Princess Diana stepped out into the House of Lords behind the queen and Charles. Everyone was watching her and not the queen or the Prince of Wales.

"Stop stealing the show," Charles whispered to her.

The ten-minute ceremony was brief but very exciting; a new fillip of glamour had been added to the usually staid and somewhat pompous proceedings. There was, of course, a reason for the difference.

The queen was an old hand at ceremonials. Through years of experience, she had learned all the tricks of pacing herself through endless crowds and lines of officials. She made it a point early on never to hurry, never to expend more energy than was required by any given situation. She had learned one trick of royalty: there were always more people at the end of the line; another line after the last line; and another day after tomorrow.

But Diana was just getting used to it all; and her own excitement became part of a more dramatic ceremonial.

The difference was not lost on the press. Even the staid old gray London *Times* went completely overboard. The next day it printed a huge photograph of Diana in her white gown and tiara—in the middle of page one! A tiny picture of the queen was inset down in one corner of the layout.

Even the text accompanying the pictures was somewhat out of this world. It called Diana "a glamorous concoction almost beyond description, shimmering from head to toe."

But all was not serene everywhere. The world was going on its bloody, mad, and self-destructive way. News came through that Egyptian President Anwar el-Sadat had been assassinated. When Diana heard this, she simply collapsed in tears. She remembered vividly the dinner aboard the yacht; he was the first head of state she had entertained. She had been very impressed by his wife.

"It is terrible," she said. "So terrible. How can people behave like that?"

She insisted on accompanying Charles to Sadat's funeral in Egypt; she wanted to console his widow, Jihan. Charles did not feel that Diana should risk it. Her own detectives from Scotland Yard's Special Branch advised strongly against attendance. She continued adamant against any such warnings, but eventually gave in and stayed home.

Charles went to the funeral alone. Diana drove down to Heathrow with him and wept as she kissed him good-bye. Sadat's death made her realize that "death can come at any time." Her original antipathy to the two full-time bodyguards who were always around her began to abate somewhat.

But it was not to be all grief and sadness. On November 6, 1981, came the big news. In fact, the announcement emanated from Buckingham Palace—short and to the point.

"The Princess of Wales is expecting a baby in June."

After that headline, the announcement continued in a more sedate vein.

"The Prince and Princess of Wales, the Queen and the Duke of Edinburgh and members of both families are delighted by the news. The Princess is in excellent health. The Princess hopes to continue to undertake some public engagements but regrets any disappointments which may be caused by any curtailment in her planned program."

That last comment referred to planned visits scheduled for 1982 to Australia, New Zealand, and Canada that would now have to be canceled.

With the news of Diana's pregnancy, the royal routine seemed to settle down somewhat. But the press continued to pester Charles and Diana for pictures. They were safe nowhere. Once as they were standing out in front of their house at Highgrove on a weekend, someone took a long-distance picture of them from the public road in front of the house. Diana had her arms around Charles's neck and was smiling up at him. It hit all the papers.

When Diana went into town with her detective to shop, the paparazzi appeared as if from nowhere and followed her everywhere she went, snapping pictures of the most insignificant scenes.

The queen had had enough. Press secretary Michael Shea called a special meeting of the editors of London's newspaper and broadcasting networks.

"We expected that, following the honeymoon, press attention would wane somewhat," Shea told the editors, speaking for the queen. "But it has in no way abated. The Princess of Wales feels totally beleaguered. The people who love her and care for her are getting anxious at the reaction it is having."

The frequency of these pictures diminished, but at the same time speculative stories appeared sporadically—stories of "rifts" and "spats" between Charles and Diana.

Typical was one printed about them in an argument over going out on a shoot. Diana was dead against it.

"Charles told her not to be so childish," an unnamed "insider" reported, "and Diana got dressed to join the hunt." However, the informant noted, "Diana is not the vivacious, carefree girl who married the Prince. The rows have taken their toll on her."

Then one day Diana accidentally fell down a flight of stairs at Sandringham. The details were hazy. Although it was an unnerving experience, and everyone around was immediately concerned, Diana had a quick medical checkup, and was discovered to be perfectly healthy. News eventually leaked out and in February, Buckingham Palace confirmed the rumor.

"This incident did happen," a spokesman said. "The princess was not hurt."

Shortly after that event, Diana rested in bed for a few hours, and joined her husband for a barbecue on the royal grounds.

Both Charles and Diana decided they had to get away from the pressure and fly to a secluded spot in the Bahamas for a two-week vacation. They left Heathrow under the names of "Mr. and Mrs. Hardy." For a while the disguise worked—but not for long. When the plane landed on the island of Eleuthera, Fleet Street had the word.

Eleuthera is a weirdly shaped island—ninety-miles long and no more than two-miles wide for much of its length. Located about two hundred miles directly east of Miami, the island has great beaches and is noted for its water sports.

Charles and Diana were staying there at the very secluded Windemere Island, not far from the center of Eleuthera. With their long-lens cameras, the paparazzi began prowling about in the palmettos, shooting pictures from far off of the couple whenever they appeared on the beach. By the time the local Eleuthera authorities discovered them, the damage was done.

Several shots of Princess Diana in a bikini appeared in the newspapers—revealing her obvious pregnancy. Four photographers were arrested and held nearly a day before they were flown back to Nassau. Meanwhile the pictures hit all the front pages.

The switchboard at Buckingham Palace was jammed with calls complaining about the pictures. The queen was said to be furious. Michael Shea said that the queen thought the pictures to be in the worst possible taste. Even in the House of Commons, a statement came down condemning the *Sun* and the *Daily Star* for running the pictures. The papers apologized and pulled their remaining journalists out of the palmettos and sand.

"It was never our intention to offend," the *Sun* said. "If we have done so, then we are deeply sorry."

The *Star* apologized to Diana. "If we have upset you, we are deeply sorry."

The London *Mirror,* which did not have any pictures to print, blasted its rivals for stooping so low as to print them: "The pictures were squalid in conception, furtive in execution and grubby in publication! We are not in the business of taking sneak shots of pregnant women bathing, whether they are princesses or not."

One could imagine the gleeful gleam in the eyes of the writer as he raked over the coals his successful rivals.

Within a few days of the blowup, Charles and Diana cut short their stay and flew back to England.

During Diana's pregnancy, Their Royal Highnesses had been working at staffing Highgrove and in furnishing their apartment in London. Although they planned to establish their real home at Highgrove, they knew that they needed a place in London where they could keep close to the palace for appearances and functions of one kind or another.

They had selected an apartment in Kensington Palace, which had developed into a kind of in-town royal condominium already occupied by Princess Margaret, the duke and duchess of Gloucester (Charles's cousin), and Prince and Princess Michael of Kent (another cousin). And for that Diana would need to hire a domestic staff for the household.

But for Diana it was a time of waiting.

And dreaming.

VIII

SARAH FERGUSON

8

OVER THE MOON

WITH THE WHOLE NATION—AND INDEED THE WORLD—SWEPT UP IN THE excitement of Lady Diana's marriage to Prince Charles, everyone and everything else was forgotten for a while. But quite soon things began to calm down as the Prince and Princess of Wales settled into their new life.

Close to the center of the swirl, but unnoticed by most of her fellow countrypersons, was Sarah Ferguson. During the hectic months of Diana's romance with and engagement to Charles, one of Di's most faithful and intimate confidantes was none other than her friend Fergie.

During the excitement of the Fleet Street chase, it was Sarah who sometimes lent her support in a psychological as well as physical way. Although Sarah was only a few years older than Diana, she was somewhat more mature; she had an effervescent and outgoing way about her that Diana would have dearly loved to possess.

And the friendship thrived between these two similar yet different people. It was indeed during the high-pressure days of the engagement that they were closest, exchanging ideas, giving and receiving advice, chatting things over.

"Fergie's major attraction for Diana always has been her puckish sense of humor and her tendency to egg on the more repressed Diana into pranks and childish escapades," one observer wrote. It did help to let off a little steam during this extremely tense period.

But when she was not with Diana, Sarah continued her own flighty ways. She went right on meeting men and socializing with people in a free-swinging fashion, cutting an extremely wide swathe among the "in" London set.

She was still the terror and despair of the bosses who hired her and had to oversee her work.

"She was . . . scatty, with her head in the clouds," one said, somewhat ruefully. "She was all for parties and late nights. That's what happens when you employ someone with good social connections."

The Princess of Wales did not forget Sarah. When it came time for her to choose her own "court"—that is, her "lady-in-waiting"—Sarah was said to have been Diana's choice. However, cooler heads prevailed at "Buck House," as they both came to call it. It was decided that Sarah was a bit too young for the heady position—one that needed cool judgment and experience rather than simply hot imagination and high spirits.

And so Diana's lady-in-waiting became Anne Beckwith-Smith. But indeed even that appointment solidified the relationship between the new Princess of Wales and Sarah Ferguson. For Diana's lady-in-waiting was a cousin of Carolyn Beckwith-Smith, and when Sarah came to search for a roommate to share her sumptuous apartment in Lavender Gardens in the "yuppie" Clapham area of London, she and Carolyn decided to go into the rental together.

The two of them seemed ideally suited. With some truth it was said that they really did not have much in common at all—except the annoying habit of being late for work no matter what their jobs were.

Nevertheless the relationship thrived. "In all the time I have known [Sarah], there has never been a cross word," said Carolyn Beckwith-Smith. "We always said what was on our minds."

In fact, Carolyn always marveled not only at Sarah's sense of humor but at her "feminine intuition"—whatever *that* was during the period of rising feminist agitation.

Sarah was uninterested in cooking. Carolyn was a vegetarian and a good cook. If the two threw a party, it was Sarah who did the organizing and Carolyn who did the cooking.

That winter—1981—Sarah was restless for something new and decided to spend her vacation in Switzerland to take up skiing. With one of her Sloane Ranger friends, Laura Smith-Bingham—the sister of a young man she had met in Argentina on her mother's ranch—she rented a chalet in Verbier, where all the "right" people skied.

Bingo! It turned out that Kim Smith-Bingham was there, too—engaged in salesmanship and fun and games. He was using his connections to sell mod sportswear to the rich and famous. And he was doing pretty well at it, too.

Sarah and Kim spent many hours on the slopes. He was a smooth skier, and Sarah—a natural athlete as has been stressed—soon caught on. The two of them were constantly on the slopes, loving every moment of it.

Kim's salesmanship did not confine itself to sports gear. Quite soon he had sold himself to Sarah. Without really intending to, she fell in love. Soon it was not Laura and Sarah who were sharing the chalet at Verbier, but Kim and Sarah. Where Laura wound up is lost to history.

Once back in London, with Kim following, the affair blossomed into a real romantic attachment, complete with glamour, fun and games, and plenty of sex. Kim was able to bring Sarah quite out of herself.

"Sarah had traditional values," he said. "She liked being given chocolates, but more especially flowers—particularly red roses. She liked men to pay for meals and to open doors for her."

According to one observer, the affair was "quite a staid romance." However, it did not run all that smoothly. Kim wanted Sarah always to be there for him, but he himself did not subscribe to the idea that he should remain in a monogamous relationship with her. If he saw a fresh face or a pair of flashing eyes—he was off and into another bed.

"She would spend half the time in tears because he was so often away. Sarah would hear he had been unfaithful to her [and] she would sit at home and suffer," a close associate said.

None of this seemed to bother Kim any. He remembered her fondly, and recalled she loved the theater, and the films, especially those that concentrated on songs and dancing acts.

It was not all a ball for Sarah, however, a close friend revealed. The friend considered Kim Smith-Bingham nothing more than "a bit of a nerd" anyway.

But Verbier was fun and she tried it the following year. By then Kim and she had more or less broken it off, and although Sarah was unhappy, she knew it was "just one of those things"—a flight to the moon with the gossamer wings coming off on the way up.

A nearby chalet in Verbier was rented out to a man whom Sarah found quite interesting. His name was Paddy McNally, the manager of racing driver Niki Lauda. McNally was a widower with two growing children. He was lonely. He was sexy. He was exciting. He was well-off, one of the top men in a very exacting but rather exotic profession.

He was twenty-two years older than Sarah—but what the hell?

What he probably did best was manage Niki Lauda. But what he did most was to throw huge parties for all the wild, free-wheeling jet setters who hung around racing heroes like Lauda in and around the skiing area.

And since Sarah was a natural management type, she began to supervise these parties, getting them going for her somewhat older consort.

She also actually *liked* McNally's two teenage children, Sean and Rollo, and got on famously with them. This was something that McNally liked—and one of the reasons he liked to keep her around. He continued to treat Sarah decently because of her importance to his life-style. Love her? Well. Love him? She certainly did. But it turned out to be somewhat the same kind of affair she had fashioned with Smith-Bingham.

It was a one-way street.

Whenever McNally saw someone who caught his fancy, he was off to the races. And, until he came back, Sarah was alone.

"Again she spent half her time in tears," a friend said, "because Paddy was constantly unfaithful to her, right in front of her eyes. Sarah [seemed to be getting] used to sitting at home, waiting for her men to come back."

McNally continued to flirt with every woman he saw. And his flirtations caused Sarah a great deal of distress.

"I wondered why someone as lovely as Sarah put up with him," one British editor wrote. When she asked Fergie that, the only answer she got from her was: "I love him."

"Fergie shone on the ski slopes of Verbier," the editor said. "She is a brilliant and brave skier, capable of beating most men on the downhill, and Paddy was impressed. But there were always crowds of available young girls clustering around him—and he made no secret of the pleasure their attentions gave him."

Sarah would dismiss any awkward situations with the

remark, "What fools they are!"—meaning the girls who were out to "get" McNally. But she admitted to herself: "I know *I'm* being a fool, but. . . ."

And she might burst into tears.

"I would comfort her," said the friend, "putting my arm around her shoulder and telling her to cheer up, which she always did."

"I'm being silly," Sarah would say, and try to laugh.

Actually, she did not confine herself to the fashionable resort at Verbier. She followed McNally to the Monaco Grand Prix, for example, in April 1985. By that time, McNally had left Niki Lauda to became a respectable "racing consultant" for the world of those professionals.

Now he and Sarah were living aboard a private yacht in Cannes harbor. Their affair had been going on at this point for almost three years. She was getting tired of the emotional beating she was taking from her lover's constant passes at other women.

And she was getting tired of the jet setters she was always with—the pot-smoking, coke-snorting, high-living hellions who seemed to exist only on man-made highs of one kind or another.

"Sarah knew all these awful people, but she never became tainted by them," one friend marveled. "But again, she spent half her time in tears because Paddy was constantly unfaithful to her."

Something had to give.

And it did.

Sarah decided that she had spent three years of her life in serving McNally, and that he owed something to her—something more than a shelter over her head and food in the larder. He owed her a commitment of some kind.

When she finally got up the nerve to ask him if he intended to continue their relationship as it was forever, or if he wanted to marry her, or if he wanted to get out of her life immediately, he was unable to answer her.

He did the usual thing. He tried to placate her by helping her get into a good job. He knew a lot of people and among them were many rich and famous types. One who was a former racing driver was named Richard Burton—not to be confused with the internationally famous actor Richard Burton.

This Burton had made a great deal of money racing, and had started a printing and publishing company in Geneva. It had a branch office in London. And it was Burton whom McNally persuaded to take on Sarah as a kind of overseer of the London office.

Actually, the place was only a fourth-floor attic office next door to Sothebys—the famous auction house—with little more than a telephone, a tea kettle, and a desk in it.

But Sarah was thrilled when Burton told her she could have the job. And so she became the "director" of the office—the kind of managerial chore she did so well. In fact, she really was a picture researcher and archivist. She was to handle writers and photographers putting together "fine arts" books. She was to help with the printing contracts.

"She is a girl in a million," McNally once said, "level-headed and highly intelligent."

And so Sarah was happy for the moment. She printed up cards with her title as *"directrice"* of BCK, the company owned and operated by McNally's friend Burton. She felt the French word for female director would add a little class to the job description.

But her willy-nilly affair with Paddy was bothering her more than anything else. She was being eaten apart. There was no future in being a part-time spouse—when all it meant was all work and no security.

It was the constant abrasiveness of his affairs that got to

her. It was impossible for her not to evince signs of jealousy during these brief flirtations.

"She would never shout or sulk when Paddy was talking too long to another girl, but she would go over and introduce herself, and engage the girl in conversation," a friend said.

One of these potential "overnights" remembered vividly exactly how Fergie's conversation went.

"You got the 'Stay away!' message—loud and clear!" she said.

Finally Sarah Ferguson put her foot down.

"Marry me or we split," was the way she might have put it, but probably did not.

McNally stalled. He did not believe at first that she would leave. Then, finally he realized she *would*. They all did. It was part of the game.

Later on McNally recalled those days and how it affected him.

"It was an adult situation," he said. "Any man would be lucky to marry Sarah."

But, obviously, it was not going to be McNally. It was simply not in the cards for him. Perhaps he understood the age difference between them too well to fall into that waiting trap.

In the end she packed up and left.

She continued to work for BCK, however.

The breakup was on a very friendly basis.

Whether or not the Princess of Wales had anything to do with Sarah's splitup with Paddy McNally matters little. What does matter is that it was at this point that the wily Diana—by now the mother of two healthy children—had a brilliant idea.

She had been frustrated when "Buck House" had prevented her from selecting the bouncy Sarah Ferguson for her lady-in-waiting. To a degree, anyway.

There was another way she might form a close relationship with her good friend Fergie.

Now that the Princess of Wales had begun to settle down into the general routine of princesshood—having babies, catering to her husband, contending with the rigors of home life, learning all the royal ropes, as it were—Diana's "honeymoon" with the press was pretty much over.

And with it, the media's "honeymoon" with royalty was waning as well. The excitement of Prince Charles's romance, marriage, and immediate fatherhood was gone now. Fleet Street had to work out something new to stimulate the imaginations of its avid British readership.

A new attack on the royal family was soon conceived—as was indeed inevitable. This time the target selected was the third of the queen's children, Prince Andrew.

Most everything about Andrew was upbeat—his attractive good looks, his naval bearing and military professionalism, his penchant for running around with women—but upbeat only to a degree. The press chose to rev up his obvious popularity with the women one step further, making him look like some kind of Charles II Redivivus.

"Randy Andy" had been aptly nicknamed. The way the media saw it, he was *too* much a womanizer. Anyway, his exploits sold papers—and he was if nothing else an obliging performer in the boudoir arts.

It was obvious that the press on Randy Andy was getting out of hand. The queen was not happy. And Princess Diana thought she had a way of cooling off the heat Fleet Street was applying to the soles of Prince Andrew's bare feet.

Charles and Andrew had never been all that close as children. In fact, some twelve years separated their birth dates. In addition to that almost unbridgeable gap, each was a completely different type of human being, with entirely different interests.

Andrew was born on a bitterly freezing February 19, 1960, at Buckingham Palace at half-past three in the afternoon. Later he was christened Andrew Albert Christian Edward Mountbatten-Windsor by the archbishop of Canterbury in the Music Room of the palace.

From the beginning, his upbringing was different from Charles's. Things were more relaxed in the family now. None other than his father, the duke of Edinburgh, once remarked: "People want their first child very much. They want the second almost as much. If a third comes along, they accept it as natural, but they haven't gone out of their way to try and get it."

And so the strictures were very relaxed on Andrew. He was not thrust into the limelight immediately, as Charles and Anne both were. He was reported to be a "jolly" baby, "always full of smiles," and one who "rarely cried." He resembled more than anyone else his father—with ash-blond hair and deep blue eyes. He was a robust and sturdy child, one who soon grew to getting his own way whenever he wanted it. He was "popular" with the Buckingham Palace staff at first, but as he grew up, this popularity decreased markedly. He cultivated a kind of "little boy" charm, which concealed a stubborn, opinionated, and selfish interior personality. He was, in fact, an obstinate and determined little devil.

A male insider at the palace described him as "a troublemaker since he was a little boy." But, he added, with all that, Andrew was "enormously likable."

"He was always hitting someone or something, including the nursery corgis, poor relations of the queen's dogs. He would go through a dressing-up box, which the royal children have had for generations, and get himself into a cowboy outfit, leaving a trail of disaster behind him. Then he would expect someone to clean up."

His nanny, Mabel Anderson, would yell at him to get things in order again, and he would do so, but with a mutinous countenance. In order to take out his aggression against his nanny, he would pound on the dogs.

It was during this period that the Charles-Andrew relationship was more or less consolidated. They simply did not get on very well together. Charles was always trying to be a good big brother, but Andrew was having none of it. It was obvious that Andrew—a naturally extroverted and outgoing person—found his brother hopelessly stuffy.

The queen once remarked, "Andrew isn't a bit shy." No. Arrogant would be the right word. Arrogant and bossy. Besides that, he loved playing practical jokes on members of the family. The queen again: "He is not always a little ray of sunshine about the house."

At the age of eight and a half, Andrew started school at Heatherdown, which had thirty acres of gardens and grass, and even a swimming pool. The idea was to let Andrew lead as normal a life as a schoolboy could. Apparently the surroundings suited him well. He came across as "a lively, cheerful boy with a touch of the daredevil in his glance."

During the last of his five years at Heatherdown, Andrew played rugby and cricket. "The staff at Heatherdown were not sorry to see Andrew leave," one biographer said, "but they wished him luck when he left."

In 1973 Andrew was enrolled at Gordonstoun, where Charles had gone before him, and their father long before the two of them. But Gordonstoun had changed in one aspect. It was now a coed institution, rather than the Spartan and austere school it had been earlier.

The toughness of Gordonstoun put him off at first. He was unable to assume the low ranking that every first-year student was required to. He kept pointing out that he was royalty. His supreme self-confidence irritated those around him. He was, in fact, very unpopular.

"There was a bit of 'I am a Prince' about him when he

first arrived," one of his peers said later. "But you can't get away with that sort of thing at Gordonstoun and it was soon knocked out of him. The ribbings he got were unmerciful and he caught on fast. He had to."

Soon he knuckled down to it and thoroughly enjoyed it. A member of the staff said, "He has no time for sycophants and if anyone tries to take the mickey out of him, he fights back. He's just as good with the verbalistics as with his fists."

During his enrollment at Gordonstoun, he joined in an exchange visit for three weeks in France—the group was composed of ten men and five women from the school. The idea was to brush up on their French.

In France they stayed at a Jesuit College near Toulouse in the southwest of France. While there, Andrew called himself "Andrew Edwards"—a pseudonym composed of his first and last Christian names.

He lived with a doctor and his family in a suburb of the city. He did manage to pick up a little French, although his teacher at the college said that "he can hardly be said to speak fluently after only three weeks in France. But he made very considerable progress while he was with us."

The abbot at the college remembered him as "a lively boy with the good and bad points of any fourteen-year-old." The man in charge of the whole party of students later declared: *"Mon Dieu,* he was certainly a handful!"

It was during his stay at Gordonstoun that Andrew became interested in flying. He enrolled at the Air Training Corps at the Royal Air Force Station at Milltown Airfield, Morayshire, not far from the school. His instructor, Flight Lieutenant Peter Bullivant, found him "quite fearless and quick to learn," and pointed out that he was a "very good and enthusiastic young pilot."

Only fifteen when he started learning to fly, he had to wait until he was sixteen before he was able to fly solo. He did so in July 1976, with three four-minute flyovers of Milltown Airfield. And he thus earned his wings.

The Olympic Games were held in Montreal in the summer of 1976. Andrew accompanied his sister, Anne, who rode the queen's horse Goodwill in the games, and the queen, who opened the games. But Andrew was popular with the young women in Canada, and officially squired one named Sandi Jones, the daughter of a retired Canadian army officer.

It was during this stay in Canada that Andrew became interested in Lakefield College in Ontario, which operated an exchange of students with Gordonstoun. In the end, Andrew decided to spend two years there where he was introduced to canoeing through the wilds of Canada and to the game of ice hockey.

"The school is quite excellent," Andrew said later, "and so are the facilities it offers. But it is not just that—the boys here are terrific, really great." He also noted, "Everyone in Canada is incredibly friendly. You can say that life out here is very good indeed."

Andrew was not at all bad at ice hockey, the Canadians' favorite game. "He quite surprised me," said a member of the team, David Miller. "He was quite vicious, too, and you need to be a bit vicious to be good at the game."

His skiing, largely because of practice he had picked up on excursions with his father to Germany, earned him a place in the second downhill ski team.

He also played rugby for Lakefield. The team traveled to Pittsburgh in the United States, where Andrew was immediately surrounded by young women attracted to his persona and his position in life.

"He really attracts the ladies," said Al Pace, a member of the team.

Indeed he did. And his attraction seemed to be growing by leaps and bounds. In 1977 the queen celebrated her first twenty-five years on the throne. During this Silver Jubilee, there was a reception aboard the royal yacht *Britannia,* attended by Andrew and by Marie Corrigan, cofounder, with Betty Williams, of the Northern Ireland Peace Movement. Corrigan said, "He is a really handsome young man with charming manners and I was swept off my feet. Betty Williams embarrassed me by asking him if he was spoken for as 'I was still single and available if asked.' "

He was invited back to Canada that same year by the city of Vancouver, British Columbia, to celebrate its 110th anniversary. Young women would come up to him to meet him, declaring, "He's cute!" One said, "Even better than Prince Charles!"

Later, at the Calgary Stampede, one of the most famous events in Canada, he joined his brother Charles to witness the intricacies of roping and bulldogging steers.

Gillian Newman, who had been assigned to the two brothers to explain the things they were seeing at the rodeo, was struck by Andrew in particular, calling him "a real Prince Charming."

At the end of his stay, Andrew joined a Lakefield party on a three-hundred-mile canoe trip down the Coppermine River to the Arctic.

On his return to Gordonstoun, Andrew found his younger brother, Edward, there to start his own college career. And by now there were more and more young women interested in Andrew. A group was formed at school called "Andrew's Harem."

Sue Barnard was one of the first of these women. She was an American. Later on, she was displaced by Clio Nathaniels, who usually went home on holidays to Nassau in the Bahamas, where her parents lived.

Both these women were invited "home" by Andrew to "meet the queen." But there were more of these—an endless list, if you will.

One of the "Harem" explained later: "He knew how to spread himself around. One minute he's making your feel really great that you're the only one that matters. The next minute, just as you really think you're getting somewhere, he's off with somebody else."

Another admitted, "He knows how to make a girl feel special."

In 1979, Andrew enrolled in the Royal Naval College at Dartmouth after being accepted as a potential naval cadet. He signed on for a twelve-year commission as a helicopter pilot.

Basic training was tough—but Andrew had learned the meaning of tough at Gordonstoun, and he was able to cope with the spit and polish of the Royal Navy. Up at dawn for a run, cleaning his dormitory, shining his shoes. He passed his preliminaries without trouble, and then put in some sea time on the HMS *Hermes,* an aircraft carrier on which his brother Charles had also served.

Although quite successful in his naval duties, he was criticized by his associates more for his attitude than anything else.

"He was very conscious of being royal," one of his shipmates said.

Even though he did not inspire his male companions, he certainly did inspire the ladies! There were long parties aboard the *Hermes,* with Andrew the star attraction among all the visiting women.

He finished his helicopter training, and celebrated his twenty-first birthday, February 19, 1981, with dinner at Windsor Castle—learning there that his brother Charles was engaged to marry Lady Diana Spencer. In April 1981 he graduated, winning his wings and a "silver salver" in recognition of having come in first in his class. It was based on merit rather than on his rank in life, won by "his genuine aptitude for helicopter flying and a determination to succeed." His father presented him with his wings.

Returning to the navy, Andrew was officially promoted

to sublieutenant in September 1981. His first posting as an officer was aboard the HMS *Invincible.*

Hardly had he settled into that job than Argentina attacked the Falkland Islands on April 5, 1982, and the ship he was on was sent to the south Atlantic on war duty. His helicopter was fully operational throughout the action.

On June 21, he was regaled by his shipmates over the fact that he had slipped down a notch in rank—referring to the fact that although he had started the voyage in the number two spot as heir to the throne of England, he was now number three with the birth of his nephew William.

In combat, Andrew had fought as was expected of him. "It simply never occurred to me that, because I'm a member of the Royal Family, I wouldn't take part if it came to fighting or seeing it through," he told a reporter. "I was jolly glad that I was here throughout with my squadron: they are absolutely fantastic."

One of the critics of Andrew's personality—a member at one time of the Buckingham Palace staff—commented:

"The British public was impressed [about Andrew's service during the Falkland War] and on the strength of that he'll probably get away with his antics for a long time to come!"

In fact, it was his attitude that was still one of his basic character flaws. It was not long afterward that Prince Andrew was at Windsor with the family, refusing to send out any Christmas cards at all and refusing to buy any presents for anyone. The queen was upset, and asked Prince Charles to discuss the matter with him.

"Speak to him, Charles, and see if you can get him into the family Christmas spirit," she said.

Charles and Andrew met, and later Charles sighed and told a member of the staff: "I give up!"

Yet Andrew did indeed go into Windsor and visit the shops, with his bodyguard at his heels. Apparently

Charles had gotten to him more than he had thought he did.

One of the main beefs of the staff was that Andrew never wanted to join the family during the royal outings to Sandringham or Windsor but would stay around in town to entertain his girlfriends at the palace. Because of this, the palace steward would have to keep on a skeleton staff just to look after him!

And the list of his girlfriends was formidable at best! His "puppy love" affair with Sandi Jones in Canada had made plenty of headlines in the tabloids in its time, along with his group of "Andrew's Harem" at Gordonstoun, but since Sandi there had been plenty of other new ones.

The first and foremost of these charmers was an American named Kathleen Stark, better known by her film name "Koo" Stark. The two films in which she had appeared were nothing more than bits of hard-core erotica; she was seventeen at the time she had played in them. When she began running with Andrew she was twenty-five, but dark and pretty in spite of her background.

Introduced to Koo by the impresario Michael White in February 1982 at Tramps, a London hangout, Andrew's next move consisted in taking her on a Caribbean holiday with him and several other friends. To throw off Fleet Street, Andrew and Koo disguised themselves as "Mr. and Mrs. Cambridge" on the travel manifests.

By the time they got to the Island of Mustique where they were to stay at Aunt Margaret's house, *Les Jolies Eaux* (Pleasant Waters), the news leaked out somehow. Pretty soon there were more newspaper people on the island than the island could safely hold.

There were pictures, there were stories. For example, one of the headlines read: SECRET LOVE OF THE PRINCE AND A NUDE STAR!

Another had this: I SAW ANDREW LEAVE HER FLAT IN THE MORNINGS. HE ALWAYS LOOKED RATHER TIRED.

Or, how about: QUEEN BANS KOO.

And: IF NOT KOO—WHO?

The whole Koo Stark thing fizzled out eventually when she married in 1984, but it was grist for the Fleet Street mill for some time.

Following Koo there was a woman named Vicki Hodge, who was almost twice as old as Andrew; she admitted to thirty-nine at the time. Vicki made the liaison worth quite a bit of fattening in her bank account.

A Briton and daughter of a baronet, Vicki went on a holiday with Andrew and two female friends. Three women and a prince, you see. There were pictures—plenty of pictures—of all of them romping about.

And there were words—words that Vicki herself wrote. The headlines under which her "love story" appeared went like this: WE MADE LOVE AMONG THE SCENTED TROPICAL FLOWERS.

There were pictures of the prince skinny-dipping in the surf, swinging his trunks triumphantly up over his head. There were shots of him and the three women riding the waves onto shore—all four topless.

In the story, Vicki announced that she had "seen the royal bum." In fact, she said that she had even "claimed the crown jewels."

There was another named Katie Rabett—really!—who was the daughter of an obstetrician. Things were going well for Rabett and Andrew when suddenly, lo and behold, members of the media dug up a whole set of nudie photographs of her. Andrew retreated in disarray.

Before those headlined days, Andrew had taken out such people as Carolyn Seaward, who had been dubbed Miss United Kingdom of 1980. Sadly, he had to drop her when she began talking to everybody, including the scribblers from Fleet Street, about what it was like to have a date *inside* Buck House.

He even dated Gemma Curry, the daughter of the pilot who had taught Andrew to pilot a chopper.

And so on and on.

Anyway, as the list got bigger and the headlines got warmer, heads were shaking amongst the members of royalty. Actually, the queen herself was much less worried about Andrew's indiscretions than others. She felt that it was all right to "have fun" with whatever girls he wanted to. It would, of course, be impossible for him to marry any one of them. And obviously, Andrew had really never had any ideas about doing *that!*

Now that Lady Diana was the Princess of Wales, she felt more and more a member of the family, and realized that Andrew's antics did not sit too well amongst the charmed circle. The trouble with Andrew was that he could now—and always had been able to—get away with anything he wanted. It would take someone pretty tough and able to manage him.

Manage?

The key word brought up a picture of Sarah Ferguson—and it was almost instantly that Diana decided to become a matchmaker.

As far back as 1982, in fact, she had inveigled the queen to invite Sarah Ferguson to attend Diana's twenty-first birthday luncheon at Kensington Palace. To anyone who might have seen her there and thought about it, it should have given some kind of tip to what was in the mind of the Princess of Wales.

Nobody paid any attention, of course. At that time Andrew was still riding high with Koo Stark.

It was not until June 1985 that Diana started her work in earnest.

Fleet Street, usually astute and almost extra-sensory-perceptive when it came to royal romances, was completely inattentive to the realities of a possible relationship between Sarah Ferguson and Prince Andrew. Had the members of the London media been aware of the meanings of the tea leaves at the bottom of the cup, they would have realized that Sarah's guest status at Diana's twenty-first birthday luncheon at Kensington Palace might really mean more than a simple invitation to a party.

But Diana had always been able to get away with a thing or two in her dealings with the press. This time her real intent was carefully masked—so much so that no one outside the palace made anything of Sarah's presence at her friend Di's twenty-first birthday bash.

But all that was to change in June 1985.

It was the Princess of Wales who suggested that Sarah Ferguson be put on the queen's guest list for the annual festivities at Windsor Castle during Royal Ascot Week—probably the most important of all the affairs of the year and a perfect setting for journalistic royalty watching and its attendant photo opportunities.

As for Sarah herself, if she was nervous to be at the Royal Ascot with Diana, who was by now one of her fastest friends, she did not show it. "Don't be nervous," her father advised her. "Just be yourself."

In the traditional royal procession around the Ascot racetrack that always precedes the opening of the races, Sarah Ferguson shared an open carriage with Prince Andrew—again, at Diana's suggestion. The prince and Sarah sat together at lunch, playfully pelting one another with profiteroles—rich little French pastries like tiny cream puffs with sticky-sweet centers. It was their richness that inspired Andrew to tease Sarah into eating one.

"But I'm meant to be on a diet!" Sarah howled indignantly.

Andrew apparently made no remark about her weight, and the two proceeded to skirmish good-naturedly with one another in a scene out of a film farce. Plenty of Fleet Street types who were hanging around ignored the byplay—ignored, indeed, Sarah Ferguson completely.

Even in the famed royalty-watching publication, *Royal Monthly,* there was no notice of the open carriage that carried Sarah and Andrew. In the next issue there was, instead, a story about Andrew's duty with his ship, HMS *Brazen,* during which he had taken part in a gag parody of Gilbert and Sullivan's "Three Little Maids" with some sailor companions in drag. Even a section devoted to "Royals at the [Ascot] Races" failed to show Andrew and Sarah together.

In the followup article in the *next Royal Monthly,* a story on Prince Andrew and his fading romance with Koo Stark did not mention Sarah Ferguson at all.

Actually, Fleet Street wasn't paying much attention to Andrew at Ascot—some of them apparently not even recognizing him out of his naval uniform. And, because many of them had seen Sarah Ferguson around the polo matches and considered her almost a part of the scenery—they knew who her father was—they simply made the classical error reporters sometimes make of taking her for granted.

One account published later about that day said that "when Prince Andrew and Miss Ferguson walked from the paddock to the royal enclosure they were stopped, if only briefly: he was, apparently, unrecognized out of naval uniform, and she was just unknown."

They took advantage of their relative freedom to become better acquainted. Pictures taken at that time show the two of them—Andrew dressed in typical Ascot costume with gray top hat, gray tie, and gray vest, and Sarah in a snappy white chapeau and a white dress with little blue bands and crosses on it—smiling and laughing with one another, barely distinguishable from the crowd of other Ascot-clad ladies and gentlemen.

Since they were not hounded by the press, they were able to relax in one another's company, and by the time the week was over, they had forged a rather interesting and intimate relationship. In fact, if Fleet Street's finest had been paying attention to their business a bit more, they might have been on the lookout for what Prince Andrew was up to. He himself had said that his image as "Randy Andy" was passé at that time.

"I'm a loner," he said. "I really am, yet when I say that, no one believes me. They seem to think I am always surrounded by girls, that my life is all fun and games. It isn't. I'd really like to be married, I think I'm old enough now, but I've yet to meet the right girl."

He *wasn't* kidding.

After the Ascot races Prince Andrew, on leave from the Royal Navy for a few months, made a short official visit to Canada, where he appeared in New Brunswick, Nova Scotia, and Ontario, and then flew back to London on July 13. He telephoned Sarah at her Clapham digs and invited her out for the evening. After a supper at Buckingham Palace in the prince's apartment, they went dancing on the town.

That was the beginning of a number of other Andrew and Sarah get-togethers. They spent weekends with friends—most of them Prince Andrew's—and even had a week together at Balmoral Castle. There, once again, the press seemed to have been unable to rid their eyes of the scales that blinded them.

During that period, Diana herself frequently invited Sarah to Kensington Palace in London, for dinner with Prince Andrew and other members of the royal family. And so the romance blossomed, in large part helped along by the Princess of Wales—who now realized that what she had originally thought about her brother-in-law and her friend was true. They were indeed meant for one another.

Meanwhile the press was still trying to figure out who to match up romantically with Prince Andrew. A magazine report in the winter said that there were "four young ladies with splendid pedigrees" under consideration by the palace: Princess Alexis of Greece, the eighteen-year-old daughter of ex-King Constantine; Princess Katarina of Yugoslavia, twenty-five, whose father was another former monarch; the Grand Duchess Edwina of Mecklenburg, nineteen; and seventeen-year-old India Hicks, granddaughter of the late Earl Mountbatten.

However, the queen and Prince Philip also had their eyes on "the attractive daughters of a number of peers who are close friends of the Royal Family." Still no mention of Sarah Ferguson by name.

There were members of the media who were more alert than others. When the queen invited Sarah Ferguson to the royal party at Sandringham during the New Year celebration of 1986, she was spotted by an alert photographer, out in the cold, sitting with Prince Andrew on a grassy bank in plain view of passing traffic, "cuddled up and holding hands in the cold."

She was also seen tramping through fields on a pheasant shoot with Prince Andrew and his Labrador retriever—she dressed in a distinctive Davy Crockett–style fur hat, and he in the traditional garb of the pheasant hunt.

Identified only then as a possible contender for the prince's hand, Sarah was immediately targeted by Fleet Street for further questioning and grilling. And so she thus became a number one interest of the press corps, and researchers went to work trying to dope out her background.

It was not easy to find a great many details of her life, but it was easy to burrow down into the layers of gossip about the Sloane Rangers to find out that she had dated a number of men during her London years and had in fact lived with two of them for a time in the usual "swinging London" fashion.

Her father would not comment at all on Sarah's possible interest in Prince Andrew, other than to say, "There is obviously a connection between the two of them, but it is not for me to speculate on what it is. She is a big girl now, and she's old enough to speak for herself."

And what she told them when they asked was: "I'm sorry, but you know I can say nothing."

This was all the usual grist for the newspaper mill, and Sarah Ferguson became an overnight sensation in the tabloid press. But there was still the possibility that she might be just another Koo Stark—here today and gone tomorrow. And that opinion was expressed by most of the scribes who wrote about her.

In February 1986 two incidents occurred that, taken together, were proof that this "thing" with Sarah Ferguson was based on a much more solid foundation than Prince Andrew's earlier liaisons had been.

Number one. Prince Andrew's ship, the frigate HMS *Brazen,* made port in London on the Thames for a four-day goodwill visit, with all its officers and men. Photographers and reporters were on hand to spot any royal visitors who might take the time to visit Prince Andrew in uniform. Among them was—

Young Prince William, going on four, was escorted to the ship to see his Uncle Andrew's marvelous "toys," along with his mother's best friend, Sarah Ferguson. These three were the focus of almost all the photographic attention that day. Prince William looked over the pilot house of the ship and climbed into his uncle's helicopter for a dekko. The queen and Prince Philip were aboard too.

But it was the newcomer, Sarah Ferguson, who kept the cameras clicking—and cranking. This made it almost official that something out of the ordinary was happening, that, indeed, Prince Andrew was more than interested in this latest of his "dates."

ANDREW—IS IT REALLY TRUE LOVE? one headline later speculated.

"Keep smiling, for goodness sake!" Princess Diana hissed at her friend as they boarded the ship. "Keep smiling!" And Sarah did, facing a formidable array of still cameras, hand-held minicams, and big newsreel type cameras as well.

Sarah Ferguson carried it all off as if she had been facing the public all her life.

Number two. One week after Sarah's first real appearance in public officially in the royal family entourage, she made another dashing and smashing entrance with the Prince and Princess of Wales on the ski slopes at Klosters, Switzerland. She was one of several in the royal party that rented a six-bedroom chalet at Wolfgang.

The press had been alerted to the fact that Charles and Diana were on their way to ski, of course, but were unaware of their most special guest. And so when she appeared outside with the prince and princess, it was a Roman Holiday for the photographers. All but deserting Charles and Diana, the members of the media flocked around her, showering her with questions—which she answered with aplomb and dispatch.

"The princess wondered whether I would like to join Prince Charles and herself and I said yes. I'm here to enjoy the skiing. No, I promise you Prince Andrew is not coming."

The paparazzi all but swept her off her feet as she waited to climb onto the T-bar to go up the mountain. They badgered her again about whether or not she was engaged to Prince Andrew. She laughed and gave out with a phoney cockney accent: "Cor blimey, darling! You must be joking!"

But they were not joking. They were deadly serious. And the seriousness of their intent became manifest at Heathrow, when Sarah returned to London, alone, and not with the royal party. It seemed that every newspaper, magazine, and television station in the country had representatives on hand to meet her. It was some kind of brawl.

Photographers and reporters kicked and punched each other to get the first glimpse and a word from her. Police were summoned in an attempt to keep the press at bay. It did no good. The yelling and shouting and fisticuffs increased. A flying wedge of policemen finally gathered her up and ran her through the gauntlet to her car.

Nothing was going right that day. Her car would not start. The press was onto her once again, like waves lapping at a sinking ship. Finally the engine kicked over, and she was able to drive away from the surging mob.

"That was the longest five minutes of my life," she confessed to an airport worker, and she finally zoomed away up the ramp.

Speculation, in the cliché of the news business, was indeed rife over an upcoming announcement of some kind.

But now Andrew was back on board ship, and Sarah was back at work in London. Photographers and reporters could see her there, arriving and leaving each day. How could two people carry on a romance when they were miles apart? It was not easy.

Nevertheless, when Sarah went to work on Conduit Street in the West End of London she was accompanied by an escort of three policemen—an inspector and two constables—called in by Buckingham Palace as a result of the brouhaha at Heathrow the day before.

And of course the reporters were there, in greater numbers than usual. "Sorry," she kept saying. "I can't talk. You know how it is."

They continued to dog her footsteps, even when she would go out to lunch at a favorite Italian restaurant nearby with a girlfriend.

"Speculation continues about an announcement of her engagement to Prince Andrew," the papers said.

Oddly enough, the truth of the matter was that Prince Andrew *had* proposed to Sarah during the Klosters holiday, but she had asked him for just a little quality time to think about it. And of course he did allow her time; there wasn't much else he could do.

Soon, however, she made her decision.

Floors Castle is the largest mansion in Britain that is inhabited by a single family living its day-to-day life. Located outside Kelso, just north of the Scottish border, it is a huge eighteenth-century castle, rambling over a grassy hilltop. With its high Norman towers and flying pennons, it seems like something out of a costume film or a novel by Sir Walter Scott.

For years the duke and duchess of Roxburghe, who live at Floors Castle, had been friends of Prince Andrew and the royal family. He was in the habit of visiting the area for the wonderful shooting and fishing on the Tweed River that flows nearby. The duchess of Roxburghe is the sister of the duchess of Westminster, incidentally, one of the Princess of Wales's closest confidantes.

Somehow Sarah Ferguson was able to disguise herself as a "Miss Anwell" and fly from Heathrow to Newcastle for the weekend of February 22 and 23 without anyone the wiser. From Newcastle she was driven the fifty-odd miles to the castle to be welcomed by her host and hostess.

Meanwhile, Prince Andrew had secured a forty-eight-hour leave from his ship, docked at Sunderland, and was on his way to Floors Castle himself. Actually, both Prince Andrew and Sarah Ferguson had been there at the castle two years earlier in the same large party, but that was before their romance had blossomed—and few people there had seen them together much at that time.

As their private weekend progressed, it became obvious to Sarah that the time was now ripe for action. And she was prepared. When it happened, it was not exactly the way she had envisioned it—but it was worth it all nevertheless.

Prince Andrew later admitted to the world that he went

down onto both knees on the carpet of Floors Castle to ask Sarah to be his wife.

"Do you remember the exact words that the prince used to ask you to marry him?" someone questioned her.

"Absolutely!" she replied. "But I'm not telling you!"

And so . . .

Whatever those words were, they certainly did the trick, for no sooner had he asked her this time, than she replied that she would.

"I was surprised," Prince Andrew later admitted, probably referring to the fact that the first time he had asked her she had begged for time to think it over.

"Now," Sarah said after she told him she would marry him, "when you wake up tomorrow morning, you can tell me that this is all a huge joke."

But next morning he did not.

It was time now for the world to hear—but, wait a moment! Was it?

It was *not*. The queen and the duke of Edinburgh were on a tour of Australia and New Zealand, and would not be back for some days. It was, in fact, almost three weeks later that the world learned of the news.

But others—

The weekend over, Prince Andrew returned to his ship, and Sarah flew back to London under her assumed identity, her cover unbroken. Then, on Monday, she had lunch with the Princess of Wales at her home in Kensington Palace.

"Did he do it?" Diana asked first thing.

"Yes!" replied Sarah, and the matchmaker was overjoyed at news that she had been able to make two people she loved happy.

The secret was kept in a tight little group of people within and close to Buckingham Palace.

It was not until the morning of March 19, 1986, after the queen and the duke of Edinburgh had returned home to

London, that a member of the palace staff walked leisurely out into the front area of Buckingham Palace where the usual crowds were standing around and watching for anything of interest to happen, and slowly posted a notice on the front gates.

This was in pursuit of an ancient tradition announcing any coming wedding of a member of royalty, devised in times when newspapers, radio, and television were not even heard of, and the nearest thing to a media event was the arrival of the town crier. The time-worn tradition is not broken even in today's vastly different world of instant communication.

Those who were closest peered briefly at the announcement, and a yell went up as others crowded in to read.

"It is with the greatest pleasure," the notice began, "that the Queen and the Duke of Edinburgh announce the betrothal of their beloved son the Prince Andrew to Miss Sarah Ferguson."

The day before had been a busy one for Sarah. The "royal engagement interview," traditionally held on the day the engagement is announced, is one of the most engrossing and yet ennervating types of media event yet devised by the world press corps. It has been said that both the Princess of Wales and Captain Mark Phillips—who married Princess Anne—had never known anything like it before and had shied away from interviews for some time after their marriages into the royal family.

Sarah had been forewarned by the Princess of Wales herself. The day before the posting of the notice, she had made final arrangements for the wool crepe suit she had selected to wear during the television interview that would be broadcast all over the world. There would also be numerous photo opportunities for Fleet Street's paparazzi, and gab sessions with reporters and magazine writers from all over the world. It would be a grueling day.

And so it was that on "engagement day"—March 19,

1986—Sarah Ferguson and Prince Andrew were interviewed by a joint team of Anthony Carthew of ITN, the British commercial channel, and Michael Cole of BBC News. It took place in Prince Andrew's second-floor study at Buckingham Palace. The thing itself was fairly short—about ten minutes—and to the point.

After initial congratulations from the court correspondents, Sarah Ferguson showed her diamond and ruby engagement ring. It was an oval Burma ruby with ten diamonds set in the form of a cluster mounted in 18-carat white and yellow gold. It had been made by Garrard's, the royal jewelers, to a design sketched by Prince Andrew himself.

"They were," Prince Andrew attested as the world studied the ring, "very nice engineers."

That evoked a response from Sarah to the effect that the prince was being much too crass and light-hearted about the superb craftsmanship of her prized ring.

"Stunning!" she said of it. "Red. I wanted a ruby. Well, I didn't *want* it. I'm very lucky to have it. Certainly it's a lovely stone. I've got red hair too." The last a needless and rather amusing comment, considering the fact that the screen was filled with that red hair at the moment she said it.

Prince Andrew told his interviewers that he had been quite proper about his engagement, and had even asked for both the queen's and Major Ferguson's approval before going ahead with Sarah.

The two reminisced about when they had first begun to be interested in each other—at Ascot, of course. There, according to the prince, they had been "made to sit next door to each other" at lunch, where he had made her eat a chocolate profiterole. And she had hit him.

It was indeed the place where true love had begun. Prince Andrew: "There are always humble beginnings. It's got to start somewhere."

How many children did they want? They talked about that indecisively, admitting that they had not really discussed the point yet.

Then Sarah began talking about how the two of them felt being in love, saying that they were "good friends, a good team," and that they were "very happy."

Prince Andrew agreed. "I'm over the moon."

Sarah: "It's *we*."

"*We* are both over the moon," Prince Andrew corrected himself. "This *we* business," he muttered, "might not be easy to get used to."

When photographers asked him to kiss her as they sat there, he demurred, but Sarah smiled and said, "Oh, why not?" and gave Prince Andrew a peck on the cheek—followed by a proper kiss on the lips.

Even in America, Sarah Ferguson's waspish charm captivated the toughest of hard-nosed journalists. Jilly Cooper wrote: "It is no small achievement that by being her lovely, larky, unaffected self, she had captured the heart of not only the most eligible man in the country, but also the entire nation."

Baby Sarah in the lap of her father, Major Ron Ferguson in a family snapshot taken on the banks of the Thames.

All photos courtesy of Globe unless otherwise credited.

Sarah Ferguson at 3½ wore a look of determination and a sense of knowing what she wanted.

Mother and daughters: Sarah Ferguson (left) is photographed with her mother, Susan, and her elder sister, Jane; Sarah was then aged 9.

Below: Fergie grew up a keen and competent horsewoman. Here, at 10, she takes a jump smoothly.

G B

Opposite: Sarah Ferguson The initials reflect her patriotism for Great Britain.

Charles, Fergie and a pregnant Di discuss the outcome of a Polo match at Windsor.

Below: Fergie and sister-in-law Princess Anne.

The Duke and Duchess of York, and the wedding party.

Fergie at a Christmas shoot near Sandringham. Her labrador, Tarn, was a wedding gift from Prince Andrew. The hat her friend borrowed is in the shape of a plum pudding.

Fergie, Andrew and HRH the Princess Beatrice of York.

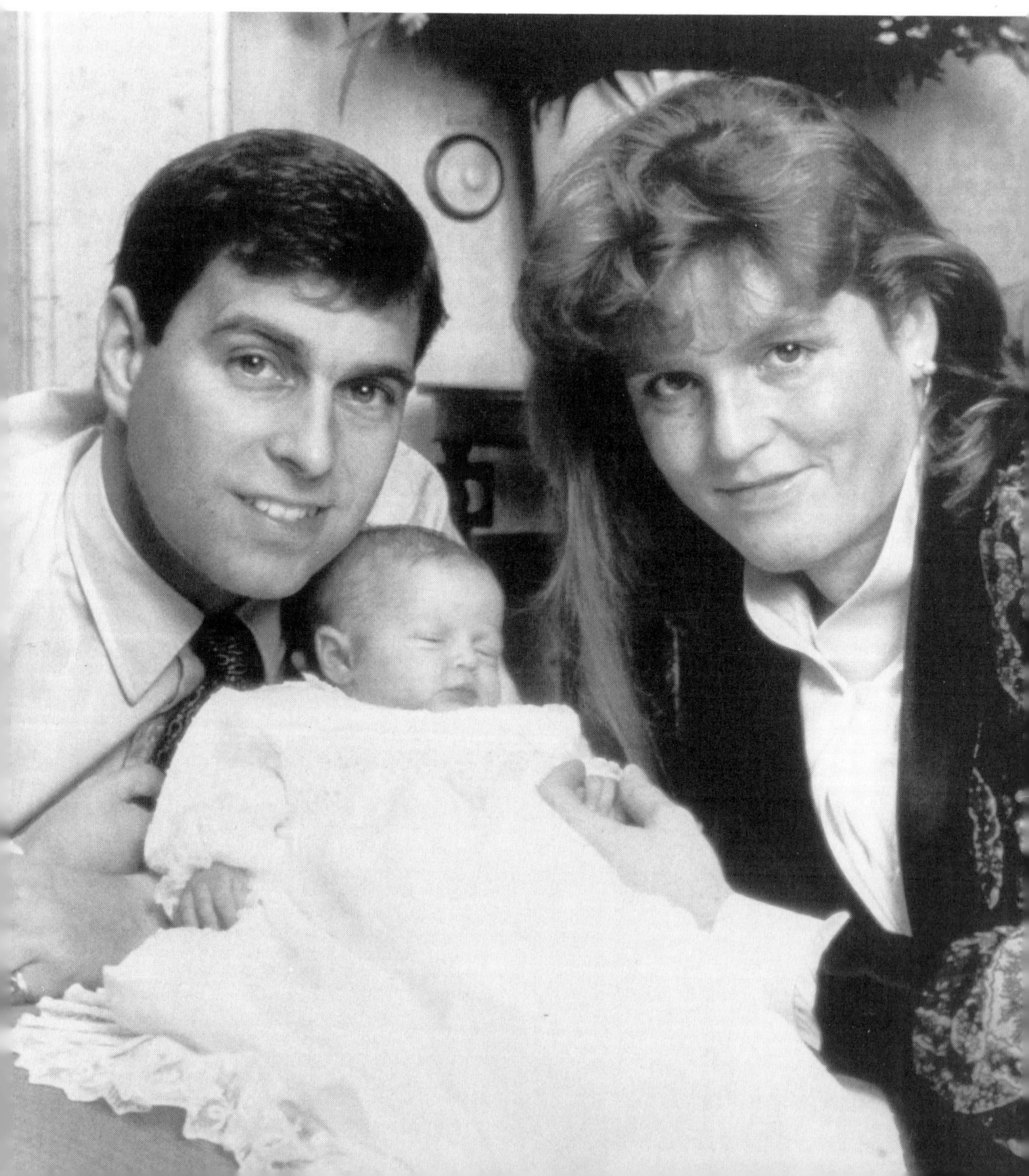

Even as a chatty 2-year-old, Diana showed hair and fashion sense.

The growing Diana showed promise of the beauty she would become.

Diana is clearly not second best to Prince Charles as she awards him the runner-up medal after his loss in the British Open Polo match.

Di watchers say she knows how to please the photographers. That's Prince Charles behind her.

Diana's keen fashion sense hasn't failed her often, but this emerald-green checked ensemble raised eyebrows on her visit to Italy.

Opposite: Diana and William the Conqueror.
Rangefinders

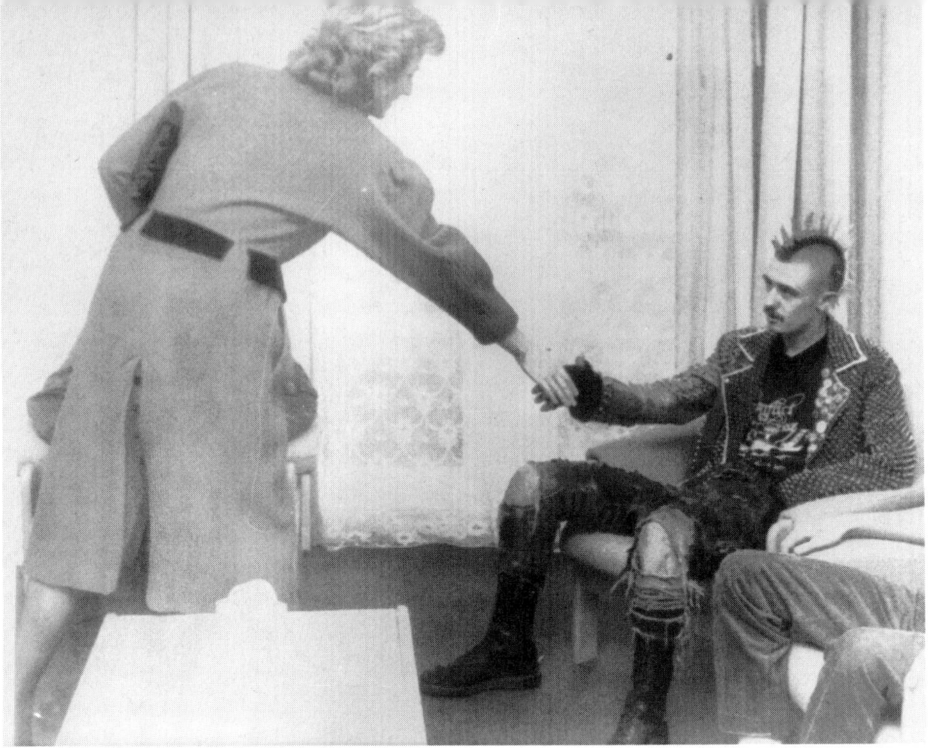

Above: The Princess and the Punk. Di greets a constituent on a visit to a youth center.

Diana's low-profile garb worn to watch Prince Charles play polo didn't fool the photographers or the crowd for long.

The Royal Harry. Diana holds her young son prior to a trip to Scotland. The princes now fly separately from their parents to prevent the family flying together.

Jim Bennett
Alpha

Diana's inspired use of some costume pearls had heads turning at a Steven Spielberg film premiere.

IX

THE DUCHESS OF YORK

9

"THE GRAND OLD DUCHESS OF YORK"

ONCE THE NEWS WAS OUT, IT DID NOT TAKE SARAH FERGUSON AND Prince Andrew long to set the date for the wedding itself. As they had averred from the beginning, it would be soon, as early in the summer as possible.

The date finally set aside was July 23, 1986. And the ceremonies were to take place at Westminster Abbey, and not St. Paul's Cathedral, where Prince Charles and Lady Diana Spencer had been married.

Then it was back to work as usual for Prince Andrew, who was still on naval duty, and for Sarah Ferguson the next Monday—and she was now accompanied as she always would be in the future by Prince Andrew's personal detective, backed up by two plainclothes officers.

When the paparazzi arrived in force that morning to take pictures of the new Princess Andrew to be, they were forced to shoot her from across the street, since the entrance to the building was guarded now by a dozen constables.

By now the pressure of Fleet Street was a great deal mitigated; most of the press corps had turned into friends because of Sarah Ferguson's natural affability and goodwill toward them. In addition, she had a quality of showing others her good points of character and personality.

"Sarah will take her role as The Princess Andrew extremely seriously," said Sarah's old roommate, Carolyn Beckwith-Smith. "She'll go far . . . very far."

Sarah's mother, now Mrs. Hector Barrantes, was on hand visiting London to see her daughter. Of course she was hunted down immediately by quote-hungry reporters.

"She is twenty-six," her mother said of Sarah, "but she is a much older woman now and there is more head on her shoulders. She is not some silly slip of a girl, some dumb Sloane Ranger, even if her clothes and her appearance might make some people think she is."

It was about this time that one of Fleet Street's minions casually asked Sarah's mother where her daughter had happened to meet Prince Andrew. Mrs. Barrantes, married first to a polo master of the Guards and later polo director of Princes Philip and Charles, and remarried to an international polo star, took that question in stride.

"On the polo field!" she said, with a "where else?" air. "Doesn't *everyone?*"

The press dutifully tracked down Sarah's boss at the publishing company. Richard Burton was found to be a great admirer of his "directrice."

"Sarah is very skilled at her work," he told the press, "showing great expertise in the business side of the art world. She has helped with a book on Impressionist painting, which has sold 105,000 copies in the [United] States. Now she is working on a book on the palaces of Westminster."

About Sarah, he said, "She is a jolly girl with a good sense of humor. She is delightful to work with and has masses of common sense. Her best quality is that she is good-humored. She deals with clients extremely well.

"One of her great loves—apart from Andrew—is her father's Jack Russell terrier. I have four, and if not for the quarantine laws, I'd love to give them one as a wedding present.

"Another big love is, of course, her father. She is really 'Daddy's girl'—like Princess Diana. And she does get on well with her mother, Mrs. Barrantes."

And he even had a word to say about Sarah's mother. "Mrs. Barrantes is as charming as Sarah."

Things died down after a few days of excitement, and Sarah's efforts were directed toward getting her wedding dress started and learning some of the palace "ropes" that she would have to know by heart sooner than later.

Even so, along about the end of May, she was able to get away from the cold, wet weather of the typical English spring to visit the West Indies for a week's holiday in the hot and steamy sunshine of the Caribbean.

With her detective at her side, she flew down to Antigua to be with one of her old school friends, Florence Belmondo, the daughter of Jean-Paul Belmondo, the French film star.

There she tried to lose a little weight, but spent most of the time luxuriating in the sunshine and swimming in the warm Caribbean waters. She learned to love the light, tasty food that was so easy to get in that island paradise: fresh fruit and fish.

Not surprisingly, the paparazzi were everywhere, just as they had been whenever Princess Diana had tried to elude them. But Sarah found it much easier to fob them off with a wisecrack and a grin that took the sting out of the "no comment" so easy to come to the tongue.

One evening she was eating a big grilled kingfish with

her friend at the famed Admiral Inn Restaurant, when she turned around to see a whole table full of reporters and photographers looking over at her.

With a smile, Sarah sent over two pink lilies by a waiter, with a note to the journalists.

"Please accept these flowers from the lady with her love."

When they waved acknowledgment to her, she called over, "Sorry I can't run to champagne!"

In turn, the reporters sent a bottle of champagne to Sarah's table, which she sipped happily, raising her glass in a toast to them: "Enjoy yourselves!"

As Sarah and Florence left the restaurant, she handed a half-empty bottle of the champagne to the reporters with an apology. "We can't finish it."

That brought cheerful laughter from them. One of the reporters said they were sorry for disturbing her meal out, but she laughed and responded:

"There was no problem. We anticipated we would run into each other sometimes. We had a very enjoyable meal and I appreciated the way you handled it."

She was a natural charmer—and she charmed Fleet Street into almost loving her even when she was trying to elude them.

Next day, tanned and rested, Sarah was on her way back to London for a reunion with Prince Andrew.

The press was full of quotes about the wedding, and one of them appeared in an interview in the magazine *Woman's Own,* in which the duke of Edinburgh said that he had been misquoted when he said that he was "extremely grateful" his son Andrew was going to marry Sarah Ferguson.

"That sounds as if I were afraid he had not been going in the right direction, which is absolutely not true," the duke said.

"I'm delighted he's getting married, but not because I

think it will keep him out of trouble because, in fact, he's never been in trouble in the sense the popular press would have it."

He said that "they seem very happy. I think that Sarah will be a great asset."

As might have been expected, the days just preceding the wedding were filled with a great deal of horseplay and nonsense—mostly instigated by the irrepressible Prince Andrew, and in some cases, by his younger brother, Prince Edward. This was well within the tradition of the family that had always been great at playing jokes and pranks on one another—and always would be.

For example, at the final wedding rehearsal, Prince Edward—acting as best man for his brother Prince Andrew—arrived with his arm in a sling, as a funny gag. He had flown in from New Zealand for the wedding, he said, and claimed that he had been "bitten by a kiwi."

A "kiwi," of course, is British slang for a New Zealander.

That was only one of the jokes that might seem incomprehensible to the outsider. "There was so much laughing and carrying on that it was difficult to hear a word," one witness to the rehearsal said. At one point in a rehearsal earlier in the week, Sarah Ferguson had kicked off her shoes and sat down to play the Westminster Abbey piano in a kind of impromptu prenuptial recital.

Two nights before the wedding, Major Ferguson mounted a massive bash at Smith's Lawn at Windsor Great Park. Seven hundred guests were invited—and all attended—including such luminaries as Michael Caine, retired race car champion and renowned TV commercial star Jackie Stewart, Elton John (said to be Prince Andrew's favorite singing performer), and Anthony Andrews, of *Brideshead Revisted* fame. In addition, Katie Rabett, one of Prince Andrew's former girlfriends, was on hand as well.

But the big celebrating took place the night before the

wedding. It was Prince Andrew's bachelor party—his final good-bye to his many girlfriends and the kiss of death to his swinging singles–hood. Twenty intimates, including his brother Prince Charles, Elton John, and David Frost, came to dinner at the Kensington Castle home of Peter Dineley.

Unfortunately, the paparazzi had somehow managed to rumble the entire operation, and were suddenly there in force. Police were summoned. While Robert Peel's finest held the media types at bay across the street from the palace, the celebrants ate their meal and drank champagne on the garden terrace well out of sight of the dreaded paparazzi. The party droned on and by 12:45 or so, it simply died of its own weight. Not quite the swinging affair it had been hoped to be.

The arrival of the newshounds was bad news to another faction of fun lovers. In the time-honored tradition of high jinks, the bride-to-be and her friends had dreamed up a little plot to crash the bachelor party in disguise.

And who else was in the trio of party-crashers than Sarah Ferguson (of course), Princess Diana (huh?), and a comedienne friend of Princess Diana's named Pamela Stephenson. These three were all waiting to stroll into the party and break it up.

Their disguise would have probably worked out all right had it not been for the presence of the crowds of Fleet Street regulars outside, being held back by the cops. The women had decided their best disguise would be to go in as policewomen—but now that would hardly be logical, with cops all around the place who would immediately see that they were fakes.

Now, all dressed up and no place to go, the three women decided to stop in at Annabel's, one of their favorite London night spots nearby. Swaggering in in their very nice disguises, the three bewigged bobbies took their places on bar stools and ordered drinks. They sat there drinking and giggling among themselves—quite unlike cops.

One slightly tipsy Londoner offered to buy them a round.

"Sorry," Princess Diana declared, shaking her bewigged head. "We never drink while on duty."

By now patrons of Annabel's were beginning to look at these three policewomen a little more closely. And, because both Princess Diana and Sarah Ferguson were constantly in the headlines with their faces in front of the public, some of the people in the boîte began to take a good second look.

Voilà!

By the time several more had sidled up to them offering to buy them drinks, they decided they had been made and got out of the place quickly.

End of caper.

Next morning, however, the press was onto them. The London tabloid the *Daily Mirror* had the most fun with the headline. "Fergie and Lacey," they called the pair of them.

Later on, the Princess of Wales talked about the escapade at a garden party given at the palace by the queen for a number of police wives. She admitted that it was never much fun, really.

"The wig was hot and uncomfortable and the black shoes were two sizes too small." But it was an interesting diversion. "It did cause a stir—sometimes you just have to laugh."

July 23, 1986, dawned in a rather petulant and ambivalent manner—half overcast and half brilliantly sunny—and yet London was ready to accept the sunshine as it was, with intermittent overcast. Even early on, the streets along the way from Buckingham Palace to Westminster Abbey—a good half mile in length—were lined ten-deep with people of all ages, shapes, and sizes.

The queen had actually began the day at eight o'clock in

the morning by drawing aside Prince Andrew and naming him the Duke of York, Earl of Inverness, and Baron Killyeagh—the traditional titles of the second in line to the throne. That despite the fact that Andrew was now fourth in line because of the presence of Princes William and Harry.

Elizabeth II's father and mother had been the duke and duchess of York, and she, before the abdication of her uncle, Prince Edward, had been the Princess Elizabeth of York. And so before he was even married, Prince Andrew had become much more than merely a prince of the realm—he would be His Royal Highness the Duke of York. It was a much more important title than Prince Andrew.

Thus now Sarah Ferguson would become by her marriage to him Her Royal Highness the Duchess of York rather than simply Princess Andrew—as everyone had thought she would be.

Less than two hours later, the queen and the duke of Edinburgh climbed into a semi-Landau to begin their ride from Buckingham Palace to Westminster Abbey—the queen wearing delphinium blue silk crepe with a matching hat and the duke in his naval uniform.

Eight minutes later, Prince Andrew, now Lieutenant His Royal Highness the Duke of York, Royal Navy, accompanied by his younger brother, Prince Edward, left the palace in another State Landau. Edward was to act as Andrew's "supporter"—the Royal British term for "best man."

As Andrew's carriage arrived at the west door of Westminster Abbey and the two brothers alighted, the crowd, alerted to the fact that Andrew's title had changed, burst into a rousing nursery rhyme: "The Grand Old Duke of York."

The four bridesmaids were waiting in a side chapel. They were Zara Phillips, Princess Anne's daughter; Alice

Ferguson, the bride's half-sister; Laura Fellowes, the niece of the Princess of Wales; and Lady Rosanagh Innes-Ker, the daughter of the duke and duchess of Roxburghe.

With the bridesmaids were the page boys—Prince William of Wales, and Seamus Makim, both nephews of the bride and bridegroom. They were dressed in sailor suits modeled after those worn in 1846. Peter Phillips and Andrew Ferguson, also in the party, wore midshipman's dress, based on a uniform of 1782.

Prince William was the one everyone in the marriage party was sweating out. At the age of four, he was a precocious handful, and a show-off to boot. It was thought that he might upstage the bride and groom on this, their big day. But other than fidgeting a bit and looking around at everything in a curious, penetrating manner, he kept his cool and behaved well.

Now the curtain was going up on what might be termed the beginning of the main event. From Clarence House—diagonally across the parkland from Buckingham Palace—emerged the traditional Glass Coach, carrying the bride, at precisely 11:15 in the morning. Fifteen minutes late—but didn't a bride *deserve* a little extra time?

This was the first public view of Sarah Ferguson's bridal gown—seen through the glass window of the Cinderella coach. It had been designed by Lindka Cierach, who had created it to express the personality of the bride. The gown was made out of ivory duchess satin, champagne in tone, tapering from full crowned shoulders to a point at the elbow and waist. The designer's hallmark—heavy beading—showed up dramatically on the dress.

The train was seventeen feet six inches in length and contained the thistles and bees of Sarah Ferguson's newly adopted coat of arms, together with anchors, waves, and hearts.

Her bouquet was a mix of gardenias, lilies, lilies of the

valley, veronica, and myrtle, created by a florist named Jane Packer, surprisingly only twenty-six years old and in business only four years.

Sarah was riding in the Glass Coach with her father. She waved to the crowds on the way, and when the coach stopped at Westminster Abbey, she descended on the arm of her father. After her train was arranged, twenty-two Royal Marine trumpeters sounded a fanfare.

And Major Ronald Ferguson and his daughter began the long four-minute walk up the nave of Westminster Abbey, joking and chatting together as they passed under the organ screen covered with creamy-white madonna lilies.

On the Persian-carpeted sacrarium, on the north and south sides of the altar, the families of the bride and groom stood facing one another. Prince Andrew gave a wide grin as he caught Sarah's eye at her approach, and they moved toward the prayer desks where they would be exchanging their vows.

Sarah Ferguson folded her hands in front of her as the archbishop of Canterbury, Dr. Robert Runcie, gave the usual warning of any "impediment" to the marriage.

After the traditional pause—since there were none to declare such an impediment—he continued.

"Andrew Albert Christian Edward, wilt thou have this woman to thy wedded wife?"

As the words continued to roll out in the stillness of the vast cathedral, it developed that Sarah Ferguson had opted to "obey" her husband as was decreed in the traditional 1662 marriage service rather than merely to "cherish" him, as Lady Diana Spencer had done.

Later, this drew protests from Clare Short, a Labour member of Parliament. "If she wants to give a lead to modern women in Britain, this is *not* the way to do it!" Short snapped.

Sarah was later able to explain: "I was thinking of

obeying in moral terms, as opposed to physically obeying. I am not the sort of woman who is going to meekly trot along behind her husband."

She said that in any kind of conflict she would look to her husband for the final, decisive word. In all other respects, she and her husband would continue to work in unison or as the "good team" she had said they were at the time of their engagement.

During the service, the only time Sarah stumbled was in pronouncing Prince Andrew's third name, Christian. Once she got that straight, everything went along like clockwork. The couple said their vows, and Dr. Runcie then blessed them as husband and wife.

The Prince of Wales read the lesson from Ephesians and the choir led the congregation in the hymn "Lead Us, Heavenly Father, Lead Us."

When the sound of the national anthem had died away the bride and bridegroom entered the Chapel of St. Edward the Confessor and there, to the singing of Mozart's "Laudate Dominum," followed by "Exultate Jubilate," the royal couple signed the marriage registers, and the veils and flowers that covered the bride's face were removed.

Their Royal Highnesses the Duke and Duchess of York moved back into the sacrarium, the bride curtsying to the queen, and the duke bowing.

It was all over, and they climbed into the Landau to make the trip back to Buckingham Palace. After the wedding breakfast of diced lobster and prawns the couple appeared on the balcony in a traditional salute to the nation.

"Kiss her, kiss her!" yelled the crowd below.

"Can't hear you!" joked the duchess of York.

And then, to whistles and cheers, the couple embraced and bussed each other resoundingly. The whole family congregated on the balcony, and then it was back inside for the newly wed couple.

"The French would not do it so grand," said a French student who was watching below. "It was beautiful and magnificent," he went on, describing the wedding inside the cathedral, and the processions to and from the palace.

"We don't have this in Germany," said another onlooker.

An Italian observer went all-out in praise for the event. "It was better than 'Dynasty'!"

One exceptionally embarrassing situation had apparently been passed over without comment by the media or any of the guests—who had come, as always, from all over the world. That possible "situation" was the presence of Hector Barrantes, the bride's stepfather, at the ceremony.

Although the queen had pondered considerably on extending the invitation to him to attend the wedding, in the end she did so—in spite of the fact that the man who was going to marry Barrantes's stepdaughter had risked his life fighting against her stepfather's country, Argentina, during the invasion of the Falkland Islands.

In finally extending the invitation, the queen had hinted to the world-class polo player that if he decided he was feeling ill at the time of the wedding, perhaps everyone everywhere would be happier. Apparently Barrantes enjoyed robust health and decided it would be a sham to call in sick for the wedding ceremony.

And then, several days earlier, he was playing a polo match in Greenwich, Connecticut, and had been smacked square in the nose by a caroming polo ball—and those things are heavy! Swelled nose or not, he decided he was feeling fine and flew to England.

In any event, there he was, seated in the second row of noted visitors, not far from Mrs. Ronald Reagan, and just behind his wife, Sarah Ferguson's mother—throbbing nose and all.

By tea time that afternoon the crowds of Londoners had reassembled in front of Buckingham Palace to cheer on the bride and groom as they left for their honeymoon somewhere in the Azores.

Just after four o'clock a storm of rose petals was released from above—more than twenty-four thousand roses had been gathered for the event—and the thirteenth duke of York and his bride rode into the cloud of petals out of the palace in the Landau, decorated with flags, masts, and a model satellite dish with a slogan that read: PHONE HOME.

Waving at crowds everywhere, the duke and duchess rode through Victoria and Pimlico to the Royal Hospital in Chelsea, from where they flew by helicopter to Heathrow Airport. There they jetted out to the royal yacht *Britannia* to embark on their cruise to that secretly guarded destination where their honeymoon would be celebrated.

About the couple the archbishop of Canterbury said: "They both have a fine sense of humor. They are blessed with an unusual mixture of exhilaration and steadiness. It should stand them in good stead in their marriage as well as in their public life together."

Amen.

The duke and duchess of York spent the weeks of their honeymoon in the Azores—a group of islands in the Atlantic that lay west of Lisbon and are owned by the Portuguese. Tanned and glowing, they returned to England for a few days before setting sail with the queen on the royal yacht *Britannia* for the royal family's traditional "western isles" cruise.

At the end of that cruise, they continued on with the queen's party to Balmoral for the traditional August and September stay there. Although the official Scottish residence was Holyrood House in Edinburgh, the queen spent little time there, living instead at Balmoral Castle on the banks of the River Dee in Aberdeenshire.

Arriving about the middle of August, the family devoted itself to the various outdoor activities available—shooting, fishing, and deer stalking. There was even a golf course. Sarah and Andrew spent some of their time walking about in the gardens and the conservatories dotting the estate, and going on the regularly scheduled picnic-shoots once in a while.

The Balmoral picnic-shoot was peculiarly royal; at the same time it was intimately familial. A heavy tartan rug was spread out on the ground, with the party sitting on their shooting sticks. The typical picnic usually lasted about four hours—until dusk—when the group then headed back to the castle loaded down with birds.

The duke and duchess of York sailed on Loch Muick several times, but the waters were too cold for swimming. They walked over the heather-clad hills, poking into hidden attractions: scattered wooden huts, many dating back to Victorian days.

Nevertheless, the schedule at Balmoral was rigid: breakfast at 8:45, then away for the shoot with Prince Philip by 9:30. For the women, it was breakfast in bed, and a free morning—but only until one o'clock, when they were required to join the picnic-shoot.

Dressing for dinner was obligatory, beginning about five o'clock after the return from the picnic-shoot. Drinks at six until dinner was announced. A piper played at the end of the meal, and everyone retired to the drawing room—the women ahead of the men, who stayed to drink port.

Games later on tended to be the favorites of the royals—scrabble, charades, or the new and exciting Trivial Pursuit. And perhaps a film—at least once a week.

After Balmoral, it was back to London for the duke and duchess of York to begin their married life together as members of the royal family.

Unlike the Princess of Wales, the duchess of York had

decided not to give up her nine-to-five job in London but to work it in around her royal duties, which were not yet under full steam. The reason for that was that the duke of York was still serving in the Royal Navy and would spend most of his next few years in uniform and in the service, with only weekends and holidays with his wife and family available.

The schedule of visits in England and in other countries could be easily controlled so that both the duke and duchess could name their own times for their royal duties.

And so Sarah Ferguson, now the duchess of York, became the first royal family bride to remain a "working girl" after her wedding.

Luckily, her job was such that her employer, Richard Burton, could utilize her services when they were available. As a result, she had no set working hours. Some weeks she was on duty for the royal family and could devote only a few hours to her job. At other times she would put in as much as a forty-hour week, and sometimes she would be able to work weekends. Again, this schedule was easy to follow because of the duke of York's service in the navy.

One of her first projects after returning from her honeymoon was to work on a book on the houses of Parliament. She became a coauthor with a one-time member of Parliament, Sir Robert Cooke. Cooke said about her: "The Duchess has been a terrific help in organizing everything surrounding this book. A vast amount of work has gone into it. She even sent stuff down to me from Balmoral when she was [still] on honeymoon. She's very efficient."

Quite soon Sarah was at work on a new project—a book about George III's collection of two thousand Italian architectural drawings, housed in the Royal Library at Windsor. With the queen's permission, Sarah coordinated and organized the task of sorting out the drawings with

Howard Burns, professor of the history of architecture at Harvard University.

She would soon be doing a book based on exhibits in the Israel Museum in Jerusalem. During the work on this book, she was planning to visit Israel—making her the first member of the present royal family to make a trip to Israel, an event that might prove somewhat controversial with the media and the public.

"She is a great asset," her boss, Richard Burton, said, "but will she be able to continue as my London representative? There is no doubt in *her* mind that she will, and she has managed to persuade everyone that she should."

The only one who might cast doubts on this decision of the duchess to continue working was her husband, the duke of York. With his tongue only half in his cheek, he once said, "Doing this job is fine, but it must *never* interfere with putting me first."

Hah!

During the first months of their married life—after returning from the long honeymoon—the duke and duchess of York settled down into a luxurious apartment in Buckingham Palace, not at all eager to begin the arduous search for a residence.

The practicalities of their life-style—he away all week and only home weekends and holidays, and she working in London nearby—precluded immediately moving out into the country to some remote and stately household, or even emulating the Prince and Princess of Wales and living at Kensington Palace where a large number of royals lived.

They took up their life together in two apartments. One had been occupied by Andrew during his bachelor days. This digs had been inherited from Prince Charles when Charles moved out to Kensington Palace. The other apartment was that lived in by Diana before her marriage.

During the first days after their return they were offered an apartment in Kensington Palace next door to Diana and Charles. Sarah did not feel that she should be quite that close to Diana. Obviously they were fast friends—but living right on top of one another would be a bit too much; at least, so she felt. And so she and Andrew opted to remain at Buckingham Palace and do their looking around from there.

In spite of the fact that from the beginning, Sarah and the queen and Prince Philip had got on very well, she knew that she could not remain forever at Buckingham Palace, and so she and Andrew did finally begin to do some shopping.

Days of Andrew's weekends and leaves were spent running around the countryside looking for housing. The word went out that it was Andrew who was the fussy one about where to live; Sarah saw a dozen places where she would have been happy to settle down.

What she wanted was a place close enough to Andrew's base so that he could get home more often—say, every night. The Royal Navy was based at Portsmouth Harbor, just to the east of the Isle of Wight, some sixty miles south and slightly to the west of London.

"Even if Andrew has late duty," she once said, "I want him to be able to get back to me at night. I think this is very important."

In January 1987 they finally found a house in a village named Chideock—population eight hundred—about a hundred and fifty miles southwest of London in Thomas Hardy country. The house even had a name—as most houses of that size do in England. It is called Chideock Manor, and was of Regency design. (The British pronounce it "Chidduck," incidentally.)

There was also a built-in ghost from the old days. The original house had been razed by Oliver Cromwell during those troubled times of the Commonwealth, and the present structure, erected in 1810, contained some of the original stones—which, apparently, came equipped with the ghost that was now rumored to stalk the stately towers.

A beautiful and typically English country home, it was hidden from the main road on thirty acres of grounds. It had a huge living room, a formal dining room, a library, a sitting room, five bedrooms and—unusual for England—a swimming pool. It also had a croquet lawn and stables for the family horses, plus an old burned-out Roman Catholic church whose relics included the hair shirt worn by Sir Thomas More, executed, as one should remember, by King Henry VIII for sticking stubbornly to the tenets of Rome.

Proximity to Portsmouth Naval Base? Very close for Andrew. Actually, all he had to do was to hop into his navy helicopter and make a ten-minute flight from the base. If one was a duke of York, one did have certain privileges.

Sarah and Andrew did not purchase the house, however. They took out a two-year lease on it with the rent running at about $350 a week. What happened was that in spite of the fact that they considered it their "real home," their basically commuter-type marriage made it somewhat impractical to settle down in the countryside.

What they finally worked out was an arrangement somewhat like this:

Sarah would spend most of her time during the week in London at her Buckingham Palace apartment. Then, on Friday afternoon, she would drive the four-hour trip from London by car. Andrew would fly in from Portsmouth on Friday and during the weekend the two of them would keep to themselves, often sleeping in until noon or so, and then messing about the house, watching television or old movies on their VCR.

Then on Sunday night the schedule would go into

reverse and both would return to their respective careers.

"You'd think they would have put in an appearance [in Chideock] by now," the manager of a local hotel said a bit ruefully to some visiting journalists. "People thought they'd see [the duchess] come down to the butcher, but she doesn't."

Meanwhile, Sarah Ferguson was changing her image as well as her residence. Physically. There had been nasty noises about her weight at the time of her marriage to Prince Andrew—she was a hefty size 14—and she took it to heart. Sticking to a diet high in protein and citrus fruit, she shed twenty-five pounds rather quickly and pushed herself down to a size 10. She did it strictly by dieting, and not by exercise—although her own energetic approach to life supplied its own weight-reduction mechanism.

Sarah Ferguson's first official foreign engagement as the duchess of York took place in October after she and Andrew had returned from Balmoral. This was a trip to Holland to visit the opening of the Scheldt flood barrier that had been built after almost two thousand Dutch had been drowned during the floods of 1953. It was a typically formal affair.

The duke of York plunged into the project with all the enthusiasm of a natural-born engineer, explaining the intricacies of the workings of the new dam, while the dignitaries, including Sarah, began to nod and blink to keep themselves awake. Sarah admitted later that she smiled her way—somehow—through the day.

On Sunday, they were off to a church service when disaster—or almost-disaster—struck. Sarah and Andrew left The Hague, where they were staying in the palace home of Queen Beatrix of the Netherlands, to drive to Rotterdam to worship at St. Mary's Anglican Church.

During the high-speed drive the royal cars shot through red traffic lights while local policemen kept the intersections clear. As they arrived in Rotterdam, the lead police car slammed on its brakes as a set of lights changed, and the royal car carrying the duke and duchess smashed into its rear.

Nevertheless, the duke and duchess, slightly pale and shaken, put on a brave front and entered the church some minutes later. As a visiting dignitary, the duke was given the lesson to read, and he did so without showing any sign of stress.

Sarah was learning how to let the show go on, no matter what happened backstage.

For some time the duchess of York had been nursing a secret ambition to fly a plane just like her husband. And she had enrolled in a course in Oxfordshire at the Oxford Air Training School. She made her first solo in a fifteen-minute circle of the field at Oxford in a Piper Warrior trainer early in November 1986.

After that it was simply a matter of flying forty hours solo before getting a bona fide license to fly. And so finally, in March of 1987, with her chopper-expert Prince Andrew, the duke of York, at her side, riding shotgun as it were, Sarah Ferguson, the duchess of York, now known as the "Flying Duchess" by the media, winged her way across the Oxfordshire countryside in her Piper Warrior to complete her last hours of solo work to qualify.

Thus when she climbed down from the cockpit in a brown sheepskin jacket, white silk Snoopy-type Red Baron scarf, and gloves, she became the first female member of the royal family ever to receive a private pilot's license.

She thanked her "wonderful husband" for encouraging her to take her forty hours of flight training, and got a bouquet shaped like a helicopter, although she was still unable to fly one of *those.*

"We are now a two-plane family," she said, holding hands with her husband.

"What is your next challenge to be?" one of the Fleet Street observers wondered, notebook poised in hand.

"Concorde," grinned the duchess in her best "Fergie" fashion.

Laughs all around.

During the summer of 1987, Sarah and Andrew were scheduled to make a twenty-five-day visit to Canada. It turned out to be a triumphant one, with crowds out everywhere and plenty of news coverage. Although the press had at first dismissed the visit as nothing more than an exercise in flag waving, they covered the two visitors, and seemed to sense that they were something to be proud of as well as to like at first sight.

"For the past six years Diana has had the stage all to herself," wrote Andrew Morton in the *Star,* a London tabloid. "Now she's found that a woman who used to be a cheerleader is vying for top billing." He meant Sarah, of course, in her official position as the duchess of York.

Harold Brooks-Baker wrote, "Historians will point to Canada as the turning point in their [Diana's and Sarah's] careers."

Not everybody was gracious about them. A columnist for the *Toronto Sun* called the duchess "a giggling disco queen," and the *London Evening Standard* headlined a supposedly hostile press reception in Canada: FAT GIGGLER FLIES INTO STORM. Someone called her "Big Red," and another paper declared that she was a part of the "Queen's off-the-wall family."

But Sarah was learning how to take care of herself and was also getting a bit sharper about the press. While the London scribblers followed the duke and duchess through Canada, they continued to set little traps for her.

A housewife named Enid Phillips asked Sarah out of the blue if she liked to wear furs.

"Who asked you to say that?" Sarah asked suspiciously, scenting some kind of setup.

Phillips pointed to nearby James Whitaker of the *Daily Mirror.*

"Oh, he would!" snorted Sarah.

The athletic duke and duchess even embarked on a private two-week canoeing holiday in the Northwest Territories. At the kickoff of the canoeing expedition, Sarah and Andrew, in full canoeing regalia, clowned around in front of the paparazzi and reporters for pictures and quotes. At one point Sarah read a sticker pasted on the canoe: "Never underestimate the strength of this woman."

She grinned, "I've adopted that as my motto for the holiday."

The British press reacted in predictable fashion. Four London tabloids carried identical headlines: FERGIE CROCKETT—QUEEN OF THE WILD FRONTIER.

But the usual worries about the "imperiled royals" were expressed as well. "As the Royals head east," wrote *Today*'s Martin Phillips, "they will pass woodland where moose lurk. In the Barren Lands, the danger will be from grizzly bears, wolves and caribou."

They made a three-hundred-mile trip down the Thelon River to Baker Lake, just two hundred miles west of Hudson Bay. It was a spectacular voyage—"but," said Douglas Heard, a Canadian government biologist, "it is not a walk in the park. The water is cold, cold, and they'll have to negotiate fast rapids and three monster lakes." Nevertheless, "if they exercise good judgment they should be okay."

And they were.

All in all the Canadian jaunt was a triumph in a public-relations sense.

Somewhat later, the two visited the tiny United Kingdom island of Mauritius—called the "Island for Lovers." For the reader without an atlas handy, Mauritius is a tiny island republic in the Indian Ocean, south of the equator almost directly south of the bottom tip of India, in a group of islands called the Chagos Archipelago.

Talk about isolated!

It was Sarah, as always, who was the focus of the attention, but it was Andrew who seemed to radiate more unaffected happiness than observers usually noted on his tours of duty. Once again Sarah was tested and found unalloyed gold. By the time the Mauritius tour was over, she was said to have entered the "Big Leagues" of royalty, alongside the Prince and Princess of Wales.

And it was the tremendous success in Canada and Mauritius that inspired the queen to engineer another overseas trip, in 1988, for the duke and duchess of York—this one to Los Angeles, California.

Meanwhile rumors had been emerging in the popular press for months—throughout all of 1987, actually—that the duchess of York was—oh, happy day!—pregnant. However, most of these "rumors" proved to be exactly that, and without a grain of truth in them. Fleet Street had always figured that they could endlessly leak "secrets" like a pregnancy among royalty—until one rumor finally coincided with the truth.

With Sarah Ferguson, of course, the matter of pregnancy was somewhat a historic first. She was probably the first member of high royalty to have lived on the pill during her unmarried and free-roving days. Thus instant pregnancy, according to medical fact or old wives' tale, sometimes was out of the question until the body adapted itself to being *without* contraception pills.

The rumors persisted.

In the early winter of 1987 it was known among her friends for some time that Sarah was "sick a lot," and therefore might quite possibly be pregnant. Still, she said nothing. Still, no one asked.

"We all knew she was desperate for a baby," one friend said, "and she was normally never ill, so we put two and two together, and kept very quiet."

Well, the time came when it was true that she *was* pregnant. And so she decided to announce it.

One evening around the New Year at Sandringham, where the royal family traditionally gathered to ring out the old and ring in the new, everybody went out on a pheasant shoot. Nobody really noticed that Fergie was wearing a hat shaped a bit peculiarly. It was, oddly enough, designed in a kind of lumpy shape that might resemble a rather dowdy Christmas pudding. And then one sharp-eyed member of the family suddenly did a classic double-take.

And the word was out!

Word? What word?

In English idiom, the term "to be a member of the pudding club" means that one is pregnant. And so, the fact that Fergie was wearing a hat in the shape of a Christmas pudding—however dowdy or not it seemed—meant that she was announcing to one and all that she *was* at that point a member of the famed "pudding club."

Expecting.

Late in January 1988, Buck House issued a laconic statement to the effect that the duchess of York and her husband Prince Andrew were expecting a child to be born sometime in August 1988. That child, of course, according to the reports, would be the fifth in line to the British throne. And so on.

Ironically enough, on the day the announcement appeared in the papers the duchess was taking a flying lesson in a helicopter—a type of craft she had not yet gained proficiency in. And, interestingly enough, she and Andrew had just returned for a short trip to Klosters in Switzerland for some action on the slopes.

And so the pregnant duchess of York made ready in the first months of 1988 to visit Los Angeles at the end of February. The ten-day tour began when the royal yacht anchored off Long Beach and the couple were flown to Los

Angeles International Airport to land in an obscure corner away from the paparazzi and TV cameras—but just to add a little spice to the affair, security men had found a mysterious briefcase only a block away from the royal yacht and had detonated the thing in a blast of smoke and flame.

And found . . . Some poor fool's office homework shredded, scorched, and rendered totally useless.

In Chinatown someone had inscrutably mounted a huge sign: WELCOME FERGIE AND WHAT'S HIS NAME. Security types roaming the area decided that the sign was not inscrutable enough and just wouldn't do. The sign came down. But everybody knew all about it the next day in the papers.

The "visit" included schools, where all the kids were drilled on how to act with the duke and duchess until one student, exhausted by the strain even before anybody showed up, groused: "I don't even like them already."

On Saturday the vintage Rolls Royce carrying the visitors developed a water-pump problem and the duke and duchess were hastily and ignominiously switched to a—gasp!—Cadillac halfway between the airport and Long Beach.

In one classroom they visited, Andrew was asked about the number of dungeons still in use in England. "There is no use for dungeons nowadays," he answered stoically, and pointed out that the one in Windsor Castle had "been brought up to date and is now a disco."

Sarah described the bathroom fixtures in the palaces and castles. "There are very good old-fashioned loos that actually work really well," she said. "You don't flush [them], you just pull it up from underneath."

At a fund-raising affair a British subject of the duke and duchess—the actor Roger Moore—handed over a coupon for disposable diapers in celebration of their August expectations. In riposte, Sarah presented the Los Angeles

Central Library with a specially bound volume, *British Heritage,* commenting, "We decided, all three of us"—obviously Andrew and the coming baby—"to present the book."

On Sunday, a minister, during his sermon to the royal pair, said that their visit was "the biggest thing that has happened in this city since the Richfield oil refinery exploded, and that was in 1933."

The duchess was un-put-downable in ad-libbed repartee. At one point when she was introduced by the duke at a UK/LA Gala at the Biltmore Bowl, an irrepressible politician, State Senator Art Torres, began to shout, "Bravo, Fergie, bravo!"

When he finally quieted down, the duchess said, "At last I have the turn to talk. All these men—"

Once again the senator shouted out: "We love you, Fergie!"

Without batting an eyelash and in perfect timing the duchess wisecracked, "I'll see *you* later."

While on a visit to a film studio, Sarah was experimenting with a prop whiskey bottle used in western fights. Her private secretary, Lieutenant Colonel Sean O'Dwyer, was at her side. "Does it really hurt?" Sarah asked, turning to him and smashing the "bottle" over his head, then helping him brush off the splinters.

"It's quite all right," murmured the long-suffering O'Dwyer with excellent English sangfroid.

Discussing the fact that they were "future parents," Andrew told a student on the Westwood UCLA campus, "I have not yet made a choice where to send" his coming child for an education.

"It's not *I,* it's *we!"* Sarah said, stepping forward into the act.

Back home, royalty watchers were nonplussed. The *Star,* which usually took pot shots at dignity and tradition, suddenly got very uptight and pretentious. "She is a

Royal, so she should act like one," it said of Sarah. "And that doesn't mean . . . gigglingly revealing the secrets of the royal water closets." (The *Star* meant toilets—"loos" in British slang.)

The *Sunday Times* was most upset about Sarah's clothing. Craig Brown said that her wardrobe made her look "as if she'd just won third prize for her Carmen Miranda impersonation," and accused her of "grabbing every opportunity to chirp inane and coquettish remarks." As for Andrew, it said that he appeared to be "an overanimated young man with a carnivorous grin." It dubbed the couple "the Duke and Duchess of Yob."

Generally, Angelenos applauded them. "As a Californian," said the president of the UCLA graduates, "it's hard for me to be critical of having fun and being spontaneous."

At the end of the trip, Andrew returned to the Royal Navy and Sarah shopped in London for a day before flying to Klosters for some spring skiing with Prince Charles and Princess Diana.

X

THE PRINCESS OF WALES

10

DIANA SUPERSTAR

It goes without saying that the first year of marriage was one of gradual and sometimes painful adjustment for the Prince and Princess of Wales. The idea had been spawned in the press and in the minds of the British population that this was a marriage made in heaven—or if not in heaven, at the very least within the covers of a fairy tale.

To foster that image, the Prince of Wales invited photographers to Balmoral Castle in September 1981—just after he and Diana had returned from their honeymoon trip in the Mediterranean—to take pictures of the happy couple. In tartans and smiling broadly, they appeared in newspapers and magazines as the happiest of newlyweds.

Charles's move was a sharp one: it allowed the couple the rest of their days at Balmoral in relative seclusion, protected from the milling mob of reporters and paparazzi. Charles was allowed to get into his waders and fish in the river without prying eyes, and Diana lounged about the castle grounds in happy isolation.

But this happy distancing from the press was not to last

long at all. In her naïveté Diana had apparently believed that the public would lose interest in her once the honeymoon was over and would walk away. Such was not the case. After the momentary lull in publicity, pressure began building up once again for a look at the princess. And of course, the scheduling of the royal couple was such that being in public was one of the most arduous of all their duties. There was to be, Diana found to her dismay, no time for any private life of her own at all.

Her first scheduled tour in Wales occurred in foul wet weather, with Diana dressed too lightly. In appearance, she was a brilliant success. But she was not a natural show-off, not one who could appear before thousands of people and *be* pleased with the adulation. She returned exhausted and almost ill.

As if that wasn't enough, there was still the hassle of getting settled in their home. Actually, it was not simply a home—it was *homes*. Once things calmed down the prince and princess finally established a kind of schedule. The two homes were located in London and Gloucestershire.

After some searching around, Diana finally settled on a London residence at Kensington Palace—with which she was familiar and where she felt she could cope better than elsewhere. Kensington Palace was to be their apartment in the city. The palace was open to the public, but their rooms were not, of course. Diana and Charles were in apartments 8 and 9—three stories of a house where Kings George I and George II kept their mistresses. The house faced onto a courtyard called the Prince of Wales's Court.

In the apartment there was a large drawing room, a sitting room for Diana, a study for Charles, a kitchen, a dining room, bedrooms, a playroom, and accommodation for their staff.

Kensington Palace served for the weekdays. Charles

had offices not only at Kensington, but in Buckingham Palace as well, about a mile away.

But the weekends were spent in Highgrove House in Tetbury, a beautiful royal residence in the countryside. This "distinguished Georgian house" had four reception rooms, domestic quarters, nine bedrooms, six bathrooms, a nursery wing, and full central heating.

Once the schedule had been established, rumors persisted that Diana hated Highgrove and wanted to move to some other country area; the rumors were determined by some to have been untrue. True or not, there were no more words to be heard from her about that after November 1981.

It was on the fifth of that month that Buck House issued the announcement that the Prince and Princess of Wales were expecting their first child the following June.

What had been a moratorium on press pressure was now dissolved like snowflakes in July. Swarms of paparazzi hid in the bushes outside Kensington Palace to snap her; they followed her in the streets when she was sighted. Her life, as has been related, was reduced once again to hide-and-seek exercises.

On June 21, 1982, Prince William was born—seven pounds, one and a half ounces. Wrapped up, and tagged "Baby Wales," he was handed to Charles. At Buckingham Palace word was posted: "Her Royal Highness the Princess of Wales was safely delivered of a son at 9:03 P.M. today. Her Royal Highness and her child are both doing well."

In the crowd that surrounded Charles when he appeared two hours after the birth someone shouted: "Nice going. Give us another one, Charlie."

Charles laughed. "Bloody hell! Give us a chance!"

Diana had proved equal to the task of providing an heir apparent for the royal family—and for the country. She hoped it would give her a chance to settle back and catch her breath. Speaking with a disc jockey on a radio show, Diana was heard to muse, half to herself: "Isn't it nice that people can just be themselves? Most of life is not being able to be yourself."

About this time it was noticed that Diana was losing weight. Was she on a diet? Could she not help it? Immediately the press tagged her as "anorexic"—and stories multiplied about a royal illness. It was no surprise that Diana reacted to these gossipy rumors with denials—and some of them were heated.

Nigel Dempster decided: "Shy Di has become a willful and spoiled girl. . . . Suddenly, getting this enormous power, having people curtsy and bow and do everything she wants, she has become a little monster."

By the end of 1982 it became obvious that she *was* thinner, that she *was* short-tempered. In the fall of 1982, on the night of the Festival of Remembrance at the Royal Albert Hall—an important event on the royal calendar—Diana quite suddenly told Charles that she had "opted out" for the public appearance and had invited some of her own particular friends over for dinner.

Charles blew his top. There was a great deal of shouting and pacing about.

Charles: It was her *duty* to go to Albert Hall. She was part of the royal family. She *owed* it to her subjects.

Diana: She was simply too tired to go. She did not *want* to go. She wanted to be with her friends.

The Albert Hall officials were advised that the Princess was unable to attend the performance; such an announcement was made public. The royals appeared.

Suddenly—*after* the queen arrived—Diana put in an abrupt and unexpected showing. Arriving later than the queen was a breach of royal etiquette. The false announcement of her illness was an embarrassment to the ceremony. Charles was annoyed. The queen was unhappy.

Rumors surfaced that the Princess of Wales was proving to be "difficult."

To defuse these rumors, Charles and Diana appeared on television in December 1982 to disport themselves and to show off Prince William, then six months old. The prince sat on his mother's knee, and then on his father's. Diana shook his teething rattle and rubbed his tummy. The parents seemed relaxed and cooperative. It was nuptial bliss.

The idea was to stroke the press and keep them off the premises during the upcoming Sandringham New Year's holiday. However, public interest had been stimulated by the television appearance of Prince William, and Sandringham was under siege from the beginning. "Fifty photographers," Press Secretary Michael Shea moaned, "and the worst harassment ever."

On January 9, 1983, Charles and Diana flew to Zurich, Switzerland, for a skiing holiday. Within hours the hotels around them were booked solid with reporters and photographers. Not only the professionals, but people with their own instamatics got into the act. The slopes were unskiable. The crowds pushed into the royals. Even in the restaurants they were unable to eat but had to pose for pictures.

Diana hung her head, distraught.

"Please, darling," Charles said, "please," trying to get her to relent and smile. She pushed him away, and held her head away from the cameras.

"Sorry," Charles said to the photographers. "Please, be reasonable."

The press built this up into some kind of squabble between Charles and Diana. On television, one journalist opined that Diana had become "a spoiled little monster" who was "making her husband's life a misery."

From this seed grew the rather quick-growing weed of "marital difficulties," and the press made the most of this, strictly on speculation. The marriage was on the rocks, they said. Articles appeared about how a divorce could be obtained by Charles or Diana if either wanted it.

A break in the hostilities came when the two of them left London on March 20, 1983, for a tour of Australia. In this instance, at Diana's insistence, Prince William, nine months old, went with them, watched over by his nanny, Nancy Barnes. This was an unusual thing at best—most times royalty at that age was in the full charge of a nanny and definitely at home and not on the road.

They landed at Alice Springs in the south of Australia where about a hundred townspeople appeared to greet them—along with sixty-odd reporters, photographers, and television crews from all over the world. Then Prince William arrived in Nancy Barnes's arms, and the family stood there smiling at the cameras. It was a fine domestic scene.

For a month and a half Diana traveled thirty thousand miles, shook over six thousand hands, and was photographed a million times—and did not once complain. The word went out that she even ate everything that was placed in front of her. The tour was a huge success. For Diana personally, it was a triumph.

She was absolutely great with the kids who swarmed around to see her.

One small boy asked her: "Do you like dead horse?"

"What on earth's that?" Diana asked.

"Tomato sauce!" hooted the boy in great glee.

Later a little girl failed to get close enough to Diana to hand her a bouquet of flowers—and burst out sobbing. Diana bent down to take the flowers from her, reassuring her with: "Agony over."

Even when she overstepped herself or committed what might be considered a conversational gaffe, Diana was able to carry it off.

On a walkabout seeking out the disabled for a special

word, Diana was chatting with a one-armed man. "I'll bet," she said, strictly on impulse, "you have fun chasing the soap round the bath!"

It could have been a brick dropped. But it was not. By the way she put it, and the smile she gave the man, any tension was neutralized. And the man was quick to admit that he did indeed have trouble with the blasted soap.

Journalists noted that Charles and Diana were exhibiting obvious signs of mutual affection for one another—something that had been missing for some time now . . . his hand on hers, her glances at him, and so on.

There was more. The presence of Prince William, if it was a risk, was a calculated one at that. Charles admitted it to one of his audiences: "I hope his presence here will revive that family feeling which I know my wife and I think is so important."

It did.

Another point was made obvious during that tour. Charles was changing as much as Diana was changing. She had started transforming him on the outside—getting him to buy better-looking suits, for one thing, and shoes—and was now working on the inside.

The earlier Charles was assailed by self-doubts; the new Charles no longer had many. He seemed to have more purpose to life—something he had lacked in the 1970s. Of course, the fact that he was no longer in thrall to that long search for a wife gave him a lot more self-confidence.

His entire public demeanor was changing too. He was less apt to display the nervous tics of his youth, and less apt to show that awkwardness in meeting people.

In fact Anthony Holden, a longtime royal-watcher who particularly focused his work on Charles, wrote in 1984: "All his life, after being dubbed a late developer, he has seemed much younger than his years; now, he looks and acts like a mature monarch in the making."

The age gap between Charles and Diana continued to be

a problem in the years after their marriage. Diana chose her own friends, not particularly liking Charles's older acquaintances. He chose his own friends, too, not particularly liking her younger ones.

In June 1984 Diana had a second child, this one also a boy, at St. Mary's Hospital in Paddington. After nine hours of labor, a son was born, "fair of face and blue-eyed like his brother"—according to the papers. He weighed fourteen pounds. Known officially as Prince Henry Charles Albert David—"Harry" to the family—he was shown to the crowds when he was thirteen hours old by a beaming Charles.

Moments later a town crier, in white-plumed hat and red knickers, rang a big bronze bell: "Her Royal Highness the Princess Diana has issued forth a second son." Although this seemed quite traditional—it was *not*. A Japanese television company had hired an actor to whomp up its coverage of the event. No one seemed to mind.

What television did *not* show was the interesting scene at the birth itself—Prince Charles in green hospital gown and surgical mask, watching at his wife's side throughout the natural birth, just as he had during William's arrival.

Outside the crowd began chanting: "Let's have another one."

Charles sighed. "We've nearly got a full polo team now."

With the two children now safely ensconced as the second and third in line to the Crown of England, Diana seemed to relax a bit.

She began building her own inner circle—among them, of course, Sarah Ferguson. But while she was spending more time with her children, her public appearances did not diminish any, and she seemed more in control than she had been between the two births.

Nevertheless, Fleet Street felt it had to do something to liven up the news. All the old shibboleths were once again examined: She was dieting too much. She was exhibiting terrible traits of bossiness. She was spending four thousand dollars a week on clothes alone. She was spoiling Prince William, letting him run wild. She did not get on with the queen.

And so forth and so on.

One by one all these rumors were squelched—but slowly and laboriously. Yes, she had indeed lost weight after the birth of Prince William. But she began to gain it back soon. It never became a medical problem.

Yes, she was strong-willed; no, she was not tearing the family apart by being that way.

No, she did not overspend her allowance. And: "Her clothes are not paid for by the British government," said Michael Shea, the queen's press secretary.

About Prince William: "Wills," their name for him, was "just a normal little boy," one palace source said.

Indeed she got on famously with the queen too.

But she was making her own way with the staff that worked for her and around her. Not that they were disappearing like flies, but they were departing, and in numbers.

The casualties—if they could be called that—were the following:

Edward Adeane had been Charles's private secretary for six years. A barrister by profession, he saw his role as guiding the Prince toward his kingship. Adeane, some rumors had it, was annoyed by the incessant foofaraw made over Diana. Diana, it was said, felt that Adeane was too straitlaced. He left in 1985.

Stephen Barry had been Charles's valet for twelve years. Apparently his 1982 dismissal—if indeed it was a dismissal—was engineered by Diana. Diana was said to be annoyed that he continued to enter Charles's bedroom without knocking even after Charles was married to her.

"I think I was too close to the Prince," Barry said

afterward. "Diana is very determined. She's rather like a young actress who goes to Hollywood, makes a few films and then becomes a star."

Barry became a sort of stereotype on his own: he wrote a book about his experiences with Charles and then turned out another about his experiences with Charles and Diana.

Oliver Everett was an old polo sidekick of Charles's, who became Diana's personal secretary in 1981, sacrificing a diplomatic career in the move. After setting up complicated schedules for her, he found she would simply ignore them; she decided that he had too much control of her life. "Why won't you get rid of this bloody man?" she was reported to have said to Charles. He departed soon enough, upsetting the queen who thought him a valued employee.

Alan Fisher was a Kensington Palace butler who spent sixteen years working for Bing Crosby before he came to the palace. He found the royals dull by comparison.

"They are wonderful people, but incredibly boring," he said. "They never did any entertaining and there was absolutely nothing for me to do. Charming as they are, I couldn't stand it anymore." He took the money for two years and then ran.

Roseanna Lloyd was a cook at Kensington Palace, and was hired away from a restaurant in Wales by Charles and Diana. She found the work boring.

Paul Officer was Charles's guard for fourteen years. When Diana was engaged to Charles, Officer became Diana's guard. Some weeks after the wedding he became a London police superintendent.

John Brownridge was another guard who lasted less than a year. Kensington Palace, according to the word, had earned a new name among security people: "the Minefield." "You don't have to do anything wrong to find yourself kicked out these days."

David Robinson was a protection officer who made Diana nervous during her shopping expeditions. He left to guard Princess Anne.

Harry Alsop was the head gardener at Highgrove, but he quit in 1982 when Charles—not Diana—began interfering with his work. Charles apparently was interested in becoming a gentleman farmer.

But these changes were inevitable and seemed mostly interesting to the press, for what it could make of them. At the same time, Diana was building up her own inner coterie of friends.

These included:

Anne Beckwith-Smith was Diana's only full-time lady-in-waiting. She soon became the Princess's closest confidante. Emotionally, the word went, she had become a substitute for Diana's three former roommates. On her return from the Australian trip, Diana gave Anne a pair of diamond, sapphire, and gold earrings inscribed: "I couldn't have done it without you."

The three other ladies-in-waiting were Lavinia Baring, Hazel West, and Sarah Rose Campden. Baring was an old and close friend of Anne Beckwith-Smith. She was married, with two sons and a daughter. West was the daughter of the late Sir Thomas Cook, the travel tycoon. Campden was the daughter of Colonel Thomas Winnington and Lady Betty Winnington, members of the fox-and-hounds set.

Diana's foursome with her three roommates simply did not survive the marriage and her elevation into the royal circle. She procured another trio of personal friends—Carolyn Herbert, Lady Penelope Romsey, and Catharine Cameron Soames. Herbert was a Diana look-alike—used sometimes when Diana needed a decoy to avoid crowds. Diana's sister Sarah introduced them. Romsey was an old friend of Charles's—one of his early "romances." She helped Diana through the social labyrinth during her first years of marriage. Soames was one of Diana's bridesmaids at her wedding; she was married to Nicholas Soames, a close friend of Charles's.

By 1985 there was a great deal of gossip in print about the royal family, and especially about Diana—including a supposed rift between her and Charles. Buck House dreamed up a major counteroffensive in a carefully packaged lengthy interview with the Prince and Princess.

One of the major rumors Charles wanted quashed was the idea of some people that he get a "real" job. Another was the story that Diana spent all her time shopping. The show—forty-five minutes on British television—was taped at the couple's Kensington Palace drawing room one Sunday evening.

Britain's own Walter Cronkite—Sir Alistair Burnet—handled the interview, after Diana had been coached by none other than Oscar-winning director Sir Richard Attenborough.

She appeared dressed in an understated blue-and-white dress, giggling at times, but playing a flawless role of the doting mother, affectionate helpmeet, and conscientious do-gooder.

About her clothes, she said: "My clothes are not my priority. I enjoy bright colors and my husband likes to see me look smart, presentable. . . . I do think there's too much emphasis [by the press] on my clothes."

She said she checked with Charles, asking him if she looked right in this or that. "But the chances of turning up in what he says are absolutely nil," she said.

"Why do you ask me?" Charles wondered.

"I don't know," Diana admitted.

About being a domineering wife, Diana said, "I don't think I am. I'm a perfectionist with myself, but not necessarily with everyone else."

About her rumored anorexia, Diana said that she had

never gone on what could be called a diet. "Maybe I'm so scrawny because I take so much exercise."

And no, she and Charles did *not* even occasionally indulge in marital scraps.

"I suspect most husbands and wives find they often have arguments," Charles mused diplomatically.

"But we don't," Diana said firmly.

"Well, we *occasionally* do," Charles averred.

"No, we don't!" snapped Diana.

It was a huge success. Fleet Street cooed like doves in their cotes.

"She appeared to be egoless, genuinely interested in things other than herself," the *Daily Mail* wrote.

In the words of one national American magazine, it was "the most mesmerizing Sunday evening TV event in Britain since 'The Forsyte Saga' eighteen years ago."

Shortly after their self-cleansing on British television, Charles and Diana visited Washington—and wowed the Americans. After a private dinner and dance for eighty people at the White House, they were driven off in a silver Rolls Royce.

"I've danced with John Travolta," said Diana. "I've danced with Clint Eastwood. I've danced with Tom Selleck. It was wonderful!"

A young woman, visiting from Michigan, said about Diana: "She is a fairy tale come true. She was working and living a life like other girls her age, and then she upped and married a prince. It's like a dream!"

Even the *New Republic* was gentle in its barb. "The current hysteria over the visit of Prince Charles and Princess Di," the magazine editorialized, "is less a matter of Anglophilia than of simple celebrity. If a celebrity is defined as someone who is famous just for being famous, then Britain's pea-brained royals are in some ways the original celebrities of the English-speaking world."

Things settled down for a while, but in January 1987

there was another rhubarb in the royal family. For some reason Nancy Barnes, who had been the nanny of Prince William, and then also Prince Harry, since 1981 suddenly left.

Barnes, by then known familiarly as "Baba" to the family, went her own way for reasons unknown. There was plenty of speculation. The *Daily Express* said that the queen was responsible because she was so "dismayed at Prince William's scallywag antics." It concluded that the queen told Charles "to find a new nanny."

The *Daily Mirror* claimed that it was because Baba would side against the Prince and Princess at times. "When the boys were naughty, Barnes gave them a cuddle. But their parents preferred . . . a good hiding."

XI

THE DUCHESS OF YORK

11

FERGIE SUPERSTAR

MEANWHILE THE LOGISTICS PROBLEMS IMPLICIT IN THE DUKE AND DUCHESS of York's arrangement to reside in Chideock on weekends and at Buckingham Palace during the week had created havoc enough to put an end to the regular hundred-and-fifty-mile commute. With Fergie's pregnancy, the weekly ride was obviously out. And with Fergie's insistence on not living permanently at Buckingham Palace it was mandatory that *something* be done.

They had heard about a seven-bedroom mansion located on a couple of acres not too far from Windsor Castle that might do the trick. The place, called Castlewood House, was owned by King Hussein of Jordan. The Yorks put in a bid to rent it and were immediately taken up on the offer. It would give them an escape valve, allowing them to live without the close scrutiny of Buck House.

They were to have exclusive use of it for as long as they needed. Meanwhile, Fergie was thinking about the future—the future being for the three of them, not just the two. A house was called for, a house of their own.

Queen Elizabeth had given them the right to a residence as a wedding present. Now the Yorks finally got their heads together and came up with the idea of building their own place, rather than taking on some old country house already on the royal list.

Immediately plans were begun for the house, which it was estimated would cost on the order of $2 million. It was finally decided that it would be designed in mock-Tudor style—a model of which was later facetiously compared to "Dallas"'s Southfork. It was finally decided that construction would begin in the spring of 1989.

Its sixteen rooms would be furnished with the Yorks' huge collection of wedding presents: sixteen Persian carpets, eight sofas, 308 vases, eighteen complete breakfast sets, and a thousand crystal wine and water glasses.

Building a brand-new house—this one would later be dubbed "Sunninghill Park"—was a radical departure from the tradition of the royal family to select one of the beautiful old English houses available for royal residence.

And so this move was not lost on the press and on watchers of royalty. The decision to choose new over old created controversy from the onset within certain groups. These were the royals who thought the Yorks should adhere to tradition. The Yorks ignored the uproar caused by their decision to build new.

Fergie selected a firm of interior decorators to do the furnishings of her new home, a move completely within acceptable limits. However, the firm she chose would again bring down a storm of criticism on her.

It was during a trip to Greenwich, Connecticut, with her mother that Fergie visited the home of a polo-player friend of her mother's Henryk de Kwiatkowski—where she noticed a very vibrant decor that she liked.

She asked her host who was responsible for the interior decorations for his home, and he told her that it was done by Parish-Hadley Associates, in New York—a firm founded by Sister Parish and Albert Hadley. De Kwiatkowski owned four homes decorated by the same firm.

Fergie got in touch with Parish-Hadley and was soon talking to Sister Parish on the phone. "I'm sitting here in this wonderful chair," she told her, and followed that up by explaining that the work was exactly the kind of thing the Yorks wanted for their new place near Ascot. "We're only number two," she said. "We don't have much money."

That didn't matter, and Parish-Hadley began preliminary designs. However, as the plans took shape, and news of Fergie's selection was made public, another uproar ensued. Eventually, as the royal family looked on and studied the effects created by the American firm, it became evident that changes would have to be made.

It was reported in the British press that the queen considered Parish-Hadley's plans too costly. Whatever the reason was, the Yorks finally switched to a London company located in the Knightsbridge section. And so it was that Nina Campbell, who had been running her own business for twenty years, became the interior decorator for the Yorks' new home.

Campbell's designs, usually featuring floral chintzes, painted furniture, horticultural prints, and floor-length curtains, were quite popular among the Chelsea and Mayfair sets in London. She said that she considered her appointment "jolly exciting," and tried to keep it secret for some months.

Of course it all leaked out. But the reaction was good.

"She's very clever with her combination of being both practical and stylish," Stephen Calloway, a curator at the Victoria and Albert Museum was quoted as saying. "She's in the great English tradition of being able to make things exciting by making them over a bit."

In other words, she was very good at post-modernism in design. Using the old in a new way.

"She will almost certainly become rich and famous as a result of this. It's a stamp of approval money can't buy," said Harold Brooks-Baker, of *Burke's Peerage*.

Fergie meanwhile was still fighting the battle of the bulge during her pregnancy. "Fortunately," she confided once, "I don't have a kitchen in our rooms at [Buckingham] Palace." When Andrew was away on sea duty, she would concentrate on salads and fruit sent up from the palace kitchen. She was still valiantly trying to get her weight below a hundred and forty-five pounds. She was never able to imitate her friend Diana in dieting willpower. Her blouse size was twelve, her skirt fourteen.

Her gynecologist, Anthony Kenney, finally told her to give up drinking—and she did so, with the exception of champagne. She almost lived on cheeseburgers. But despite this she did gain pounds over pounds, and when she was seven or eight months through her pregnancy it was found that she had gained thirty pounds in weight!

Some unkind humorist dubbed her the "Duchess of Pork."

She was no longer steadily employed in 1988. In point of fact, she had lost her job at Burton's. What happened was that the company went out of business at the end of 1987. Richard Burton was declared bankrupt and left his Swiss base in Geneva for California.

It was a nasty blow to Fergie, in spite of the fact that royalty was never supposed to worry about money. The job had paid her a nice fat $45,000 a year, and she had worked hard at her job as acquisitions editor. She had been Burton's employee since 1984 and had played a valuable part in creating a book that had become *The New Painting, Impressionism 1874–1886,* which sold 155,000 copies and generated over $7 million in revenue. In addition to that title, she had also helped produce *The Palace at*

Westminster, which she had commissioned the late Sir Robert Cooke, a member of Parliament, to write. She was working with him from Balmoral estate just after her wedding and honeymoon was over.

In November 1987 the book appeared in print. With its debut, Fergie agreed to help Burton publicize it with radio and television interviews—nothing at all new in the world of promotion and publication.

However, her successful appearances were criticized by many people in England who felt that a member of the royal family should not be involved so blatantly in commercial enterprises. Whatever animosity might be building up in the public mind against Fergie's so-called conflict of royal interest was neutralized by the sudden failure of Burton's BKC Publishing Company at the end of 1988. That was the good news. The bad was that Fergie was out of a job.

And so the sniping returned to her clothing. Once again she was being compared unfavorably with her friend the Princess of Wales (with her model's figure and her motion picture starlet's features).

Clothing? "I'm a workaholic," Fergie said. "I don't have the time to spend thinking about clothes. There are not enough hours in the day for me. I don't think people realize just what I do put into the day."

Once her publishing job was over, she began building up her royal contacts—becoming the patron of at least eleven organizations by the middle of 1988. In addition to these specific groups, she had to deal with the hundreds of requests for her time that rolled into Buckingham Palace every day. And she also had to take care of mandatory official entertaining responsibilities as well.

In spite of the collapse of BKC, Fergie still entertained the hope that she would be able to return to publishing. "I have some good ideas up my sleeve," she said, "but they're secret. If I don't start working on them straight away someone might pinch my ideas."

And then, quite suddenly, Fergie became involved in an "incident" that basically involved her brother-in-law, the heir apparent, the Prince of Wales. In March 1988 she decided on one last bout of skiing in the Swiss Alps. She and Diana were with Charles, staying at the chalet in Klosters used by the royal family for skiing visits.

Although she had been warned by friends about the possibility of a miscarriage—and miscarriages did tend to run in her family—she pooh-poohed the idea. "If it's going to happen, it will," she said about miscarrying. "Skiing or riding won't make any difference."

Fergie was skiing at top speed down a rocky gulley when she lost control and smashed into a stream at the bottom of the slope. She was lucky—oh, how lucky! But she was seething with rage and angrily rejected an offer of dry clothing from a member of the royal party, Patti Palmer-Tomkinson.

Instead, she determined to go up the mountain again before returning to her chalet to change into dry things. And she did so.

That afternoon, Fergie opted out of more exercise on the slopes and stayed at the chalet with Diana, who, unlike Fergie, was never one to rush out into the snow without very good reason. It was Charles who went out that afternoon with several companions—among them Major Hugh Lindsay, a close friend and former aide to the queen, and Patricia (Patti) Palmer-Tomkinson—and their Swiss ski guide Bruno Sprecher and a Swiss policeman.

The skiing holiday had started on Tuesday, March 8, with no fanfare, and continued through Thursday, the day Fergie had fallen in the creek. That afternoon—with Fergie and Diana in the chalet—disaster struck.

The group had decided to ski off the main track between

the treacherous Gotschnawang and Drostobel trails at an altitude of about 5,800 feet. In fact, their decision to do so was made against the advice of officials in the area who had warned them of the danger of avalanches at 5,200 feet high and higher.

They were skiing, as Charles said later, at their own risk—every member of the party accepting "that mountains have to be treated with the greatest respect and not treated lightly."

Suddenly there was a tremendous roaring and a shaking of the hill. An avalanche had obviously started high up on the slopes. Charles skied out of harm's way.

"Major Lindsay and Mrs. Palmer-Tomkinson," Charles said later, "just failed to ski clear [of the slide] and were swept away in a whirling maelstrom as the whole mountainside seemed to hurtle past us to the valley below."

Within seconds it was all over.

Sprecher, the Swiss guide, immediately located Patti Palmer-Tomkinson by the sound of the electronic beeper she wore on her body. She had been buried in the snow. Charles and Sprecher rushed to help dig her out. The incredible force of the avalanche had broken both her legs. Sprecher gave her mouth-to-mouth resuscitation. She revived slowly.

"I sat with Mrs. Palmer-Tomkinson while [Sprecher] went to try to locate Major Lindsay," Charles said. "He found him about fifteen yards above Mrs. Palmer-Tomkinson, but tragically he had been killed outright during the fall."

The Swiss policeman with them immediately sent for assistance from below using his walkie-talkie, and soon Patti Palmer-Tomkinson had been removed from the slope to safety and to a hospital. Major Lindsay's body was recovered.

The group, dressed in black, flew back that same afternoon to Northolt Air Base near London.

"Why was he there?" the *Sun* demanded, referring to the heir apparent. "Charles has consistently risked his life by going on increasingly deadly slopes."

The *Daily Mail* was more moderate. "Please, Your Majesty, can you ask your offspring, for the nation's sake, to show just a little more care?"

It was dramatic evidence of the danger that constantly clustered around royalty of any kind. The princesses were very close to death during that March skiing holiday. Fergie felt it in her bones. She made a promise to herself to take it a little easy until the baby was born.

Her father, Major Ronald Ferguson, had made no such promise to himself. In early May 1988 he made such a splash in the public prints that he almost wiped himself completely off the royal map forever. To Fergie this was a humiliating and embarrassing interlude in her life as well. However, it was comic and bizarre at the same time. In this case, it did not have to do with her, but with the major.

He was now fifty-six years old, but apparently much younger than that in spirit. He still loved to have a good time. One of his recreations was unknown to most of his immediate family, although there had been rumors for some time of a tiff between him and his second wife over—well—"other women." But nothing ever came of it.

Then, suddenly, on May 8, 1988, Major Ferguson was on all the front pages of the country's tabloids. A photograph showed him marching out of what was euphemistically called a London "massage parlor." The term was used as a cover for a house of ill repute at which he had frequently given women gifts of perfume and lemon bath oil purportedly used by the royal family—in exchange for their sexual favors to him.

The scandal that broke was the talk of the town. Major Ferguson had been a member of the Wigmore ("health")

Club, which he had visited at least six times in 1988 already. More than "health" was included in the favors granted at this club.

"As soon as you pay your entrance fee," a regular customer was quoted as saying, "you know what you're going to get. There are steam boxes available. But I was only there for the sex."

While most of London's well-heeled Wigmore clients masked their identities, the major enrolled under his own name. One of the club's employees was asked how she liked working with royalty—that is, Major Ferguson—and she responded, "He's not exactly cautious. In fact, I think he is rather stupid. He has talked to me about his problems. He often pops in for a massage and chat, and I usually finish the session off with a sexual act."

When the Buckingham Palace phones began ringing off the hook for Fergie, she was luckily absent, attending a christening with her husband. She had already been contacted by her father. "Keep your chin up high, and don't let them get you down," she told him, somewhat tearfully.

He did so. Next morning, the major appeared for his regular weekend polo match, playing on the same team with Prince Charles. Diana and the two children were there cheering from the sidelines. Talk about solidarity!

When Charles was questioned by reporters about the Wigmore affair, he scowled at them. "You must be out of your tiny minds! I'm not saying anything!"

The queen was away in Australia. Charles said that he would do nothing about firing Major Ferguson, unless the queen herself demanded it. The major, asked if he would go on his own, responded: "No way. If the Prince of Wales asks me to resign, that's another matter."

Chins up, heads high, chests thrown out. That was the way the royal family walked through that murky mine field. Major Ferguson did indeed sum it up when he told a friend of his with some chagrin: "I've been a fool."

By the end of June, the palace relieved the duchess of York of her official royal duties. This was to allow her some time to relax and be by herself before the birth of her child.

It was about this time that she leaked out the fact that this was an "unplanned" pregnancy. She had really wanted to wait until Andrew finished his tour of duty aboard the HMS *Edinburgh*—and that would be sometime in October 1988. But that was not to be. Nevertheless, she was planning to take a trip to Australia with her husband in the fall, either with or without the baby.

A routine medical examination then showed that she had high blood pressure and was experiencing excessive retention of fluid—and that was bad news indeed. Fergie did what she could to cope. Andrew, of course, was on the high seas, afloat somewhere on the opposite side of the globe.

The day for the birthing finally approached, and, as expected, the English media zeroed in on London's Portland Hospital, where Anthony Kenney, Fergie's gynecologist, practiced. A big banner was unfurled in front of the hospital: *Any Moment Now!*

But it *wasn't* any moment now. Time kept dragging along.

The queen, who would be a grandmother for the fifth time with this birth, was opening a new soap plant in northwest England and, when asked about the baby, responded testily:

"We hope it is soon. We are fed up with waiting." And she elaborated on that: "These wretched babies don't come until they're ready. They don't come to order!"

On Sunday, August 7, 1988, it looked as if the event was about to occur—when, indeed the father, the duke of York, arrived by plane from Singapore, where he had been offloaded from the HMS *Edinburgh* to make the flight. But it wasn't to be Sunday, either.

Then finally, at 8:18 P.M., August 8, 1988, the duchess of York was "safely delivered of a daughter," as the palace notice announced. The daughter weighed six pounds, twelve ounces, with the mother doing fine. "All members of the Royal family are very pleased with the news," a palace spokesperson said.

Soothsayers and astrologists read excellent portent into the time of the birth: eighteen minutes past eight on the eighth day of the eighth month of 1988. 8/8/88! All those eights. Very good news, indeed. Andrew, incidentally, was twenty-eight, and so was Sarah—to continue the lucky pattern.

Andrew had been with Fergie throughout her four-to-five-hour labor—quite short for a first pregnancy. The new arrival was now the fifth in line to the British throne—behind Uncle Charles, cousins William and Harry, and father Andrew.

Fergie's own father was in the crowd outside waiting. One photographer took it upon himself to shout out jovially to him. "Off to the Wigmore Club, Major?"

On Friday, August 12, Fergie and Andrew finally left the hospital with the baby in her arms. They pushed through the crowds and finally made their getaway to Balmoral Castle in their blue Jaguar.

Two weeks later the name followed: Beatrice Elizabeth Mary—to be called Her Royal Highness, the Princess Beatrice of York.

Beatrice?

"Queen Victoria's youngest daughter was Princess Beatrice," Brooks-Baker of *Burke's Peerage* pointed out. "Princess Beatrice married a member of the Battenberg family. The name was changed to Mountbatten in 1917 when the British royal family wished to appear more English instead of German."

Over two hundred people were contacted in the royal family to approve the name, he said. And the name proved to be eminently suitable.

"It's a dignified, old-fashioned name that was very dear to the heart of Queen Victoria. It's a name that, for no particular reason, went out of vogue. Many people felt that the duchess of York would choose a rather controversial modern name. She has chosen a name that is different, yes, but a name that is elegant and old-fashioned and still capable of being used in the modern age.

"And you can predict thousands of little girls being born in the next two or three years will be called Beatrice."

As for Beatrice herself, she faced a splendid life. As Fergie's stepmother, Susan Ferguson, said:

"Sarah always gives children a jolly good time. She's forever romping with my three. But she's also a disciplinarian and likes to see children well behaved."

XII

THE TWO PRINCESSES

12

BEST FRIEND AND . . . ENEMY?

As the Duchess of York's media star soared, the Princess of Wales's dipped. Or so it seemed to the public tuned in to the BBC news, ITN's specials, and Fleet Street's effusions.

"While Sarah and Andrew still bask in a rose-colored honeymoon glow (or at least the remnants thereof), the Queen's 'other' daughter-in-law, beauteous Diana, has hit a time of troubles with her husband, Charles," pontificated one American publication.

It went on to point out that Diana had become simply a shadow of her usual sparkling self, quoting some "firsthand observer." She was losing her enthusiasm and zest for life, another royalty watcher said, and was feeling isolated, alone, and "up against it."

No longer the queen's favorite, as she was when she first married Charles and bore his two children, Diana had been cast aside by the monarch, who had taken up with the easygoing, amicable Sarah Ferguson (as she was).

Yet, ironically enough, the two friends—the open and bouncy Sarah and the complex intense Diana—*remained* the best of friends, and, if anything, spent more and more time with one another, attending functions as a part of each others' life-support systems.

In a way, they were the "new" and "mod" pitted against the "old" and "trad"—two spirited young women coming of age during a revolution of women's liberation (a revolution repeated, admittedly, from earlier revolts during the nineteenth century in which the leaders were also women of England and America). And these two liberated females found themselves opening wide the windows of the ancient castles in which they were fated to live and letting in a bit of the free and fresh air of the late 1980s.

The younger media professionals saw them as a breath of fresh air too; the more ensconced and conservative watchers saw them as scandalous and radical iconoclasts. They were—and are—neither.

The public? Ah, the public. Indeed, the public was still on Diana's side no matter how emphatically the star of Sarah was on the rise. Londoners knew that even the sight of that dark-green, chauffeur-driven Bentley pulling in to the curb near, say, Westminster Abbey, would draw a tremendous crowd.

"Megacrowds," a London bobby reported recently. "It's always like this when the Princess makes an appearance."

Picture the scene:

With the Bentley's door opening, the crowd gasps in excitement, watching the leggy, chic, svelte Diana emerge from the car, wearing a sapphire-blue suit and matching hat to cover her well-coiffed blonde head.

Breathless and beside itself, the crowd holds its breath as Charles climbs out and the two vanish inside Westminster Abbey. A moment later the crowd has dispersed and nothing remains of the magic of the "appearance."

This is not exactly a scene that prophesies a falling off and decaying of Diana's public allure. In fact, it reinforces the impression of ferment over and interest in the monarchy held by every good British citizen—and citizen of America, too, for that matter. A large number of tourists, mostly from the United States, crowd around the royal couple whenever such a sighting is made.

And yet, and yet . . .

Royalty-watcher Wendy Leigh put it this way recently in *New Women:*

> Diana's august mother-in-law, England's beloved queen, shudders at her daughter-in-law's *Dynasty*-style glamour, her inability to submit stoically to damp autumns spent at the family's Scottish castle, and her unwillingness to embrace the queen's passion for horses, dogs, and grouse shooting.

Further, it has been reported that Diana's sister-in-law, Anne, simply loathes her. It has also been reported that the British public is freezing up in the warmth generally accorded her. And what Diana had hoped would happen—that her friend Sarah Ferguson, once married into the royal family, would become a confidante and support for her—has turned into a kind of psychological boomerang. This according to the talk, of course.

Tune in on Harold Brooks-Baker, from his elegant eyrie as publishing director of *Burke's Peerage:*

> The Princess of Wales likes being in the center of attention, and in many ways she is already being outshone by the Duchess of York. There will soon be a power play. I think there will be two separate courts, but because people enjoy so much more being with the Yorks, their court is bound to be larger.

Wow!

Even psychologists and personality therapists have gotten into the act. Consider this statement from Abigail Hirsch, M.S.W., a New York therapist: "Fergie and Di were unable to support and be nurturing to each other. . . . Each may have sought in the other the mothering they needed."

"Since her marriage," *New Woman* reported, "Fergie seems to have eclipsed her old mentor in every area. Diana craves publicity. Until now, it always had been Diana who had done the upstaging, and Prince Charles had resigned himself to Diana's stardom. Since the advent of Fergie, however, the situation is reversed. Every time Sarah gets in the headlines, Diana tries to upstage her. In fact, royal observers believe that Diana's recent flirtation with banker Philip Dunne was just her way of making sure Fergie didn't grab too many headlines."

And there are very good reasons to assume that indeed Fergie is on the up and Diana is on the down. Diana had never really endeared herself to the queen or to the family. Her sudden appearance and her quick ascent to superstardom garnered her a large percentage of the press coverage normally allotted to the entire royal family. In fact, she reduced the rest of the royals to a kind of dowdy support role. Perhaps they did resent it just a bit.

Then, when Fergie came along, she managed to grab the headlines for a while herself, but she wasn't as dominant in her superstardom as Diana had been—and, in fact, continues to be. Fergie was a lovable kind of teddy bear toy. Diana had always been the ice maiden, cool and aloof and—well—untouchable. Fergie was a team player, no question about that. Diana had always been a loner. Fergie's talents were in playing the royal family's favorite game—charades—and she had proved herself to be quick-witted and fast on the uptake. Diana's talents had never run along that line; there was no wit or sparkle of any kind in her talk—her *mots* were definitely not *bon*—and she had always resigned herself to being as "thick-headed as two planks" in her very own words.

In addition to that, their attitudes and personalities were quite different. Diana from the beginning had rather resented the country, and loved the city. She had always been shy of riding and she had never really taken much to tennis, skiing, polo, or hunting (which of course entailed riding).

On the other hand, Fergie from the start had been sports-oriented, with riding in her blood, so to speak. For that reason, she had become very good friends with her new sister-in-law, Princess Anne. And she even found rapport with the rather remote Prince Philip. The queen herself spent time with Fergie teaching her the finer points of grouse hunting, a sport that Fergie took up handily from the beginning. The two of them began to take long rides together on horseback—something the queen had been unable to do with her other daughter-in-law.

Of all the members of the palace involved, it was said by insiders that Fergie had won over all hearts but one—that of Prince Charles. The message from inside Buck House was that for the sensitive Prince Charles's taste, Fergie was much too loud and crass minded. Nor was he too happy over the fact that Fergie had become the media favorite that his wife suddenly was *not*. He also felt that it was Fergie's presence and influence over Diana that caused his own wife to involve herself in mindless pranks—japes that made British royalty look not only common but air-headed as well.

Another bit of gossip was beginning to surface once again. Actually, it had always been there, just below the skin, festering somewhat, like some kind of low-grade infection. It was simply that Diana had always really been in love with Andrew—*not* Charles. In school she had worshiped Andrew in her heart of hearts.

When she was a very young teenager, Diana had confided in the Spencer cook, Rose Ellis, that she was saving herself for Prince Andrew. "When she was a teenager," Andrew Morton of the *Star* once said, "she had a crush on a certain Prince Andrew, and she never thought she would capture Prince Charles. As a teenager, she thought that Prince Andrew would be her future husband."

Later on, when she was originally invited to the royal retreat at Sandringham, Diana was brought into the picture to be paired off romantically with Andrew—*not* Charles.

Andrew and Diana are, in the words of several insiders at the palace, as alike as two peas in a pod. They are both glamorous in person and in public, and they are very close in age. Besides that, both of them love to play the same kind of empty-headed practical jokes.

Nevertheless, this loose talk about Diana and Andrew tended mostly to be speculation of a rather wide-ranging sort. Actually, Diana herself had changed in her married years. She had even managed to achieve a certain kind of maturity—especially in her attitude toward the many former girlfriends of her husband.

At first, according to insiders, she had insisted that Charles break it off with all his former playmates of the female persuasion, but after a while Diana allowed him to reestablish some of those relationships. Growing security in her marriage had obviously allowed her to loosen up in her own attitudes about her husband's companions.

Directly after her marriage she had banished many of his women from the royal social circle. For several years no one from the old pack was allowed around the place. But then, along about the fifth year of her marriage, Diana began reestablishing the lines of contact between Prince Charles and Kanga—Lady Tryon, the Australian-born clothing boutique entrepreneur who ran Beauchamp

Place, a Sloane Ranger favorite. Diana even encouraged Kanga to organize a party for her and Charles after the London premiere of *Out of Africa*.

Later, Diana went out of her way to patch up her friendship with Camilla Parker-Bowles, a polo-playing friend of Prince Charles.

Of course, in spite of all the sophistication and understanding that the Princess of Wales was achieving in her dealings with the palace gang, she was still having her troubles with the press—the media people who had once loved her and made her a princess and then turned on her.

There were nasty rumors of liaisons with other men—those discussed briefly in the opening chapter—balanced by stories of Charles and his liaisons with women.

Typical headline: CHARLES SPENDS WEEKEND WITH MARRIED WOMAN WHILE DI FRETS AT HOME.

And so, typically, there was a lot of loose talk about what a divorce would do to the royal family.

"A divorce would not cost Prince Charles the right of accession," one American newspaper reported sanctimoniously. "Princess Diana would probably be given a house of her own and a generous financial settlement for the remainder of her life—provided she agreed never to write her memoirs."

The report went on to opine that Diana could marry any man of her choice, but that she would have to give up the care and control of her sons to the royal family. She would get visitation rights, and so on.

In spite of the thrust of the piece, the writer did finally admit: "Princess Diana is a child of divorce who was reared by her father. Experiencing firsthand the trauma that it caused, she no doubt will do anything to avoid a divorce—even to the point of permitting her husband to take a mistress or two, if it ever comes to that."

Bravo!

Charles? Mistress? Huh?

It seems obvious that this was all pure speculation—speculation based on a desire to underline the nonfact that *something seems to be going on here, doesn't it?* It's a kind of backward logic. Since there is a discussion of a divorce, even though the words in the story underline the fact that it probably won't happen, by backward reasoning one is forced to admit that indeed there must be some *reason* to talk about divorce; therefore, Charles and Diana must separately be making their own way through the forests of deception to that secret goal.

And that kind of thing.

Andrew Morton went on national television in America on—of all things!—the "Geraldo Rivera Show," November 23, 1987, to add fuel to this kind of fire.

"Prince Charles on walkabouts, on tours," he said, was always "very loving towards Diana"—in the past, that is. He was "affectionate, cuddling—patting on the backside, putting his arm around her." He continued, "Nowadays, you look at them on a walkabout, and . . . there's no conversation, no interaction at all. It doesn't seem as though either of them are making the kind of effort which should be made in that position. And, for example, when they went off to Wales, asked to go there by the Queen Mother, to visit certain areas, they could have stayed the night together at Kensington Palace. Instead, Charles chose to go straight to Balmoral, and Diana just stayed on her own."

On the same show, James Whitaker, another reporter and royalty watcher, opined:

> The sparkle has gone out of their marriage, there's no question about it. . . . What I think is sad now is that this great passion that was there is now come down to an arranged marriage. I think you'll find that in the way it is with Princess Anne and Mark Phillips, they lead a life together when it's important for family life, but when

> they're on their own, doing their own things, then they are just not together. And I find that absolutely dreadful, because I was with Diana the day she asked me about getting married to Prince Charles, and it meant so much to her, she wanted to do this from the age of about fifteen or sixteen, and she was absolutely alive with excitement. She said, "What do you think?" And, "Is it going to be all right? I'm sure I'm going to be able to cope." And she really adored him. Now I see an air of indifference. It's not dislike . . . but it's just rather going through the motions . . . without really caring. And I find that very sad.

But as for having an affair with anyone, even those two seasoned Fleet Street journalists would not admit that. "She's a great flirt," Morton has said. "She loves to flirt with guys. She has those incredible powder-blue eyes. . . . And half the guys who have ever met her have fallen for her and swooned for her. And it doesn't mean anything. [She just] enjoys flirting with guys, especially good-looking ones."

And so on examination it all looked like a big puff of smoke sent up by Fleet Street in the exercise of its duty to entertain and bemuse the British public.

But then in the course of 1988 there appeared to be a bit more than mush-mouthed headlines like that and smarmy opinions on television about unspecified trouble in Paradise.

In 1988 alone, Charles spent five holidays without his family around, including an Easter fishing expedition at Balmoral with Lady "Kanga" Tryon—that old ex-flame. Along for the ride, however, were her husband and other friends. Hardly one of those undercover rendezvous.

In May 1988 Charles went on a holiday to Florence, Italy, where he usually stayed at the house of the Marchesa Bona de Frescobaldi. Rumors went flying that something was going on between the two of them. They—the rumors—got so hot that the marchesa's brother-in-law looked up Charles, pronounced the word *"Basta!"* several times, and added the Italian version of "read my lips," finally suggesting that the Prince of Wales should decamp and find somewhere else to lay his head. Bad vibes quivered everywhere.

But then, quickly, in July 1988 Charles and Diana were seen in public in tandem, watching Michael Jackson at Wembley Stadium; the two of them laughing and smiling together throughout the concert. What was real? What was unreal? No one really knew.

"Things have leveled out," said Ingrid Seward, editor of *Majesty* magazine and the author of the biography *Diana.* "They've sort of reached a compromise. They're doing their own thing. But it's rather sad. When they got married seven years ago, people *loved* their being together and rather hoped that they'd always be together."

Oh, well.

About the media's new star attraction—the irrepressible Fergie—reporters Morton and Whitaker had a quite different story to tell. Things were still *up* with her, to hear them tell it.

Morton: "Sarah is a great girl, and I won't hear a word said against her. She's great fun, what she's done is she's brought Diana, as it were, away from all these appalling fuddy-duddies who inhabit Buckingham Palace, all these old colonels and majors, and all these dreary, dreary characters, and taken her out to the clubs, and why not? She's twenty-six, her kids are growing up, she's got nannies. Why shouldn't she have a good time?"

As for her husband: "Prince Andrew is something of a brat," Morton admitted. "And Prince Charles doesn't particularly get on very well with him. He's one of these rather 'Hooray Henry!' types who throws rolls at dinner parties, he's a bit of—oh, I don't know, he's not the sort of character that Prince Charles would get on with very well.'' Even if they *were* brothers, Morton failed to mention.

Besides, of course, Prince Charles rather envied the fact that Prince Andrew had fought in a real war—the Falkland affair—and was a skin diver, a parachutist, and a chopper pilot.

His wife, the duchess of York, had her own protectors—the most powerful and the most protective of whom was her own father. Talking about his daughter's adjustment to her ''new'' life, Major Ronald Ferguson said:

> Anybody would find [marrying into the royal family] daunting. Sarah has a great deal of courage and determination. Everything she does she wants to do to perfection, not only for herself but also because she is married to Prince Andrew. She doesn't want to let him down. There is nothing peculiar in that.

In spite of Sarah's change in life-style, Ferguson said that the two of them continued to be very close. He found his daughter to be very caring about him. ''There can't be many daughters who ring up by radio phone on the night of their wedding, which she did. Funnily enough, I probably speak to her more now than before—about four or five times a week when she's not traveling.''

He said that he felt she would like to be even more natural than she already was. But she could not be, now that she was a member of the royal family with all its traditions and regulations.

''One difficulty is that she doesn't have the same freedom now as she did in the past,'' Ferguson said. ''Everywhere she goes, whether it's out shopping or to restaurants with friends, she is accompanied by a bodyguard. . . . In the past she could dress whatever way she liked. Now, whenever she steps outside, the eyes of the media are upon her.''

Perfect for the job she undertook, Sarah Ferguson

would be able, he felt, to make herself into a model wife for a royal prince. "Sarah . . . has been accepted into the royal family for what she is. She does get on very well with all of them. There is no reason she shouldn't. She is very upfront. She is a good listener and is the sort of person who, if she wants advice, will ask for it. Whether she will accept everyone's views is a different matter."

She and the Princess of Wales, Ferguson said, were "great friends, incredibly close"—not "best friends" in *that* sense of the term. "They have completely different roles. One is married to the future king, and the other to Prince Andrew. . . . They are not trying to compete as to who wears the smartest dress, or who attends the most functions. At the same time, they have a great deal of fun together and carry on accordingly. . . . The press says you can't behave like that, which is ludicrous."

About the story that the two princesses tend to drink too much and carouse about, Ferguson said that it was "absolute rubbish. They both might have a glass of wine, but they have never drunk to excess." As for reacting to criticism about them, he said that "they cannot ring up the newspapers. They just laugh and carry on as normal. Sarah has given up reading all the rubbish they write, which is a good thing."

As for him, he admitted that he read everything that was written about Sarah. And, of course, he would get extremely angry—especially about the nonsense that Sarah supposedly was taking fertility drugs to become pregnant—which, he said, was patently and undeniably "untrue."

In all this swirl of controversy, gossip, and public envy, the two princesses continued to do just about what they wanted to do—within the especial parameters of their peculiar life-style.

But something very important about the two princesses seemed to be starting to make itself evident. They were in a crucial stage of development. They were both in the process of taking on more responsibilities than they had ever had before. They were being forced to cope with a number of very adult situations that they had never had to face before.

To be effectively blunt about it—they were both mothers now, maidens no longer. Life was moving on for them. A plateau had been scaled. New horizons were in view.

The teenage princess had become a woman in her twenties, and was now a woman approaching the end of her twenties—facing, indeed, the dreaded . . . thirties! The bumptious duchess who had rollicked about wherever she chose was now facing the prospect of becoming a . . . mother! Sigh.

For good reason the flower children of the 1960s had chosen as the watchword of their era: "Never trust anyone over thirty."

Thirty marks the dividing line between youth, with its fun and games, and adulthood with its responsibilities. It is a watershed year, not only for the common person, but for a royal as well. Charles had long since passed it. He was over the hill. Andrew was waiting to cross the divide; after that it would be all downhill.

For the princesses it was a time of radical change.

Would it be good-bye to pranks and high jinks?

Hopefully—no.

The princesses were—and are—very special cases. They glamorize a dull and unimaginative breed. One does it with a svelte beauty that the camera lens makes love to, that people idolize, and that the world takes to its heart. The other does it with an irrepressible sense of humor and fun, and a drive to live life to the hilt—and enjoy it at the same time.

More power to them both—if indeed *power* is the proper word.

Best of *luck* to them both.

BIBLIOGRAPHY

Periodicals

"After the Princess of Wales Takes to Dotting the Di, Britain Breaks Out in a Fashion Rash." *People,* July 14, 1986.

Alan, Ray. "Buckingham Dallas." *The New Leader,* October 6, 1986.

———. "The Long March of the Prince of Wales." *The New Leader,* January 12, 1987.

"All about Diana: The Private World of a Princess." *People Weekly Extra,* Spring 1988.

"Alone at Last." *Royalty Monthly,* September 1981.

Ames, Katrine. "Let's All Play Queen for a Day." *Newsweek,* January 11, 1988.

Anderson, Judith. "How the Royals Keep Fit." *Chatelaine,* March 1987.

———. "Royal Switch: Now Anne Outshines Diana." *Chatelaine,* August 1986.

"Andrew Loves Her . . . and So Does His Royal Family." *McCall's,* June 1986.

"Andy, Fergie Reunited." *Stamford Advocate,* September 24, 1988.

Anthony, E. C. "Princess Diana Plans for Her Next Child." *McCall's,* July 1984.

Arnold, Sue. "Delicious, Delively Diana." *Cosmopolitan,* February 1985.

Austin, Victoria. "The Day the Snow Princess Came to Visit. . . ." *Royalty Monthly*, January 1982.

———. "Diana: The Brightest Jewel in the Royal Family." *Royalty Monthly*, June 1983.

———. "The Duchess as Working Woman." *Royalty Monthly*, February 1987.

———. "Going Dutch." *Royalty Monthly*, November 1986.

———. "Good on Yer, Chas 'n' Di!" *Royalty Monthly*, May 1983.

———. "Her Heart's in the Highlands." *Royalty Monthly*, October 1981.

———. "How the West Was Won." *Royalty Monthly*, August 1983.

———. "Ma Che Bella! Fashion and Friendship on the Grand Tour." *Royalty Monthly*, June 1985.

———. "Out of the Ivory Tower and Back on the Road Again." *Royalty Monthly*, March 1983.

———. "A Ray of Sunshine in Norway." *Royalty Monthly*, March 1984.

———. "To Have and to Hold." *Royalty Monthly*, August 1981.

———. "What Ever Became of 'Shy Di'?" *Royalty Monthly*, May 1982.

———. "With Andrew and Sarah in Paradise." *Royalty Monthly*, November 1987.

———. "A Year in the Life of a Princess." *Royalty Monthly*, August 1982.

Backlund, Laurie. "Arrest of 'Armed' Man Stirs Royal Fuss." *Los Angeles Times*, February 29, 1988.

Barber, John, "Going to the World's Fair." *Maclean's*, May 12, 1986.

Barber, John, with Thomas Suddon and Paulette Roberge. " 'Fabulous Fergie.' " *Maclean's*, July 27, 1987.

Bardens, Dennis. "A Cause for a Nation to Rejoice." *Royalty Monthly*, July 1982.

Barry, Stephen P. "Upstairs at the Palace." *Good Housekeeping,* February 1985.

"Beginning in Britain." *New York Times,* January 31, 1988.

Bernstein, Fred, reported by Laura Healy. "Now Playing at the Palace . . . Fergie and Di, the Best of Friends and the Toast of the Town." *People,* October 13, 1986.

Bernstein, Fred, reported by Terry Smith. "Rebellion at Kensington." *People,* July 22, 1985.

"Boo Hoo, Koo! Diana's Pal Sarah Ferguson Wins Andrew's Heart and the Queen's Approval." *People,* January 27, 1986.

Booth, William. "Living Hell?" *Texas Monthly,* April 1986.

"Born to Be King—but When?" *Time,* November 11, 1985.

Botham, Noel, and John Collins. "Desperate Di's Last-Ditch Effort to Save Marriage." *National Enquirer,* November 17, 1987.

Burnet, Alistair. "At-Home Exclusive: Prince Charles, Diana, and the Children." *Good Housekeeping,* November 1986.

———. "A Royal Photo Album." *Good Housekeeping,* January 1986.

"The Cannes Film Festival Is a Grade B Movie with No Good Parts for Charles and Diana." *People,* April 20, 1987.

Chambers, Andrew, reported by Logan Bentley, Garry Clifford, and Jonathan Cooper. "Doing Europe Right." *People,* May 20, 1985.

"Charles and Di: The Past that Haunts Them." *Redbook,* July 1988.

"Charles Escapes Injury: Avalanche Kills Friend." *New York Times,* March 11, 1988.

"Charles Lays Claim to a New Title: Prince of Break Dancing." *People,* April 15, 1985.

Clarke, Mary. "Princess Di's Nanny Remembers . . . The Custody Battle for Diana." *Redbook,* August 1987.

Collins, Dan. "Birthday Bash at Harvard." *U.S. News & World Report,* September 15, 1988.

Concini, Chuck. "Personalities." *Washington Post,* November 10, 1986.

Cooper, Nancy, with Tony Flicton. "The Royal Family's Gothic Shocker." *Newsweek,* April 20, 1987.

Cooper, Nancy, with Nikki Finke Greenberg. "Trying to Join the Few." *Newsweek,* October 28, 1985.

Cooper, Nancy, with Gerald C. Lubenow and Donna Fook. "Wanted: Less Pomp, More Circumstance." *Newsweek,* March 7, 1988.

Courtney, Nicholas. "Guess What's in Princess Di's Suitcases." *Redbook,* June 1985.

"Daddy's Little Princess." *New York Daily News,* August 23, 1988.

Dallas, Mary. "How the Princess Passed the Test." *Royalty Monthly,* September 1980.

———. "The Press—When the Queen Was Not Amused . . ." *Royalty Monthly,* August 1984.

———. "A Princess for Wales." *Royalty Monthly,* November 1981.

———. "Prince William: The Royal Wanderer." *Royalty Monthly,* August 1984.

———. "Waiting for the Happy Event . . ." *Royalty Monthly,* April 1982.

———. "Welcome Home, Andrew!" *Royalty Monthly,* October 1982.

———. "With One Bound, Will the Daredevil Duchess Be Free?" *Royalty Monthly,* November 1987.

Denton, Herbert H. "Her Majesty's Man in Toronto; Lincoln Alexander, Playing Host Today to Andy and Fergie." *Washington Post,* July 15, 1987.

Diamond, S. J. "Colored Stones: Quality's in the Eye of Beholder." *Los Angeles Times,* August 10, 1987.

"Diana and Charles's Visit to America in November." *Good Housekeeping,* October 1985.

"Diana: Her Private Photo Album." *Ladies Home Journal* July 1988.

"Diana Is Special Enough for a Special Issue." *Newsday*, May 17, 1988.

"Diana, No Dipso, Knocks Those Risible Bubbly Rumors Flat." *People*, August 10, 1987.

Dilberto, Gioia, reported by Terry Smith. "Harry and Di Are a Hit on Camera, but the Prince's Papa Is in the Palace Doghouse." *People*, October 28, 1984.

Dilberto, Gioia, reported by John Wright. "Hello, Harry!" *People*, October 1, 1984.

Dillon, Sheila. "Good-Bye, Shy Di!" *McCall's*, March 1985.

"Dinner of the Decade." *Ladies Home Journal*, March 1986.

"Di's Little Lone Ranger Flies Like an Heir with the Greatest of Ease." *People*, April 8, 1985.

Dobovay, Diana. "The Rumors That Plague Princess Diana." *McCall's*, October 1984.

Donaton, Scott, "Cover Story." *Advertising Age*, October 19, 1987.

Durkee, Cutler, reported by Jonathan Cooper. "Di: Birth of a Saleswoman." *People*, November 11, 1985.

Eady, Brenda. "Unforgettable Faces of Our Time." *People*, April 30, 1984.

Edwards, Anne. "Diana and Her Friends." *Ladies Home Journal*, November 1985.

"Etc.'s Fall Preview." *People*, September 2, 1985.

Fairlie, Henry. "Washington Scene: The Second Coming." *The New Republic*, December 2, 1985.

Fearon, Peter. "An Intimate Embrace in the Back Seat of a Limo—and Those Royal Rift Rumors Are History." *Star*, November 17, 1987.

"Fergie and Andrew Do Niagara, and Canada Falls." *People*, August 3, 1987.

"Fergie and Andy Name Their Baby Bea, and All Britain Is Abuzz." *People*, September 5, 1988.

"Fergie, Duchess of York: The Toast of Britain, Spirited

Sarah Ferguson, Takes Happy Title to Prince Andrew." *People,* December 22, 1986.

"Fergie Wins Her Wings and Andy's a Backseat Pilot." *People,* March 21, 1987.

Filler, Martin. "Less Is No More." *House & Garden,* October 1985.

Fincher, Jayne. "Did the Fashion Princess Get It Right?" *Royalty Monthly,* July 1985.

———. "How the Snood Made a Royal Comeback." *Royalty Monthly,* March 1987.

"The Flying Duchess on the Piste!" *Royalty Monthly,* March 1987.

"For the Prince and Princess of Wales, a Time of Troubles." *McCall's,* June 1987.

"From the Empire Comes News of an Heir, New Hair, and Maggie on a Roll." *People,* October 8, 1986.

Garcia, Guy D., reported by Helen Gibson and David E. Thigpen. "Who's Who on the Wing." *Time,* November 30, 1987.

Goldberger, Paul. "Should the Prince Send Modernism to the Tower?" *New York Times,* March 13, 1988.

Goodwin, Betty. "Fergie's Look in L.A.: Flair without Fuss." *Los Angeles Times,* March 4, 1988.

———. "Mum's the Word as Wedding Gown for 'Fergi' Takes Shape." *Los Angeles Times,* July 4, 1986.

Gray, Charlotte. "Royal Baby Album." *Chatelaine,* January 1985.

Gray, Malcolm, with Nancy Durham and Carol Kennedy. "The Royal Pack in Pursuit." *Maclean's,* November 11, 1985.

Gray, Malcolm, with John Howse. "Royal Welcome in the West." *Maclean's,* August 3, 1987.

Gross, Jane, "Awaiting the Royals, Amid Splendor and 'So Whats?' " *New York Times,* September 19, 1987.

———. "Duchess Warily Confronts a Wild Kingdom." *New York Times,* September 20, 1987.

"Has the Monarchy Gone to Diana's Head? Fleet Street Calls Her New Look a Di-Saster." *People,* November 28, 1984.

Hauptfuhrer, Fred (interviewer). "When the Critics Get Tough, Fergie's Major Defender, Her Dad, Rides to the Rescue." *People,* September 1987.

"Heading for the High Ground." *Royalty Monthly,* March 1985.

Hemp, Paul. "Royals vs. the Press Ends in a Hat Trick by Princess Diana." *Wall Street Journal,* January 15, 1988.

"Her Majesty Is Pleased to Announce . . ." *Royalty Monthly,* May 1986.

Hitchens, Christopher. "Minority Report." *The Nation,* November 23, 1985.

Holden, Anthony. "Andrew and Marriage: Obstacles and Options." *Royalty Monthly,* October 1980.

———. "Andrew, the Perfect Uncle." *Royalty Monthly,* February 1985.

———. "Can Diana Beat the Italians at Their Own Game?" *Royalty Monthly,* April 1985.

———. "Can Diana Knock 'Em Dead in the States?" *Royalty Monthly,* October 1985.

———. "Charles." *Royalty Monthly,* July 1983.

———. "Diana." *Royalty Monthly,* July 1983.

———. "Diana and Elizabeth." *Ladies Home Journal,* November 1985.

———. "Diana's Diamond Celebration." *Royalty Monthly,* July 1985.

———. "Diana: The Facts behind Those 'Health' Rumors." *Royalty Monthly,* January 1983.

———. "Happy Birthday, Diana!" *Royalty Monthly,* July 1985.

———. "Is It True Love at Last for Andrew?" *Royalty Monthly,* December 1985.

———. "New Man in Diana's Life . . ." *Royalty Monthly,* December 1984.

———. "Princess Diana: Royal Role Model." *Ladies Home Journal,* May 1985.

———. "Princess Di: Superstar." *Chatelaine,* July 1984.

———. "A Second Baby—and Diana's Dilemma." *Royalty Monthly,* September 1985.

———. "A Tale of Two Duchesses." *Royalty Monthly,* September 1986.

———. "To the Manner Born." *Royalty Monthly,* October 1984.

———. "A Visit to Diana's Family Home." *Royalty Monthly,* July 1985.

———. " 'We're a Good Team.' " *Royalty Monthly,* May 1986.

———. "Why Diana Became the New Royal Matchmaker." *Royalty Monthly,* January 1986.

———. "Will Sarah Be the New Royal Fashion Queen?" *Royalty Monthly,* June 1986.

———. " 'Wills,' the Mini-Tornado, Grows Up." *Royalty Monthly,* June 1985.

———. "Will the Image Makers Take Over?" *Royalty Monthly,* November 1985.

Holder, Margaret, "Fergie: Can She Bring up Her Baby—*Her* Way?" *Redbook,* August 1988.

"Hooray for the New-Look Diana!" *Royalty Monthly,* November 1987.

"How Diana's Friend Stepped into the Limelight." *Royalty Monthly,* December 1985.

Howell, Georgina. "How to Shop Like a Princess." *Travel,* December 1987.

Hull, Fiona MacDonald. "On Tour with Diana." *Ladies Home Journal,* August 1985.

"It's a Girl for Fergie and Andrew." *Newsday,* August 9, 1988.

"It's Black Tie, Blue Blood, Blondes and Bubbly as Diana's Titled Brother Turns Twenty-One." *People,* June 10, 1985.

"It's a Canadian Caper!" *Royalty Monthly*, September 1985.

Janigan, Mary, with Ross Laver. "A Right Royal Uproar." *Maclean's*, July 6, 1987.

"Jobs Too Frantic? City Living Just Too Much? Rent a Cozy Rural Hideaway Like Andy and Fergie Did." *People*, February 18, 1987.

Johnson, Bonnie. "Baba Says Ta Ta to Wills and Harry—the Question Is, Did Charles and Di Get the Nanny's Goat?" *People*, February 2, 1987.

Johnson, Bonnie, reported by Laura Sanderson Healy and Terry Smith. "Autumn of Their Discontent." *People*, November 9, 1987.

Johnson, Bonnie, with Laura Sanderson Healy, Rosemary Thorpe-Tracey, and Cathy Nolan. "Royal: When It Comes to Raising England's Privileged Little Princes, Princess Diana Rules the Roost." *People*, April 25, 1988.

Johnson, Bonnie, and Leah Rozen, reported by Laura Healy. "No Titters, You Two, This Is Serious!" *People*, July 20, 1987.

Johnson, Bonnie, with Eleanor Hoover, Kristine Johnson, David Marlow, and Melissa McCoy. "Friendly Fergie Blossoms in the California Sun, Drawing Cheers Here but Sneers Back Home." *People*, March 14, 1988.

Jones, Jerene. "Di's Kid Brother Is a Good-Time Charlie but a Restaurant Dustup Has Some Folks Dubbing Him a No-Account Viscount." *People*, June 11, 1984.

"A Joyous Occasion for the Nation." *Royalty Monthly*, July 1986.

Junor, Penny. "Charles: His Side of the Story." *McCall's*, March 1988.

Karlen, Neal, with Nikki Finks. "The Royal Treatment." *Newsweek*, November 18, 1985.

Kaufman, Joanne, with Jonathan Cooper and Rosemary Thorpe-Tracey. "For Fergie, Mum's the Word." *People*, August 29, 1988.

Kaufman, Joanne, with Laura Sanderson Healy and Rosemary Thorpe-Tracey. "Seven-Year Hitch." *People,* August 1, 1988.

Keay, Douglas. "Diana—the Royal Matchmaker." *Good Housekeeping,* August 1986.

———. *Good Housekeeping* Spends the Day with Prince Charles and Diana." *Good Housekeeping,* September 1984.

———. "Royal Secrets." *Good Housekeeping,* April 1984.

"King-Size Welcome." *Time,* March 3, 1986.

Korda, Michael. "Serene Highnesses of Celebrity." *Newsweek,* November 25, 1985.

"Lady Diana's Family Album." *Royalty Monthly,* July 1981.

Lederer, Edith M. "A New York! Fergie Gives Birth to a Girl." *New York Daily News,* August 9, 1988.

Leigh, Wendy. "Best of Friends, Best of Enemies?" *New Woman,* December 1987.

Lynch, Lorrie, Ann Trebbe, and Stephen Schaefer. "Briefly . . ." *USA Today,* December 15, 1987.

Macleod, Alexander. " 'Young Royals' Said to Lack the Dignity That Befits a Dynasty." *Christian Science Monitor,* July 6, 1987.

Martin, Ralph G. "Charles and Diana." *Woman's Day,* November 5, 1985.

Mayer, Allan, with Tony Clifton and Donna Foote. "Beyond the Fairy Tale." *Newsweek,* October 28, 1985.

McIver, Mary, with Ross Laver and Brian Jones. "Roughing It in the Bush." *Maclean's,* August 10, 1987.

"Milestones." (Birth of Prince Harry.) *Time,* September 24, 1984.

Morrison, Patt. "Britannia Rules as Royals Hit Town." *Los Angeles Times,* February 27, 1988.

———. "Even Weather Turns British for Royal Couple." *Los Angeles Times,* March 1, 1988.

———. "Royal Couple Turns to Art and Music as Sun Makes an Appearance." *Los Angeles Times,* March 3, 1988.

———. "Royals Go Behind the Scenes but Stay in Front of Cameras." *Los Angeles Times,* March 2, 1988.

———. "Royalty Meets Right Stuff on High Seas." *Los Angeles Times,* March 4, 1988.

———. "Royal Visitors Get Taste of L.A.'s Way." *Los Angeles Times,* February 28, 1988.

———. "UCLA Gives the Duke, Duchess a Royal Send-Off." *Los Angeles Times,* March 5, 1988.

Morton, Andrew. "Fergie." *Good Housekeeping,* July 1988.

"New Zealand's Princess of Wales Health Camp Stamps." *Stamps,* August 17, 1985.

Nightingale, Spencer, and Gwen Robyns. "Princess Diana." *Ladies Home Journal,* May 1984.

"No Match for a Headstrong Polo Pony, Prince Charles Winds up on a Real Downer." *People,* June 30, 1986.

"No Ordinary Fender Bender, Diana Gives Prince Charles a Pain in the Aston Martin." *People,* July 8, 1987.

Oates, Marylouise. "Fergie Plays the Crowd." *Los Angeles Times,* March 1, 1988.

———. "Loyal to the Royal Itinerary." *Los Angeles Times,* March 4, 1988.

———. "A Royal Luncheon Sets This Crowd to Dreaming of Crowns." *Los Angeles Times,* March 1, 1988.

"Only in L.A." *Los Angeles Times,* March 3, 1988.

"A Peek at the Ferguson Family Album." *Royalty Monthly,* July 1986.

Peterson, Susie, and David Thomas. "All about Fergie: Her Flair, Her Flubs, the Kind of Mother She'll Be." *Ladies Home Journal,* August 1988.

Petulengo, Eva. "Having to Conform Is Something of an Ordeal—He Likes to Be Master of His Own Destiny." *Royalty Monthly,* February 1982.

"Prince Andrew in Los Angeles." *Royalty Monthly,* December 1984.

"Prince Charles and Princess Diana: All the World Is Their Stage." *U.S. News & World Report,* November 18, 1985.

"Prince Charles Given Painting." *Nuestro,* May 1986.

"Prince Charles Tells of Role in Rescue." *Newsday,* March 12, 1988.

"Prince Charles Visits Library of Congress." *American Libraries,* December 1985.

"Prince Charles Visits Library of Congress." *Wilson Library Bulletin,* January 1986.

"Prince Henry: The First Pictures." *Royalty Monthly,* November 1984.

"The Prince's Own Princess." *Royalty Monthly,* December 1981.

"Prince William: A Progress Report on the Royal Baby." *Royalty Monthly,* January 1983.

"Princess Diana." *People,* December 28/January 4, 1988.

"Princess-to-be Sarah Ferguson Is Well-Suited in Di's Old Duds." *People,* May 28, 1986.

Raines, Howell. "Defying Tradition: Prince Charles Recasts His Role." *New York Times Magazine,* February 21, 1988.

———. "Wives of Windsor; Making Too Merry." *New York Times,* June 28, 1987.

Randolph, John. "The Warrior Prince and a Bit of Fun." *Royalty Monthly,* November 1982.

Reynolds, Barbara, and Princess Simmons. "Naming a Princess Is Tedious Work: 200 Relatives Must Say OK." *USA Today,* August 23, 1988.

Robyns, Gwen. "Fabulous Fergie Flying High." *Ladies Home Journal,* February 1987.

———. "Princess Diana: A Royal House Party." *Ladies Home Journal,* December 1984.

Rossiter, Sean. "Eight B.C. Princesses Await Their Very Own Prince Charles." *Saturday Night,* October 1986.

Roura, Phil, and Tom Poster with Patricia O'Haire. "Di's Dad: Spats, Yes, But No One Gets the Boot." *New York Daily News,* April 4, 1988.

"The Row on the Ski Slopes." *Royalty Monthly,* February 1983.

"Royal Baby Boom." *People,* May 20, 1984.

"The Royal Road to the Isles." *Royalty Monthly,* September 1985.

"Royals at War." *Royalty Monthly,* May 1982.

"The Royals' Conquer Washington." *U.S. News & World Report,* November 25, 1985.

Rozen, Leah, reported by Victoria Balfour. "Connecticut Yankees Court the Yorks." *People,* September 1987.

St. Clair, Jean. "The British Fashion Toast Is 'Diana!' " *Royalty Monthly,* May 1984.

———. "Diana Unveils Another Stunner." *Royalty Monthly,* October 1984.

———. " 'He Makes Everyone around Him Happy—Really Nice Person.' " *Royalty Monthly,* February 1982.

———. "The Making of a Man." *Royalty Monthly,* February 1983.

———. "Why the Queen Is Tickled Pink . . ." *Royalty Monthly,* January 1982.

Salvatore, Diane. "Diana in America." *Ladies Home Journal,* November 1985.

Samuels, W. S. "The Focus of a Nation's Joy." *Royalty Monthly,* August 1986.

———. "Will Andrew Become Duke of York?" *Royalty Monthly,* January 1986.

"Sarah, Duchess of York." *Current Biography,* March 1987.

"Sarah's First Highland Fling." *Royalty Monthly,* October 1986.

Schiro, Anne-Marie. "American Weekend for Royal Couple." *New York Times,* September 17, 1987.

Scott, Walter. "Personality Parade" (Prince Charles). *Parade Magazine,* March 6, 1988.

"Selling Britain." *Fortune,* December 9, 1985.

Seward, Ingrid. "The Duchess of York." *European Travel & Life,* July/August 1988.

———. "Family Secrets: How Anne and Diana *Really* Get Along." *Good Housekeeping*, November 1984.

———. "My Friend Fergie." *Good Housekeeping*, August 1986.

Shearer, Lloyd. "The Baby Goes with Them." *Parade Magazine*, June 19, 1988.

Slack, Kenneth. "Staying Away from the Pope's Mass." *Christian Century*, June 19–26, 1985.

Slazenger, Jeremy. "The Women Princess Diana Trusts Most." *McCall's*, May 1984.

Small, Michael, reported by Laura Sanderson Healy and Terry Smith. "Bundles for Britain." *People*, November 11, 1985.

Smith, R. C. "Let's Spare Charles and Diana the Cheap Shots." *TV Guide*, November 8, 1985.

Smith, Terry. ". . . And Wee Willie Is Almost Two." *People*, June 25, 1984.

———. "A Pop Crooner Tells the Royal Mom to Shake Her Fanny and She Does, Before 11,500 People." *People*, July 23, 1984.

Smith, Terry, and Laura Sanderson Healy. "Fabulous Fergie." *People*, April 7, 1986.

Smith, Terry, and Rosemary Thorpe-Tracey. "A Windsor War." *People*, January 14, 1985.

Stengel, Richard, reported by Ann Blackman, Mary Cronin, and John Duren. "A Prince and His Princess Arrive." *Time*, November 11, 1985.

Stengel, Richard, reported by Mary Cronin and Alessandry Stanley. "The Royal Couple Drops In." *Time*, November 18, 1985.

"Sweet William." *Royalty Monthly*, September 1982.

"A Tale of Two Princesses." *Royalty Monthly*, February 1985.

"Their Marital Woes on Hold, Charles and Di Wow Germany." *People*, November 23, 1987.

Thomas, David, and Susie Pearson. "Diana: Her Secret Life." *Ladies Home Journal,* February 1988.

Toepfer, Susan, with Terry Smith and Rosemary Thorpe-Tracey. "Linked to High Jinks at a Swank Sex Parlor, Fergie's Dad, Ronald, Stirs Up a Royal Scandal." *People,* May 23, 1988.

"To Love, Honor—And Obey?" *Time,* July 21, 1986.

"TRB: from Washington." *The New Republic,* November 25, 1985.

Trucco, Terry. "Finally: A Designer Fit for a Duchess." *New York Times,* November 10, 1988.

Tuhy, Carrie. "On a Royal Shopabout with Princess Diana." *Money,* November 14, 1985.

Underwood, Nora, with Nancy Durham. "The Princess and the Duchess." *Maclean's,* July 27, 1987.

"A Very Stylish Princess." *Maclean's,* November 11, 1985.

Wade, Judy. "Look at Me." *US,* November 16, 1987.

Wainhouse, Beth. "The Princess and Her Protégé." *Ladies Home Journal,* July 1986.

"The Wales Family Album." *Royalty Monthly,* April 1983.

Wallace, Carol, reported by Jonathan Cooper, Fred Hauptfuhrer, and Terry Smith. "Anxious to Dispel Those Nasty Rumors, Charles and Di Take Their Case to the Telly." *People,* November 4, 1985.

Wallace, Carol, reported by Dianna Waggoner. "The Royal Wedding; Capping Days of Pomp, Parties and Prenuptial High Jinks, Sparkling Sarah Ferguson Weds Prince Andrew." *People,* August 4, 1986.

"Waterford Welcomes the Duchess of York." *Stamford Advocate,* January 1988.

Weinhouse, Beth. "Diana Now." *Ladies Home Journal,* March 1985.

Weinhouse, Beth, and Gwen Robyns. "The Princess Who Loves Children." *Ladies Home Journal,* July 1984.

"Welcome to the White House: Charles and Diana in the United States." *Royalty Monthly,* November 1985.

"Welsh Welcome for Princess." *Royalty Monthly,* March 1985.

"We're Just Wild About Harry!" *Royalty Monthly,* October 1986.

"What an End to a Wonderful Year." *Royalty Monthly,* February 1982.

Whitaker, James. "How Diana Did It." *McCall's,* June 1986.

———. "A Triumphant Transformation: Fergie's First Year." *McCall's,* June 1987.

"Why It's Saint George for Prince Harry." *Royalty Monthly,* December 1984.

"Why the World's Most Eligible Bachelor is Lonely." *Royalty Monthly,* September 1985.

"Will Andrew's Sea Dog Days Come to an End?" *Royalty Monthly,* November 1987.

Willey, Far, with Donna Foote. " 'Dallas' at the Palace." *Newsweek,* July 6, 1987.

"The World's Most Controversial Women: Princess Diana." *Ladies Home Journal,* March 1987.

"Wow! Fergie Has *Really* Changed Since Her Marriage." *National Enquirer,* July 28, 1987.

Books

Barry, Stephen P. *Royal Service: My Twelve Years as Valet To Prince Charles.* New York: Avon Books, 1983.

Barwick, Sandra. *Diana: Princess of Wales, Mother-to-Be.* London: Pitkin Pictorials, 1982.

Burnet, Alistair. *The Book of the Royal Wedding.* New York: Summit Books, 1986.

Courtney, Nicholas. *Prince Andrew.* Boston: Little, Brown & Co., 1983.

Dunlop, Janice. *Charles and Diana.* New York: Dell Publishing Co., 1981.

Hall, Trevor. *Charles and Diana: The Prince and Princess of Wales*. New York: Crescent Books, 1981.

Heald, Tim, and Mayo Mohrs. *The Man Who Will Be King*. New York: Arbor House, 1979.

Hoey, Brian. *Monarchy: Behind the Scenes with the Royal Family*. New York: St. Martin's Press, 1987.

Junor, Penny. *Charles*. New York: St. Martin's Press, 1987.

King, Norman. *The Prince and the Princess: The Love Story*. New York: Simon & Schuster, 1983.

Lacey, Robert. *Princess*. London: Hutchinson, 1982.

Leete-Hodge, Lornie. *The Country Life Book of Diana, Princess of Wales*. London: Country Life Books, 1982.

Martin, Ralph G. *Charles and Diana*. New York: G. P. Putnam's Sons, 1985.

Maxwell, Susan. *The Princess of Wales: An Illustrated Biography*. London: Queen Anne Press, 1982.

Montgomery-Massingberd. *Diana, the Princess of Wales*. London: Fontana Paperbacks, 1982.

Morton, Andrew. *Royalty Watching*. New York & London: Fodor's Travel Publications, Inc., 1987.

Warwick, Christopher, and Valerie Garner. *Their Royal Highnesses: The Duke and Duchess of York*. London: Sidgwick & Jackson, 1987.

Whitaker, James. *Settling Down*. London: Quartet Books, Ltd., 1981.